Divorced,
without
Children

The Family Therapy and Counseling Series
Series Editor
Jon Carlson, PsyD, EdD

Kit S. Ng
Global Perspectives in Family Therapy: Development, Practice, Trends

Phyllis Erdman and Tom Caffery
Attachment and Family Systems: Conceptual, Empirical, and Therapeutic Relatedness

Wes Crenshaw
Treating Families and Children in the Child Protective System

Len Sperry
Assessment of Couples and Families: Contemporary and Cutting-Edge Strategies

Robert L. Smith and R. Esteban Montilla
Counseling and Family Therapy With Latino Populations: Strategies That Work

Catherine Ford Sori
Engaging Children in Family Therapy: Creative Approaches to Integrating Theory and Research in Clinical Practice

Paul R. Peluso
Infidelity: A Practitioner's Guide to Working With Couples in Crisis

Jill D. Onedera
The Role of Religion in Marriage and Family Counseling

Christine Kerr, Janice Hoshino, Judith Sutherland, Sharyl Parashak, and Linda McCarley
Family Art Therapy

Debra D. Castaldo
Divorced, Without Children: Solution-Focused Therapy With Women at Midlife

Divorced, without Children

Solution Focused Therapy with Women at Midlife

DEBRA D. CASTALDO

Routledge
Taylor & Francis Group
New York London

Extensive efforts have been made to protect the confidentiality and identity of individuals. Methods of disguise and release were based on principle 1.07 of the NASW Code of Ethics on Privacy and Confidentiality. Obtained releases in no way extend to other professionals who might believe they recognize a given case. They remain prohibited from disclosure by statute and or ethical guidelines of their given professions.

Routledge
Taylor & Francis Group
270 Madison Avenue
New York, NY 10016

Routledge
Taylor & Francis Group
2 Park Square
Milton Park, Abingdon
Oxon OX14 4RN

Printed in the United States of America on acid-free paper
10 9 8 7 6 5 4 3 2 1

International Standard Book Number-13: 978-0-415-95585-0 (Hardcover)

Library of Congress Cataloging-in-Publication Data

Castaldo, Debra D.
Divorced, without children : solution focused therapy with women at midlife / Debra D. Castaldo.
p. ; cm. -- (The family therapy and counseling series)
Includes bibliographical references and index.
ISBN-13: 978-0-415-95585-0 (hardcover : alk. paper)
1. Middle-aged women--Mental health. 2. Divorced women--Mental health. 3. Childlessness--Psychological aspects. 4. Divorce--Psychological aspects. 5. Solution-focused therapy. I. Title. II. Series.
[DNLM: 1. Psychotherapy, Brief--methods. 2. Divorce--psychology. 3. Middle Aged--psychology. 4. Problem Solving. 5. Women--psychology. WM 420.5.P5 C346d 2008]

RC451.4.M543C37 2008
616.89'140082--dc22 2007030586

Visit the Taylor & Francis Web site at
http://www.taylorandfrancis.com

and the Routledge Web site at
http://www.routledge.com

Contents

Series Editor's Foreword

"One person's constant is another person's variable"

Susan Gerhart

Reading *Divorced, Without Children* as a man was eye opening. At first I wondered, is this really true? Unmarried men without children do not seem to have such a stigma. When I began asking female friends if divorced childless women were marginalized, I was surprised at the solid validation of this problem. The content of this book seems long overdue for all who work in the mental health professions.

Eduardo Punset, in *The Happiness Trap*, indicates that a little more than 200 years ago, the life expectancy was thirty years in Europe. This was just long enough to learn to achieve the evolutionary purpose of reproducing. There was not much future in this life but possibly in the next one if you had strong spiritual beliefs. He states that each species has a different lifespan and lives life accordingly. Animals that have short life spans devote little energy to maintenance and a great deal to reproduction before they die. Those with long life spans use considerably more energy to maintain and to protect themselves. He indicates that it is only recently that humans have shifted from a focus on reproduction to living life.

This change in the length of life has left humans challenged about how to live life from the ages of thirty to eighty. Until very recently, most marriages ended due to the death of a spouse. Today most marriages end with divorce. Two hundred years ago, women died at age thirty whether or not they had birthed children. Today, most women do not even begin childbearing until age 30.

Divorced women at midlife who do not have children are a new "social species." Unfortunately, people are frequently marginalized and criticized when their lives are new or different. This book helps us to look carefully at the possible roles that people can live when life focus changes from marriage and childbearing to maintenance in the context of healthy relational connections and individuation. Alternative stories and narratives that allow for perceiving the population of divorced and childless women in constructive and healthy ways are provided. It is my hope that this book will open the doors needed to provide empathy and compassion to this population and others that are forging new lifestyles due to changes in living. Until that time, people need to hold on to the words of Pearl Bailey, *"No one can figure your worth but you."*

Jon Carlson, PsyD, EdD
Series Editor

Acknowledgments

It has truly been my good fortune and great privilege to be mentored by wonderful colleagues and friends over the three decades I have been a professional social worker, and this book would most likely not exist without their consistent support, encouragement, and feedback. To Dr. Carole Tosone, who encouraged me initially to study this topic and to continue on with this project, many thanks. To Dr. Alice Nadelman, who has always been a consistent source of help and friendship in numerous ways over twenty five years, thank you. A better mentor and friend one could not ask for. To Dr. Grace Sisto, thank you for your constant guidance and encouragement. To Dr. Kim Sumner Mayer, for the camaraderie, watchfulness, and feedback you provided as we completed our educations and moved on in different directions, thank you. I want to also thank my family and friends who have cheered me on when the process was slow going and seemed never ending. Special thanks to my sister Judi Blimline, and my special friends, Elsie Faul, Miriam Ashworth, and Dawn Adams Martini for the endless supportive conversations.

It is with great respect I honor the memory of the teachers who changed the course of my life's work, and taught me that possibilities and hope are endless: Steve de Shazer and Insoo Kim Berg. Special thanks to Christina Lindstrom and Judith Shaefer for the introduction!

Finally and most importantly, I want to thank all the women who have been willing to share their stories, and have provided me with a deep understanding of their struggle to forge ahead on their unique journeys as women divorced at midlife without children. Their stories of hope, survivorship, strength, innovation, competence, irreverence, and humor have undoubtedly affected my own journey as a "no marriage no kid" woman. It is my hope that in offering this book and the experiences captured within this group of women will no longer be hidden or silenced, but rather, will be seen and heard for the autonomous competent women they are.

Prologue: Fairy Tales, Myths, and Legendary Creatures

Once upon a time, there was a little girl who loved to listen to fairy tales. Growing up, she heard many magical stories of princesses, princes, and the woman who lived in the shoe with so many children. These fanciful stories told the tales of little girls who grew up to be saved by princes, ride off into the sunset to be married, and have children. In fact, riding off into the sunset with a prince was *the* thing for a princess to do. In fact, a princess really wasn't a princess of value unless a prince swept her off her feet. Unknown to the little girl, the telling and retelling of these mythical fairy tales embedded messages deeply into her very being. Through storybooks, cartoons, movies, and advertisements, she absorbed beliefs into her psyche regarding her worth as a woman. She learned this was dependent upon her ability to "catch" and keep a prince, and the mothering of children. And this is how she learned about what was "supposed to be" for a woman's life.

One day, the little girl went off to the kingdom of Academia to study important matters of the world. However, she and all the other young women knew the real, unspoken dream for a princess was to come away from Academia with the prize of a prince who would ask her to marry him. During her years in the kingdom of Academia, she continued to hear the same fairy tales from scholarly kings who spun stories about the measure of a woman's worth being connected to her ability to be a good wife and mother. Once in a while she heard of legendary princesses who didn't chase after princes, who didn't live in a shoe with a lot of kids, and who had many other adventures in many other kingdoms.

As the little girl grew, she spent many nighttimes dreaming and hoping a prince would come along. One day, a prince did come along with a shiny ring and a proposal of marriage.

The gift of the ring and the marriage that followed made her feel she had caught the ultimate prize, and she was finally worthwhile. As time passed, the princess became more and more disenchanted with her life. She began to dream of a new story for herself. In the new version, the princess ventured out from the castle into the world to see what else she could experience on her own. And thus she did, despite warnings from other storytellers about the necessity of finding another prince and living with a lot of kids in the shoe as soon as possible. You see, they warned her there was no happily ever after ending for her without a prince and children.

Eventually, she herself became a professional storyteller and scholar. She began helping other princesses find their own adventures and happiness, with or without princes, castles, kids, or living in shoes. She heard the powerful fairy tales many women wove about their lives. Believed to be truths, these stories often seemed to imprison many women in castles, kingdoms, and marriages they wanted to leave, or never really wanted in the first place. There were stories of dreams unfulfilled, silence, guilt, and shame. Even little girls knew these stories when they were very young. Discovering how powerful and hurtful these stories were, she began to question the fairy tales and myths in her world that kept women from seeing all the possibilities for their lives. She searched to uncover the beliefs buried deep within her. To her dismay, she found she was bound to the same stories that devalued women who were different in some way. She discovered within herself lingering myths from all those fairy tales of years ago. They led her to diminish her own value and judge herself and other women, in a secret way.

One day she came to realize the fairy tales she had grown up with were not truths at all. In fact, they were only constructed myths, fictitious stories of legendary deeds and creatures. It became evident to her that many fairy tales about women needed to be fractured. The mythological stories could, in fact, be debunked by altering the storyline with an unexpected twist. In such a way, new meaning of stories could take shape, altering more traditional tales into modern stories with different attitudes and endings.

As time went by, she became very curious about what the scholarly kings of Academia would say about divorced women without children at midlife. To her surprise, she found their story was nowhere to be found. Where were the tales of princesses who did not fit into the stories with the princes and the children? What about princesses who never wanted the prince or children at all?

So there came a time to break free from these untrue fairy tales and leave the destructive myths and legends about women behind. The tales that say that women without a prince or kids are not of value: They degrade women for being different in some way; they do not incorporate their deep need for connection; and they do not recognize that women's fulfillment and self-actualization can exist apart from marriage and motherhood. New stories need to be spun that honor and respect the potential in all women as human beings, first of all, of value in their own right, regardless of whether they are wives or mothers.

Introduction

No marriage, no kids. What thoughts, feelings, and images do these words evoke for you regarding a woman of this status? Do your thoughts go to:

- Negative labels such as *spinster*, *old maid*, *barren*, or *infertile*?
- An unmarried, childless woman who must be leading a lonely, unfulfilled life of misery?
- Beliefs that a woman cannot possibly be happy without a spouse or children?
- Assumptions that she is selfishly pursuing career and other narcissistic interests?
- Ideas that she is incompetent because she cannot "catch" and "keep" a man?
- Beliefs that all women must want children even if they say they do not?
- Beliefs that this is a nonissue in this day and age?

In the early 1970s, the first book I was required to read in social work school was William Ryan's *Blaming the Victim* (1972). Ryan's work challenged the process of justifying inequality by identifying defects in others who are victimized by the maintenance of inequality in society. He stated: "The generic process of blaming the victim is applied to almost every American problem" (Ryan, 1972, p. 5). He further stated that every social problem in Western society is viewed within a framework of a victim-blaming ideology. Placing blame on the deficits of various groups of society that are considered outside the norm has long been a nefarious process of devaluation of others. Ryan placed the victimization process within a context of social hierarchy, asking: "To whom are social problems a problem?" Ryan exposed the process of searching for defects within individuals, and suggested paradigm shifts were sorely needed. Such shifts would look to examine the defects of a society in which socially constructed belief systems seek to victimize others and maintain preferred norms that are institutionalized as behavioral "givens."

Although much progress has been made, the "blaming the victim" ideology is still a core process that, unfortunately, remains in the mainstream of social thought. It requires that "victims" assimilate into the norms of the preferred culture, rather than require the social environment to change to meet the needs of those who differ, suffer, are underprivileged, or require assistance to have their basic needs met. This ideology is passed on from generation to generation, creating a powerful legacy of victimization that impacts women's daily lives and life choices. Such an ideology is viewed as "truth," not to be questioned. This institutionalization of "social truths" is an ideology of exclusion and social ranking, in which those who are "different" are positioned as outsiders of less value. A simple translation: People cause their own problems and misfortune, often as a result of their own dysfunction or lack of character.

Women divorced at midlife without children are no exception to this blaming the victim ideology. Despite recent "quantum leaps" of social change, the devaluing legacy of patriarchy is still alive and well. Overt and covert paradigms that separate women into "preferred" and "other" still thrive. Many believe that these paradigms are no longer relevant, or no longer exist at all. In fact, they have simply become more covert than in previous eras. Divisive social constructions still decrease our ability to see the potential of women as complete human beings, separate from the roles of wife and mother (Dever & Saugeres, 2004).

Recent news stories continue to provide evidence that the legacy of stigmatization of unmarried, childless women is alive and well. In January 2007, U.S. Senator Barbara Boxer implied that current U.S. Secretary of State Condoleeza Rice could not have a proper perspective on the War on Terror because she was unmarried and childless. These comments were viewed by many as insults that were an attempt to diminish the accomplished Dr. Rice because she did not match up to the gold standard roles of wife and mother. Other news stories have recently reported on the perception of childless women having no hope and no future. Reports have surfaced on the selfishness of "choice moms": those who choose single motherhood before or without marriage. We need to continue examining society's need to denigrate and divide women who are different, follow their own voices, and make unique choices for their lives.

In January 2007, the *New York Times* reported groundbreaking statistics. For the first time, over 51% of American women are not living with a spouse. The trends of delayed marriage, decline in marriage, and decrease in remarriage were cited as contributing factors. Also in January 2007, *Woman's Day* magazine reported results of an informal survey reporting that over half the women surveyed regretted marriage and would not marry their spouse again.

No doubt we have entered an era of social change from which there is no turning back. As a result of the trends of delayed marriage and childbearing, increase in midlife divorce, and increased focus on higher education and labor force participation, there has been significant lifestyle change and expansion of women's options. In 2006, the National Marriage Project at Rutgers University also reported the continuing trends of decline in marriage, the stability of the high divorce rate, and increase in the number of adults living life without children (Dafoe & Popenoe, 2006). The consistent decline in child centeredness has been recently acknowledged and documented, with the number of childless women increasing to 1 in 5 by 2004. The Rutgers project authors suggested a stage of adulthood without children should be a developmental life cycle stage in its own right.

Continued preferences for women as wives and mothers are also still evident in everyday experiences. As a case in point, I was recently struck by the poignant observations of two colleagues of mine. One, an accomplished marriage and family therapist with a strong feminist viewpoint, recently became the mother of her first child at age 39. In discussing how motherhood has changed her, she recently stated:

> Now when people realize I am now a wife and the mother of a baby, they acknowledge me in a way that is very different than before. There is immediate approval, and somehow it feels like even with complete strangers, I hold some value that I didn't before. When you are not a mother, sometimes you feel invisible, like people don't know you exist. That doesn't happen to me anymore since the baby.

Another accomplished colleague who has never been married related to me:

> I stopped going to synagogue because I couldn't cope with being asked all the time why I am still not married. It's not as much as it once was, but it is still there. It might be just in my head, but you still think people are saying, look at her, she is still not married.

If there is doubt that such pressure still remains culturally entrenched, one only has to watch an episode of a currently popular television show that victimizes women by pitting a group of 25 against each other in competition for marriage to a bachelor. In patriarchal style, the bachelor controls the outcome, dispensing with the young women one by one in rejection ceremonies. I recognize that these women are hardly an unbiased, legitimate research sample, and it cannot be assumed they represent the majority of their peers. However, even if this show is simply staged entertainment, the underlying message is still evident. The pressure to be chosen for marriage has hardly been eradicated as a social expectation and standard. In my view, it is important that we continue to acknowledge the ongoing pressures for young women to marry and bear children.

The current-day relevance of these issues has been further driven home to me during the process of writing this book. Upon hearing of the subject I was writing about, some colleagues' responses included assumptions that women without marriage and children are bereft and miserable, that their unique clinical issues are no longer relevant, and that clinical work with these women should focus on facilitating their desire and ability to successfully remarry.

Surely the embedded implications of these reactions were not lost on me, and were a powerful reminder of how deeply entrenched these assumptions remain. These reactions reflect the very stereotypes that inextricably still bind women's value and well-being to the roles of wife and mother (Casey, 2007). On some core level, women who are not married and not mothers are still presumed to be miserable and lonely. Marriage and motherhood are still the preferred goals. The "marriage and motherhood mandate" is surely still alive and well, as much as we would hope to believe it is not.

One would expect recent social change has resulted in greater acceptance of lifestyle changes for women, and surely this is evident. What remains somewhat hidden, though, is a new identity crisis for women. As women seek to redefine themselves, sort out conflicting role choices, and search for authenticity, many now find themselves on a collision course trapped between "traditional" and "modern" choices. Cultural/institutional change has not kept pace with these dilemmas, thereby leaving women without the necessary supports to decrease conflict over these changing roles.

In addition to external barriers, internal barriers to women's self-directedness and complete freedom of choice also still remain. Although externally there is evidence that the marriage and motherhood mandate has become less entrenched, the internal ability to break free emotionally from constricting messages is still a major challenge for many women. Even among women who are comfortable with their lifestyle choices, many still express internalized struggles and feeling unheard and unseen. Silence, difficulty expressing "voice," and inability to act on an authentic sense of knowing still reverberate within the core of many women's experience.

Although psychological theory has been expanded significantly to frame women's development within models of relationship and connection, significant gaps still remain regarding women who are divorced at midlife without children. A literature review as of June 2007 revealed this population has still not been acknowledged or documented in a comprehensive way in psychology, sociology, or social work writings.

Undoubtedly, many professionals have incorporated these cultural changes into their thinking and practice. However, some current professional discourse seems to presume that, due to recent social change, previously dominant cultural beliefs and role prescriptions for women no longer apply in our modern world. It has been suggested that the "woman must equal wife and mother" equation has been fractured, and women's decision making regarding marriage, childbearing, and divorce is no longer value laden or stigmatized.

In my experience, there is still frequent conversation in professional circles that discounts the core dilemmas about marriage and motherhood for women. In some cases, clinical hypotheses still surface about the dysfunction and pathology of women who, by circumstance or design, are not wives or mothers. Assumptions are made that these issues are nonexistent, outdated, irrelevant, and uninteresting, and were only prevalent cultural issues in the 1950s and 1960s. Presumptions also surface regarding the lack of relevance of internalizations of social constructions about the roles of wife and mother, as in the decision making of most women.

I suggest it is premature to think that less than a half century of social change has "wiped out" patriarchal grand narratives that have been hundreds of years in the making. As we know, family and societal beliefs are transmitted down through generations, leaving a complex emotional legacy. Although significantly altered in the larger society, pervasive narratives are often transformed into institutionally hidden secrets.

Intellectually, we would like to believe that cultural scripts and prescribed roles for women have changed. In my professional and personal experience, the limiting expectations about women's roles, worth, and value are still very much alive in Western society, and still deeply embedded in the collective and individual psyches of us all. It is important that we continue to examine and challenge the apparent and hidden social constructions that have shaped our gendered world for generations.

One might ask why special clinical consideration of this group of women is needed, and what purpose the book might serve. My hopes in embarking upon this book, as well as my original research study, were to give voice to the comprehensive story of women who are divorced at midlife without children. It is anticipated that this population will increase in the coming decades. The 21st century may well be on its way to being known as the century of childfree adulthood (Dafoe & Popenoe, 2006). The complex clinical issues this group will face need to be further understood and explored as this century progresses.

I invite you to share in the ideas and beliefs I have developed over the last several decades of clinical work and research with women divorced at midlife without children, as well as women in general. By no means am I suggesting a rigid model. A fluid approach that allows for ongoing revision and customization to the uniqueness of the individual is recommended.

In the course of my research, I challenged myself to uncover assumptions that might bias the outcomes, as well as act as barriers in my counseling practice. As you begin your journey with this book, I share with you some of my beginning questions that I hope will be useful for you as well:

- What is it like for a woman who is not a wife or mother to live a very different lifestyle than most other women?
- How do women in this role cope with stressors of divorce, childlessness, and aging?
- How do they handle feelings of devaluation and stigmatization?
- What is it that I truly believe deep down in my core about women who are not wives and mothers?

- What are my most judgmental thoughts, beliefs, and narratives about women who do not desire traditional roles?
- Do I view women who are out of the norm from a strength or a deficit perspective?
- How are my beliefs entrenched in my clinical thinking, and how do they impact my work with women?
- What do I need to change in my work in order to fully sponsor women of all circumstances?

It is my belief that we can best support women's growth by paying attention to four areas of clinical focus: sponsoring women in the service of finding their own solutions and strengths, changing the narrative stories and underlying meanings of their experiences, fostering expanded connections, and supporting role innovation. In so doing, we can hopefully begin to institutionalize new paradigms that value women as "autonomous competent" human beings, free to direct their own lives in accordance with their dreams.

As you read on, I invite you to rethink, once again, beliefs, paradigms, and theories that limit one's ability to understand the experience of these women. I also invite you to join in the redesign of ideas that will enable all of us to embrace women who are out there struggling to forge new roles, ones that may be unfamiliar, but most certainly not of less value.

PART I

Overview, Trends, Historical Perspectives, and Issues

Dramatic social change of the last half of the 20th century has undoubtedly resulted in increased opportunities and diversity of available roles for women. The trends of postponed marriage and motherhood, foregoing marriage and motherhood completely, and the increased acceptability of divorce are predicted to be here to stay (Dafoe & Popenoe, 2006). A by-product of these trends has been the emergence of a growing group of women with "no marriage, no kids": women who are divorced at midlife without children.

Being divorced at midlife without children places a woman "out of sync" with the majority of her peers in a world where the roles of wife and mother are still central to the perceived worth and value of women. Whether they have entered this role by circumstance or design, these women are by and large an anomaly, living outside a powerfully prescribed norm of what "should be." In effect, most women do marry and mother at some point in their lives. For generations, women's decision making and life choices have long reflected the complex web of patriarchal role expectations that have been institutionalized into the collective unconscious. Despite significant social progress, these overwhelmingly pro-marriage, pro-natalist mandates continue to drive women's and girls' life decisions and behaviors in pervasive ways. The experience of being without a spouse and children seems to challenge emotional anchors to traditional female roles, in effect "shaking up" women's original expectations for their lives and their core sense of self.

The experience and meaning of being a divorced woman at midlife without children is an important "clinical story" of a changing social era that has, for the most part, not been told. The clinical issues for this group are unique and universal at the same time. In my view, these issues not only apply to women divorced at midlife without children, but also have larger implications for our work with women, young girls, couples, and families at various stages of development and relationship. The information that has come to light through the stories and challenges of these midlife women also reflects dilemmas for all women about marriage, childbearing decision making, and divorce. In clinical practice, these themes are as evident as ever in the lives of both women and girls.

As social change continues to evolve in the coming decades, this group of women is anticipated to increase. It is important that clinical information about this group be explored, so that mental health professionals can work from a well-informed therapeutic stance. In addition to understanding the negative impact of this role, it is also important for professionals to be informed regarding the positive impact for women who thrive quite well and enjoy a lifestyle that has traditionally been considered substandard. The experience of resilient, competent women who are successfully adapting to a lifestyle and a future without a spouse and children needs to be further understood and embraced.

CHAPTER 1

Out of Sync in a Married, Mothering World

It has barely begun, the search of women for themselves. But the time is at hand when the voices of the feminine mystique can no longer drown out the inner voice that is driving women on to become complete.

—Betty Friedan, *The Feminine Mystique* (1997, p. 378)

THE PURPOSE OF THE BOOK

The overarching purpose of this book is to give voice to the clinical story of women divorced at midlife without children. It will include a review of the social context and historical backdrop of the topic, the clinical issues, a clinical framework, and case examples. It is hoped that the content will help experienced professionals as well as young professionals and students to shape a vision for their work with these women, as well as provide an opportunity to examine premises that may be barriers to effective treatment. It is hoped this book will be useful for professionals in the fields of family therapy, psychology, psychiatry, social work, sociology, and women's studies. More specific purposes of the book include:

- Increased knowledge regarding the dilemmas, challenges, and stressors of women in this role
- In-depth understanding of the power of social context and socially constructed meanings that continue to shape women's lives and decisions
- An opportunity to understand cultural, professional, and personal paradigms, beliefs, and myths that impact clinical practice with women

The concept for this book arose out of three areas of professional and personal experiences over the past 20 years: clinical practice, the completion of a doctorate research study on the topic, and my own personal experience as a woman divorced at midlife without children. I initially became interested in this topic while working in private practice and as a director of clinical services at a small, private, nonprofit family service agency. In the course of providing individual, couples, family, and group treatment for two decades, the experiences and concerns of women and girls have consistently surfaced as universal clinical themes that seem to be relevant for all ages, stages of development, and relationship status. The most outstanding and entrenched themes center around issues of silence, inability to express true desires and needs, and the internalized, unconscious pressure to conform to prescribed expectations of marriage and motherhood. A need for women to conform to the "gold standard" roles of wife and mother is often evident. Doubt and lack of desire for those roles sometimes lurk in the shadows, waiting to be revealed as the therapeutic relationship progresses. However, voicing doubt or lack of desire for marriage, children, or both has, for the most part, been a shameful, unspeakable taboo.

Women's stories of decision making about marriage and motherhood are sometimes colored with regret and the suppression of a sense of "deep knowing" in early adulthood. Many denied their true desires and sense of self, and entered marriages that on some core level did not reflect their true wishes for their lives. If one were to listen even more closely, unspeakable whispers of ambivalence and lack of desire for children also could be heard weaving their way through the tapestry of some women's stories. The ongoing transmission of these powerful beliefs across generational boundaries to young girls is also often evident in therapy.

Due to the prevalence of these issues, I began to question how women in different lifestyles could cope and recover, given such tremendous societal pressures to stay within the norm of prescribed roles. I also became curious about the ability of women to step outside these rigidly entrenched role expectations and forge different lives for themselves. This led to a general interest in women's experience of divorce and divorce recovery. In clinical practice, divorcing women often display initial grief reactions that include feelings of depression, anxiety, desperation, hopelessness, inadequacy, panic attacks, crying spells, increased physical illnesses, excessive drinking, excessive spending, sexual acting out, poor concentration, and, in general, feeling out of control. Once past the initial crisis point, deeper themes often emerge. These include guilt and shame; perceived selfishness; self-blame for relationship failure; regrets about early marriage, childbearing decisions, and divorce; concerns about loneliness and emptiness; and fears regarding future capacity to care for oneself and be alone.

During this time, I also personally experienced divorce at midlife without children. After a 16-year marriage, I was divorced at age 38. I had continually postponed my childbearing decision throughout my marriage. I have now been divorced for 13 years, and have experienced a full range of role transitions and experiences, both positive and negative. Issues raised for me in my own recovery and transition to life as a single woman at midlife also solidified my interest and commitment to helping other women through this process. I decided to translate this interest and experience into the topic for my doctorate dissertation.

Although the emergence of new cultural trends has resulted in an increase in women divorced at midlife without children, the literature about this issue has lagged behind. Literature flourished in the 1970s, 1980s, and early 1990s on divorce, divorce recovery, remarriage, childlessness, delayed childbearing, voluntary and involuntary childlessness, and divorce adjustment for women. However, much of the divorce literature focuses on the effects of divorce on children, child custody issues, remarriage, and blended families, thus representing a gap on the specific topic of women's experience (Carter & McGoldrick, 1988). Also, much of the literature on childlessness focuses on the experience of couples rather than on individual women's experience. Although some research exists that has examined childlessness and marital satisfaction, there is little information regarding childlessness and divorce at midlife.

There is little written that captures the comprehensive experience of this specific group of women. As of June 2007, no publication other than this author's doctorate dissertation could be located in psychology, sociology, or social work literature. While the existing literature does provide important information, some of it is quite dated, and the conclusions are dated as well. In some cases, I have referenced the older literature in this book because more current literature does not exist. In other cases, I have referenced older literature due to its timelessness and the classic nature of the paradigms represented within. Since literature was nearly nonexistent, the study of the topic seemed timely and relevant. Much of the material in the book has been adapted from clinical work as well as the qualitative research study I completed in 2004.

The purpose of the study was to explore the impact and meaning of divorce at midlife for women without children. The paradox of women in this role in a pro-natalist, pro-marriage society was an intriguing story that begged to be told. The goal of the study was to convey the complex, "in vivo" experience of the women and provide information about a group about which little was clinically known or written. The emphasis in this process was obtaining women's personal perspectives in their own words and terms, via in-depth interviews. I began with an initial hypothesis that three areas of stress — divorce, childlessness, and aging — converging simultaneously, might place these women at risk for psychological distress. Another goal was to explore and identify women's recovery and coping skills utilized in this circumstance. The original interview guide utilized in the study is included in the appendix at the end of the book. The reader may find this useful as a guide for both intake assessment and ongoing therapeutic questioning.

The research sample consisted of 12 midlife women divorced without children. Criteria included an age range of 38 to 50 years old, divorced at least 18 months, without children, and not co-habitating or remarried. For the purposes of the study, midlife was defined as the age range of 38 to 50. This range corresponded with the age of diminishing childbearing capacity. The criteria of at least 18 months post-divorce was established to ensure that the women had passed through the throes of the initial crisis and were clearly in an adjustment phase.

Several limitations of the study were acknowledged. As an in-depth, small, qualitative study, the goal of the research was not to generalize the results to a large population. The sample was limited in ethnic and socio-economic diversity, with most of the women living in major metropolitan areas, highly educated, professional, and of fairly high socioeconomic status. The sample group was not as culturally diverse as was hoped for. All but one woman were Caucasian, with one woman being Latina. Also, the socioeconomic status of the women was high, with all but one of them reporting earning over $50,000, and four reporting incomes over $100,000. Nine women had earned college degrees, with six holding graduate degrees, and one in the process of completing a doctorate. All the women maintained professional careers, even those with only high school diplomas. More diversity in those areas would have been preferred, and may have produced different results.

It was determined, after the research progressed, that the age range of the sample may have been too great. Two women who were in their late 30s and who wanted children still believed childbearing was possible for them. The perceptions of their adjustment may have differed if they thought their childbearing capacity was completed. Women 40 and above seemed more resigned to the completion of their childbearing ability, and spoke from that perspective.

While I began with a broad focus of "curious not knowing," as research progressed, several unanticipated issues surfaced. These included the prevalence of low desire for marriage and children, family of origin patterns, and women's view of their mother's perception of mothering. These issues may be relevant areas for future research investigation on this group.

Due to my own status as a divorced woman at midlife without children, particular attention was paid to research techniques that would help control for bias on my part. In qualitative research, the researcher/interviewer is the primary tool through which the data are filtered and interpreted. While my status was acknowledged as a limitation of the research, it also provided me with the advantage of greater sensitivity to the in-depth experiences of the women, and undoubtedly assisted me in my ability to focus on core themes and nuances from a deeper perspective of understanding.

THE CLINICAL APPROACH

The overarching theoretical clinical approach and the techniques presented in this book are a reflection of the accumulation of my training and style of working that has developed over the past 20 years. I believe it is critical to ground oneself in a knowledge base to frame an approach to cases from an overarching theoretical perspective. This, then, provides a frame for the specific clinical models chosen to facilitate assessment and treatment planning. It is a challenge to write simultaneously for experienced and beginning professionals as well as students. For the experienced reader/clinician, the theoretical approach may be quite familiar. For students and new clinicians, it will serve as an introductory overview. I also want to caution the reader that the approach is meant to be an integrated guideline, to be used flexibly, not applied as "prescription."

Several theoretical perspectives have been critical in framing my thinking about this population. These are social constructionism, feminist developmental theory, the family developmental life cycle theory, role theory, ego psychology, and Erik Erikson's individual developmental theory. Several clinical models have also had a major influence on my work and have formed the core of my way of working and style. These include solution-focused brief therapy, the Ericksonian perspective, a multigenerational family systems approach, and narrative therapy. This clinical framework represents my deepest professional and personal beliefs about what is helpful in therapy in general, as well as what is necessary to work effectively with women, and specifically women divorced at midlife without children.

First and foremost, training and practice as a clinical social worker over the several decades has grounded me in a "strong person in the environment" perspective. I was professionally raised in the social work values and traditions of respect and honor for the client's worth, value, and right to self-determination. In the mid-1980s, I had the good fortune to train in solution-focused brief therapy with the originators of the model, Steve deShazer and Insoo Kim Berg. This perspective focuses on an inherent belief in the strengths and capacities of the client for healing, growth, and adaptation. I followed this with further training in Ericksonian hypnosis. The study of family therapy at Ackerman Institute for the Family in New York City provided me with a theoretical base in systemic, intergenerational, and narrative family therapies.

AN INVITATION TO READERS

In the solution-focused tradition, I believe that what happens in the therapy room has just as much to do with what the therapist brings as as with what the client brings. In effect, therapy is a co-created partnership through conversation and process between client and therapist. Although I view myself as a collaborator with the client, I also recognize that what I say and do holds a great deal of influence and authority with her. Therefore, it is critical for the therapist to examine what he or she brings to the therapy process. We are all victims of stereotyping and rigid expectations that limit and devalue women and minimize their worth as full, complex human beings. None of us have escaped the patriarchal messages ingrained in all aspects of our society, and we surely bring these biases with us into the room, consciously and unconsciously. They are part of who we are as therapist, enter the room with us, and are not "left at the door."

Working with women and girls over the past several decades has certainly provided me with the opportunity to continually examine, question, and expand my beliefs. It has been necessary for me to look deeply within myself to find the beliefs embedded in the core of my professional thinking. I have also struggled to examine my feelings about myself as a divorced woman at midlife without children.

While many professionals in the field work with expertise in feminist, constructionist, and intergenerational informed perspectives, unfortunately, I have heard far too many stories of women who feel blamed, unheard, and misunderstood in therapy. Women are still sometimes viewed from a deficit/dysfunction perspective when their lives, desires, and deepest core sense of self do not "match up" with the grand narratives that still organize social constructions in Western society. It is my hope that this book will provide further knowledge about limiting theoretical paradigms that are still in need of revision.

Herz Brown (1991) stated that the process of therapy is defined and limited by the therapist's vision. Therefore, I also hope this book may provide you with some useful self-discovery that will help you further shape your vision for your work with women. As you begin your journey with this book, I hope it will challenge you to examine your core beliefs about women and their experiences in a "married, mothering" world. I also hope it will bring into your awareness the thoughts and biases that inform and impact your work with women, girls, couples, and families. I share with you the vision that I have developed for my work with women divorced at midlife without children:

To help women:

- Break their silence in relationships and about their true desires and dreams for their lives
- Loosen the constrictions of prescribed roles and expectations
- Normalize a variety of lifestyle choices and diminish feelings of distress and stigma
- Develop an autonomous competent self
- Define and innovate new roles that are free of limitations
- Modify patriarchal social constructions and reconstruct positive meanings that support a diversity of choices, roles, and lifestyles

In an era when traditional gender roles continue to change dramatically, and less limiting roles and paradigms need to continue to be embraced, it is important that clinical knowledge keep pace with these changes. Concepts and paradigms need to be continually reviewed and rethought as they are further institutionalized into the once traditional knowledge base. I can only hope that someday young women will pick up this book in complete and utter surprise and say, "What an irrelevant topic. I can't even believe this was an issue."

CHAPTER 2

How Did We Get Here? Trends and Concepts

The history of women's roles in the institution of marriage illustrates that, for centuries, marriage has precluded the possibility of leading a self-directed life. Until relatively recently, women were virtually invisible, except as daughters, wives, and mothers.

—Carol Anderson and Susan Stewart, *Flying Solo: Single Women at Midlife* (1994, p. 42)

TRENDS

The experience, impact, and meaning of divorce at midlife for women without children is an issue that needs to be viewed through a "social lens." Beliefs and meanings tend to reflect the trends of the social era in which they are constructed. Rather than viewing the individual in a social vacuum devoid of political and ideological biases, it is important to view the person in the context of the interrelated web of social experiences, the meanings attached to them, and the overarching narratives that pervade our thinking. In effect, in a society in which the social preference of youthfulness and centrality of roles of wife and mother are pervasively embedded in the culture, it is important to reflect upon the impact of this social context on women outside these roles.

This group of women has increased over the last half of the 20th century due to a number of dramatic cultural shifts. These trends have eroded traditional gender roles and had tremendous impact on the fabric of Western culture, family life, and the lives of women. They include the increase in higher education and labor force participation, availability of birth control and abortion, delayed first marriage, postponed childbearing, and increase in divorce. These changes are expected to continue in the coming decades. However, institutional changes to support alternative roles for women have not kept pace with these developments. This cultural lag in support and services for this growing population of women increases their vulnerability and places them at risk for psychological distress. Risks include anxiety, panic attacks, depression, loneliness, suicidal ideation, and role strain.

Despite significant cultural changes, marriage is still viewed as a cornerstone of American life. More than 90% of women have married in every generation since recordkeeping began in the mid-1800s (Cherlin, 1992). The trends of co-habitation rather than marriage, postponed marriage, delayed childbearing, and voluntary childlessness have been dramatic changes that have shaped the fabric of young adult development over the last several decades (Schoen & Standish, 2001). Childbearing has become a much more conscious choice, rather than an unconsciously driven, mandated expectation. It is not uncommon now for women to delay childbearing into their 30s, 40s, and even 50s. Also, the trend of voluntary childlessness, permanently choosing not to bear children, has been dramatically on the rise. Married couples have become more concerned with the costs and benefits of having children, and the impact of children on marital satisfaction (Twenge et al., 2003). The increase in the divorce rate since the 1960s peaked in the early 1980s and, according to experts, has leveled off (Goldstein, 1999). The chances of divorce are still currently estimated to be between 40 and 50% (Kelly Raley & Bumpass, 2003). We can surely not deny the impact of this trend on American family life.

Two other shifts that have had an impact on the life cycle of women and their circumstances at midlife are the increase in women's participation in both higher education and the labor force. In turn, these shifts have contributed to the previously mentioned trends of delayed marriage and postponed childbearing. The number of women obtaining higher education at all levels has steadily increased from decade to decade without interruption. The steady movement of women into the labor force is also a trend that has consistently lasted throughout the century. These trends have shown no signs of reversing. It is likely that obtaining higher education and developing a career will remain a core part of many women's life cycle in the years to come (Landa, 2004; Mejumder, 2004).

These dramatic social changes have increased choices for women regarding available roles and lifestyles apart from marriage and motherhood. In effect, the trends toward education and career, and the postponement of marriage and childbearing have shifted the previously traditional stages of the woman's life cycle (Sheehy, 1995). This shift sometimes places women in the position of making decisions about marriage, childbearing, or divorce at the critical point of midlife. Women deciding to postpone marriage and childbearing are clearly vulnerable to the possibility of facing midlife divorced without children.

Due to the interplay of these major shifts in marriage, childbearing, divorce, obtaining advanced education, and labor force participation, it is predicted that one of the fastest growing household types in the coming decades will be women living alone (Fields & Casper, 2001). It has already been reported in the *New York Times*, in January 2007, that 51% of adult women do not live with a spouse. The number of childless individuals and couples overall is also anticipated to continue to increase (Dafoe & Whitehead, 2006; Letherby, 2002).

DEFINITION OF CONCEPTS

Several terms and concepts will be utilized throughout the book, and thus applicable definitions follow here as a guide for the reader.

Midlife

Midlife, or "the middle years," has been defined as the stage of life between young adulthood and older adulthood (Erikson, 1950, 1968; Wickes, 1993). The concept of midlife has been credited to Jung, who viewed it as a transitional dividing point of the two halves of adult life. For the purposes of this book, I refer to midlife as the age span of late 30s to 50, since the issue of the potential end of childbearing capacity is central for this group of women. *Midlife* in relation to couples has been defined as a unique transitional period of transformation, innovation, and evolution in which the marital contract may be re-examined. In relation to "midlife divorce," a definition sometimes utilized is divorce of a marriage of 15 to 20 years or more (Iwanir & Ayal, 1991).

Divorce Adjustment

Divorce adjustment has been defined as a multifaceted process that includes psychological, social, and financial components (McDaniel, Kusgen, & Coleman, 2003). It involves multiple tasks for the individual. Historically, adjustment had been viewed as beginning during marriage with the emotional withdrawal of one partner, and ending with remarriage (Goode, 1956).

Wallerstein (1986) suggested that divorce adjustment is the process of disengaging from marriage, resolving feelings caused by the marital rupture, stabilizing the post-divorce relationship with the former spouse, and constructing a new life pattern that includes social and economic stability and fulfilling endeavors, a new relationship, or both.

Other definitions of adjustment also include the reconstruction process as the individual shifts from coupled life to uncoupled life, detachment from the ex-spouse, perception of the self as autonomous, and ability to adapt to single life. *Divorce adjustment* has also been defined as an absence of signs and symptoms of physical and mental illness, and the ability to function adequately in the daily role responsibilities of home, family, work, and leisure — the development of identity separate from the ex-spouse or the status of being married as a hallmark (Kitson & Morgan, 1990).

Postponed/Delayed Childbearing

The interchangeable terms of ***postponed*** and ***delayed childbearing*** have been defined as those women who postpone the decision to have children until sometime in the future. Other terms utilized include ***off-time***, ***late-timing***, ***radical timing***, ***mature mother***, and ***elderly primagravida*** (Welles-Nystrom, 1997). These terms are constructed in relation to the concept of "on-time" childbearing that refers to expectable time frames and "social clock patterns." Those women who do not complete childbearing in the expected life cycle time frame are considered delayed. Several authors conceptualized postponed/delayed childbearing as an ongoing process of deferments that eventually resulted in a permanent decision to remain voluntarily childless (Houseknecht, 1987; Veevers, 1973). The optimal age for childbearing has traditionally been defined as the 20s. A variety of ages have been used as the marker for delay. These include the ages of 28, over 30, and over 40. Another definition of delay includes over five years of marriage without childbearing.

Childless

Childless is a term used to define an adult individual without children, or the absence of children. Other terms utilized in professional literature include ***child-free***, ***unprogenied***, ***nullipara***, and ***non-mother***. These terms are usually used to describe women, and are rarely applied to the status of men without children.

Voluntary Childlessness

Voluntary childlessness refers to women who choose to have no children and do not expect any in the future, although they are biologically able to bear children (Letherby, 2002). The term ***intentional childlessness*** has also been utilized (Hird & Abshoff, 2000). Two central components that distinguish an individual as voluntarily childless include conscious decision making and a lifelong, permanent commitment to the decision. A subgroup of "early articulators" has been identified by Veevers (1980), referring to those who express the conscious desire to remain childfree early in life, even before marriage.

Involuntary Childlessness

Involuntary childlessness refers to those who have no children and expect none in the future due to the inability to physically produce a biological child.

CHAPTER 3

Stepping out of Silence

The Transformation of Susan

I wish I'd known from the beginning that I was a strong woman. What a difference it would have made! I wish I'd known that I was born a courageous woman; I've spent so much of my life cowering. How many conversations would I not only have started but *finished* if I had known I possessed a warrior's heart? I wish I'd known that I'd been born to take on the world; I wouldn't have run *from* it for so long, but run to it with open arms.

—Sara Ban Breathnach, *Something More: Excavating Your Authentic Self* (1998, p. 5)

TURNING OVER A NEW LIFE

Susan: I'm crossing over to a different path in life. Actually, I'm trying out many different paths. It's like I'm finally turning over a new leaf. It's so hard to find your way out, but I'm doing it. I'm just so tired of the old way, feeling bad about my life, the silence, the being a doormat. It's so hard to find a way out of the silence. I've been doing it for so long. I'm sick of it and I'm not doing it anymore. And I'm not going to be with someone just to be with someone. I'm passed that. And I just realized, I don't think I'm getting married again, and it's okay. (*She smiles with a look of wonderment.*)

DC: I'm not sure I heard that right, did you just say you are turning over a new leaf or a new life? (*Laughter*)

S: Well I guess either applies! (*More laughter*)

DC: You just smiled like a Cheshire cat as you said you realized you are not getting married again and it's okay. Did you know you were smiling?

S: No, but it's like this lightbulb just went on — I'm really finally okay. I really believe I'm not getting married again. I'm not even dating anyone who isn't absolutely wonderful. I'm not settling and I'm not looking. It's a little bit like I don't care anymore. I don't feel that desperation I used to, to get remarried. I went out with a guy recently, and as I was sitting next to him, it was like a lightbulb went on. He talked a mile a minute all about himself, and all of a sudden it hit me, I'm not doing this with him. He didn't listen for one second to me, and he didn't ask me anything else about my life. Looking back I think several years ago I'd be like, oh great, a MAN with things in common, WOW! Now I'm like no way am I accepting crumbs! No way I'm accepting less than I really want. I don't want to slip back into a relationship that isn't what I want. There is still the loneliness at times but I'm definitely different. I'm guess I'm healed? Like some kind of miracle? (*Laughter*)

DC: I guess you are healed! MUST be some kind of a miracle!

S: Yeah, a miracle of like six years of working on it in therapy! (*Laughter*)

DC: Well, I think YOU are the miracle. The miracle was inside you all along. It's just been a matter of finding you and your strengths. I remember those first weeks when we started working together. Look how far you've come. So many things about the progress you have made are running through my mind. I remember the desperation of feeling like you couldn't manage alone, and you had to meet someone, and you couldn't be complete by yourself, and you couldn't stand up for yourself. Seems like none of that was actually true, hmmm?

S: You remember all that?

DC: Yes, I certainly do, and from sitting over here I see a woman who has grown and is so strong, and such a survivor, and so wonderful.

S: It seems like so far away in the past. It doesn't even feel like me anymore. I'm just going on this new path. It's like it finally all is coming together. I think as far as getting divorced, it's given me the opportunity to work on the underlying issues. Therapy has been a great help. I found I had a lot of inner strength I didn't know I had that certainly came out.

DC: IT SURE DID! I think you are still you, a you with more of your strengths showing, we just had to bring them out from inside and develop them. You have not only survived, you are a strong woman FOR SURE! I can remember when you struggled a lot to speak, and you used to tell me you couldn't find any words to speak up for yourself. Remember how we used to practice the words and sentences and I used to write words down for you to take with you? And look at you now! You are speaking without even giving it a second thought, to your friends, family, boss! Are you aware how much easier and strongly you are speaking for yourself?

S: I guess I am really stepping out of the silence. It's so hard to find a way out, but I am doing it. Therapy has been helpful. It feels safe, like I am learning. I think I am learning skills. I definitely feel I can handle situations now. I don't feel like I am being judged, and I have always felt that in my other relationships with people. I feel I can say anything. The feeling of being scared has gone away.

Thus ended a recent session with Susan, my client of six years. The recognition of her growth out of silence, and her realization that she was comfortable with her single life, was astounding and represented several major shifts in beliefs about her life. I could clearly recall the frightened, silent woman who entered my office a few days after her separation. Six years later, I saw before me a woman who was able to focus on her strengths and capabilities of caring for herself, had re-storied the meaning of her life experiences, and had innovated a new role for herself as a single woman at midlife without children. In some ways this interchange effectively summarized the results of our work together over six years. Therapy with Susan focused on meaning modification of the experience of loss and re-storying Susan's perceptions of herself as an unmarried woman at midlife without children. It included consistent sponsorship and solution-focused coaching, teaching her a process of solution construction that she generalized to many areas of her life. It also included reworking internalized narratives about her experiences of marriage, divorce, single life, and "voice." Fostering and expanding relational connections was also a critical part of her recovery from divorce at midlife.

HERE COMES THE BRIDE: A LIFE PREDEFINED

Susan was the middle child of three girls, with both sisters married with children. Susan identified a family belief that prohibited women from leaving marriage, even in the presence of emotional abuse. She recalled that most of the women in her extended family of origin were not happy in their marriages. She vividly remembered the verbal abuse of her grandfather toward her grandmother, and her grandmother's response of throwing dishes at a moment's notice. She believed her grandmother as well as other women in the family were extremely unhappy for decades; however, leaving was not perceived as a possibility. This constructed family expectation undoubtedly played a major role in Susan's feelings of shame and guilt regarding her separation and divorce.

As Susan began to stabilize a few weeks after beginning treatment, she was able to begin to explore the meaning of her marriage and separation. Susan was separated and subsequently divorced at the age of 38 after a 20-year relationship with her first sweetheart. Susan had known Jim throughout their growing up as young children, and they had eloped at age 20 after an "on and off" relationship throughout high school. Like so many other women, in adolescence and early adulthood, Susan automatically fell into the unconscious goal of getting married. She later viewed this early marriage as a mistake, rooted in beliefs that she should marry as quickly as possible in young adulthood. Susan recalled her beliefs about marriage in early adulthood:

> I think we got together for the same reasons everybody did. I think we were looking for love of any kind, and we were both looking to get away from our families. It's just kind of what you did without thinking about it. I didn't have a clue who he was or who I was. It was convenient, and I didn't even think about any other way of life.

In addition to an early sense of knowing in early adulthood that her marriage was not stable or fulfilling, she also recalled feelings regarding lack of desire for children. She stated:

> I didn't have a strong interest in children growing up. Then I knew in the beginning of the relationship I didn't want kids with him. I think right after I got married, I thought this wouldn't be a good idea. I remember thinking, Could he really be there for a child? Is this someone who knew he really could do what you need to do for a kid? I never verbalized it, but I do remember thinking about it, Why would I ever want to bring a child into this?

She continued on:

> I didn't want to bring them up by myself, and that is how it would have been. As equal as things are now, it is still the woman that is really going to be responsible for the kids. I think then later I didn't want kids because I knew the relationship was unstable and he wasn't strong enough to be a responsible father. Kids would run away from him in the neighborhood. I knew he wasn't good with kids. He had a sense of anger and I was ignoring it. Also, I began to see that he wasn't raised in a good way. There was hitting and a lot of anger.

Similar to many women in the research study, Susan did not feel particularly distressed regarding the absence of children in her life. Her lack of intense feelings of grief seemed to validate that having children would have been a "cognitively dissonant" lifestyle for her. Therefore, this was not a major focus of work with Susan in therapy. Periodically, she experienced brief, ambivalent, and mild feelings of sadness that dissipated quickly. She related:

> I barely think about it anymore. I don't think about it on a daily basis. There are just some times when I am around kids or people who are parents, I just feel like I am the odd man out, but it goes away

quickly, and I don't feel I am inadequate. I used to feel I was inadequate, but now I don't. Sometimes I feel there is something missing, but maybe it's something in me that is missing, that I need to work on making myself happy. The divorce wasn't because I didn't want to have children. Towards the end I cried a little about what our kids would have looked like, but it went away quickly, it was just a little.

Also similar to many women in the research study, Susan was comfortable with her life, but was more distressed by the reactions of others toward her divorced, childless status. She remembered the reaction of others when she initially became separated:

> I remember telling people. I had to tell them something. They all thought I was going to say I was pregnant because we were married so long. Then I told them we were getting divorced. People said they never thought I would be the one getting divorced because everything looked so good on the outside. I think society is very funny. People always say right away, "you'll find someone else," "you'll get married again," and "you would have been a good mother." Society labels and categorizes you. They say, "Oh, at least you have been married once." Society thinks that marriage is the ultimate. I think it is unfair. Society is like, "There is something wrong with you if you are not married." It is much better now, people don't ask as much. But it is still in your head, What are they thinking about you?

TOGETHER ON THE LEDGE: IN SPONSORSHIP OF SUSAN

Susan initially came to me in the first week of her separation from her husband, Jim. She was visibly in a state of shock and intense grief upon her arrival at my office for her first session. As she sat down, the tears began to flow profusely, and she could barely speak. Unknown to me at that time, Susan's inability to speak during her separation reflected a lifetime of silence, difficulty expressing anger, pleasing others, and "doing the right thing." These themes would become major areas of our work together throughout her divorce recovery process. I vividly recall her first words in our initial session:

S: (*Silent, visibly distressed, tearful, and having difficulty speaking*)

DC: Take your time. We can go as slow as you need to. You mentioned on the phone you are just separated a few days?

S: My husband just left me a few days ago. I totally didn't see it coming. He's already involved with another woman, someone we both knew. I can't stop crying, I can't eat, and I can't get out of bed. I am amazed that I even got out of bed to get here.

DC: I'm so sorry you are feeling so upset and going through this. It was very brave of you to get out of bed to get here. I'm glad you made it.

In the first few moments of this first session, I made mental note of Susan's constructed belief that her husband left *her*. There were already important clues from Susan that she was developing a constructed story of self-blame, shame, and guilt regarding the breakup of her marriage. Her beliefs regarding the failure of her relationship would undoubtedly become an important area of work for re-storying and meaning modification throughout her treatment.

She continued in the first session:

S: I was seeing another therapist for awhile. Actually, we were going as a couple, and he wouldn't go anymore, so I've been seeing her. When he left this week, I didn't know what to do. I felt like I was out on the ledge ready to jump. I called my therapist and she didn't call me back for days. I was losing it. I'm still losing it. I had to see *someone*.

DC: I'm so sorry that happened to you. I'm so sorry she didn't call you back. But I'm glad you found me. I know how distressing those first few days of a separation are. I will tell you right now that I will call you back.

S: I'm glad to know that. I need someone dependable right now.

DC: Have you been able to reach her to tell her how you feel about her not calling you back?

S: No, I don't have the energy to do that right now. But maybe when I feel better I will.

DC: So tell me, since you are feeling so upset right now, how can we use the time today in a way that would be most helpful to you right now?

S: I think I mostly need help figuring how to get through the next couple of days and weeks.

DC: Well, you are here, so you have made it through the first few days. How did you do that?

While staying focused on the important goal of initial sponsoring and joining, I also was mindful to work as quickly as possible to focus on solutions. In situations of trauma and crisis, this quickly imparts to the client that even in the current state of distress, solutions are not only possible, but probable, and already occurring. Finding even the tiniest seeds of strengths or solutions can provide much needed hope to the client that "this too shall pass."

Years ago, one of the most important solution-focused questions I learned from Berg and Dolan (2001) was her simple yet elegant question: How did you *do* that? In her use of this question, Berg's gift of inflection and voice tone exuded such excitement and expectation that one could not help but lean forward, as she so often did, in anticipation of a solution description by the client. Within the simplicity of these five words lies the core of solution development. The question implies that the client *did* something within her own control and coping repertoire, and she can continue to do more of what she already knows how to do. It also imparts a powerful message of competence and belief in the expectation of recovery and improvement. Susan continued on to describe how she was making it through the first few days of her separation:

S: Mostly I've been staying in bed and crying. I can't eat very much. A good friend of mine stops by every day to make sure I am okay. I feel like that is about all I can do right now.

DC: So you haven't done anything harmful to yourself or anyone else?

S: No, I don't feel like hurting myself, I haven't been drinking, and I haven't killed him.

DC: WOW! So that is all good that you haven't done any of those things, not even drinking!! Sounds to me like staying in bed and crying is a VERY wise decision you are making right now. The most helpful thing you can do for yourself right now. And that is great your friend is checking on you. She must really care about you.

S: You mean that's okay?

DC: Of course! This is a shocking experience, and you need to just take care of the basics for right now, rest, try to eat something. Don't expect too much more of yourself right now. Who else can help you right now?

S: Well mostly my best friend. She lives close by. My sisters live in Michigan and one has been calling and I can call her 24/7. I'm not that close to my parents and they don't know yet.

DC: I'm glad you have your friend and your sister.

S: But even though they are checking on me, I still feel emotionally out there on the ledge. Sometimes I can't take it.

DC: How about if I come out on the ledge together with you?

S: Wells up with tears and smiles a little smile through the tears.

DC: You see, I've been where you are, so I know. I've been through a divorce of a long relationship quite a few years ago, and I remember what those first days felt like.

S: You do? That makes me feel so much better. So am I going crazy or what? Am I going to make it through this?

DC: Well you see me here, I am in one piece, and you are still in one piece as badly as you feel right now. No, you are not going crazy. You might feel like it, but that doesn't mean you actually are. I would guess you are feeling shocked and intense sadness and confusion.

S: I think that puts a finger on it. Is it going to get better?

DC: Of course it is going to get better. Give yourself some time here. One day at a time.

Beginning from a nonvictimizing perspective enables an approach to the client that is respectful and honors the capacity to recover in the throes of a life crisis. Focusing on a diagnosis of depression or seeing Susan as suicidal most likely would have increased her fears that she was going crazy and would not recover. I chose to accept her symptoms as attempted solutions to her state of distress, and elaborate upon the things she was already doing that were good for her. The ability to normalize a person's experience of distress and begin to frame it as an opportunity for growth can provide much needed comfort in a time of crisis.

My goals for this first session were simply twofold. The first was to begin to sponsor Susan, accepting her distress, tears, and inability to speak. Susan's story and experiences would undoubtedly awaken my own feelings and experiences of midlife divorce and grieving. I chose to share in a genuine way with Susan that I could understand her experience of separation and grieving from firsthand experience. Rather than trying to cover over my own feelings and present from a "blank screen," distancing, professional stance, I opened to use of my own experience in the service of going deeply into the experience with the client. As Gilligan (2001) encouraged, we must be willing to use ourselves to go with clients to their deepest experience in order to be able to sponsor them toward health and healing.

It was important for me to use this awakening to connect with Susan's awakening of her inner core self as she responded to her life trauma. The therapist's use of self through the appropriate sharing of experiences or stories about others also is a way of connecting and joining with the client. These are often the moments when the connection in the therapeutic relationship can be deepened. In light of the abandonment by her previous therapist, establishing trust and an acceptance of her symptoms was critically important. I thought simply about "being with" her in the presence of her intense grief.

In acceptance of her tears and distress while we sat together, I chose not to offer Susan tissues, with her freely flowing tears and tear-stained face. Knowing that Susan was in a tremendous amount of distress and barely functioning, I chose not to focus on a traditional intake interview or ask her the usual questions about herself or her martial history. I also chose not to focus on Susan's symptoms or validate her feeling of "going crazy." Susan was experiencing the expectable symptoms of the very recent loss of her primary relationship. The invitation to just be and cry in my presence was well received.

The second goal of the first session was to begin to quickly establish a focus on Susan's strengths, capabilities, and potential solutions. This was critically important given the amount of distress and psychological pain she was experiencing. The hopefulness of pointing out what a client is doing that is self-protective in a time of trauma can provide a lifeline for clients at this traumatic stage of the divorce experience. Rather than spending the first session gathering detailed descriptions of her symptoms and grieving, I chose to begin to help her identify what she was already doing that was good for her and was enabling her to cope during the first few days of her separation.

From a solution-focused approach, I encouraged Susan to identify her own solutions for the coming hours and days, rather than prescribing solutions that she might find unsuitable, or not "doable" for her at a time of such great distress. From an Ericksonian perspective, it was important to view her presenting symptoms as attempted solutions in the service of her own preservation and growth. Framing her inability to get out of bed as "needed rest" and a "wise decision" enabled her to begin to view herself as capable and self-preserving, rather than "going crazy" or falling apart. Also, identifying several things she could do to get through the next few days also pointed her in a more hopeful direction. Complimenting Susan for getting out of bed to get to therapy, and for avoiding harmful, destructive behaviors was also critical. Helping the client search for the seeds of coping, self-preservation, and beginning solution development is extremely useful, even in the midst of the worst trauma and desperation.

That first day, she was able to speak just a little bit about her relationship with Jim and the reason for the separation. Mostly she just cried. My willingness to just be with her sadness that day, and to offer her the promise of responding to her should she need to call between sessions, proved to be of critical importance. The remainder of the session was spent sitting with Susan and her tears, listening to what she felt she could manage to tell me that day, and discussing a few doable self-care ideas she thought could help her get through the next week.

Throughout the first two years of Susan's separation and divorce experience, she occasionally felt "out on a ledge" emotionally. Susan never had any active suicidal ideation; rather, these were moments of increased emotional distress. Occasionally she would call in between sessions or need an extra session. An important part of my sponsorship of Susan over the years has been a quick and consistent response when she does reach out in need. These moments decreased drastically as time progressed. My initial promise to come out and be "together with her on the ledge" when she needed me formed the basis of a relationship of trust and emotional holding that, in my view, has been one of the most healing aspects of Susan's therapy.

Rather than viewing her "out on the ledge" feeling as suicidal ideation or craziness, I framed it as expectable distress in the face of major loss and grief. The solution focus is extremely helpful in the case of suicidal statements. Of course it is important to responsibly assess the client's level of risk. However, caution must also be used not to validate feelings of craziness. In these moments, focusing on strengths, coping, and reassurance can minimize feelings of fear about one's own well-being. I am extremely cautious regarding the use of language and words as an important tool in validating competence rather than pathology.

DOUBLE TEAMING: CO-CONSTRUCTING SOLUTIONS IN A TIME OF CRISIS

The breakup of Susan's marriage brought her to her knees emotionally. Susan barely functioned during the first few months of her separation, yet function she did. Even in these tough times, Susan retained a good sense of humor, and together we adopted the motto "fake it till you make it." She managed to continue to get to her job and to therapy. The rest of her time was spent in bed, not eating, and obsessing over the fact that Jim was already living with someone else. Susan could not imagine a life without Jim, nor could she envision herself as a competent single woman. The story did not fit her original internalized dream for her life. This was not the way it was "supposed to be." Although Susan always felt she did not want children, nor did she want them with Jim, her separation and divorce brought her postponed childbearing and childbearing decision-making process to an abrupt end. So here she was, facing the triple whammy of divorce, childlessness, and midlife.

Therapy in the beginning weeks and months throughout the first two years of the divorce process focused on solution development to facilitate Susan's ability to cope with the everyday challenge of simultaneously grieving and living. Many sessions were primarily grieving experiences that required my ability to sit with Susan and accept the gift of her tears, intense sadness, and anger. At the same time, we began working on self-care and coping techniques. Susan's progress waxed and waned as she experienced waves of grief. In her worst moments of distress, sessions were focused on getting past the crisis and calling forth strengths and solutions she had previously utilized to make it through periods of distress.

It was also equally important to be a relentless messenger of hope that "this too would pass." Maintaining a consistent focus on what the client is already doing that is good for her, even a little bit, even the tiniest achievement, can build confidence and reinforce the will to continue in the face of loss. Teaching the client how to search for and develop solutions can then be replicated with each subsequent crisis. Solutions are co-constructed in a mutual process. I often think of myself and the client as a doubles team, tackling each crisis with a co-constructed strategy of solution plays. The following is from a session during one of her weeks of distress:

S: (*Crying*) I feel like I'm going downhill again. All the worst feelings are back. I had a couple of good weeks. I'm back in bed and I'm paralyzed, and now I feel like I am ready to go out on that damn ledge again! (*Laughs through her tears*)

DC: Well, if you are going out on that ledge again, you know I have to go with you. That was the promise, right?

S: Right. (*Giggles*)

DC: At some point you have to stop going out there, you know I'm afraid of heights and I trip a lot.

S: (*Giggles again, as this had become a running joke between us that usually interrupted the pattern of crying and changed her mood*) It just comes over me, the grieving feelings again, I just can't control it. I'm back to being paralyzed and everything is falling apart. I can't think straight, can't get organized, and I'm crying all the time again.

DC: Now you said you had had quite a few good weeks that were going better. What was going on then that was different than this week?

S: I was keeping busy during the week, going to work, and I was feeling pretty good during the day while I was working. I felt a little bit like going out with friends. Sometimes they could drag me out of the house. I think I was feeling more hopeful too, like I could do this.

DC: What's the hopeful part about, the feeling like you can do this?

S: I know I have been through these weeks before and I think I know what I have to do. And I know how to take care of myself. I can make a list and figure out where to start.

DC: Now we know you have turned things around quite a few times before. So what way has worked the best for you to start turning your mood around?

S: Well first if I can keep myself physically out of bed so much, then I seem to stop the crying.

DC: How have you kept yourself out of bed?

S: If I have a plan of what I'm going to do and can stick to it, then I seem to get up and make the first step.

DC: So let's say you make a plan for the next few days, what will it look like next week when you look back and see your week has gotten a little bit better?

S: Let's see, I could see myself starting to clean up a little, and starting to pay a few bills. Probably if I call my friend Lynn she will get me out of the house. I can usually count on her. I have to start eating a little bit too. Maybe if I buy food and have it in the house I could make a few things. And I think staying away from thinking too much about things, that just make things worse.

DC: So you named about five things you think would make the week go a little better and get you out of bed more. Which of these would be the easiest to do today or tomorrow?

S: Probably start paying some bills, that always makes me feel like I have really accomplished something real. I'm going to start doing that when I get home. That should give me some energy to keep going and do other things.

DC: Sounds good. Now you mentioned about not thinking about things too much. How do you do that, besides keeping busy?

S: Well, I think of it as a choice. I can sit there and feel horrible and abandoned about my divorce and think about him living with her, and all the scared feelings of "How am I going to make it through this?" Or I can try to get rid of the thoughts.

DC: What ways have you been able to get rid of those thoughts?

S: I try to picture other things, like him being miserable when he realizes he is stuck. I try to picture that relationship turning out really bad, and me being happy. I try to make it different in my thoughts. Like one time I thought of myself taking a huge paintbrush and painting the picture of him all black until it disappeared. (*Giggles*)

DC: Oh really! How did that work out for you?

S: GREAT! I just made it disappear. Made them disappear! (*Laughs*)

DC: (*Laughing also*) Have you thought of any other ways to make them disappear in your thoughts? Any funny or ridiculous ways?

S: Well, yes, you might think this is stupid ...

DC: Stupid is good! Stupid can keep you from sad thoughts, plus I'm sure knowing you I'll think it is funny, not stupid.

S: Well I saw this Star Trek movie once, and I think they put Spock in a pod and sent him out to space, out to the stars. The pod got really small, tiny, till you couldn't see the pod anymore, it disappeared into the universe. Well I pictured putting Jim in there and pushing a button to send him away. (*Laughs*)

DC: Sounds like a good solution! What else have you tried that has worked?

S: Well, I've thought of other ways of making the picture and the thoughts disappear — like pushing a button and have him go through a trap door or something.

DC: These sound great! How are they helpful to you?

S: Yes, they crack me up and they just change my mood totally. I start laughing to myself and I can't even cry anymore.

DC: It's like you are an expert at disappearing acts! What a magician! So can you spend time practicing these disappearing acts over the next few days?

S: Yes, that and starting to do a few things and pay my bills, I'm going to start there.

DC: You know I am also thinking of someone else I know who changed her ex into a cartoon character every time she thought of him and started to feel upset. I believe she started picturing him as Bullwinkle with a Mickey Mouse head. (*We both laugh.*)

S: Oh my god! That is so funny. I'll have to see what cartoon I could turn Jim into. I think that would work for me. How could you keep crying then?

DC: Right! So can you keep practicing these magic tricks and cartoon scenes?

S: Yes, I'm going to try to do that a lot. It totally changes my mood.

Co-constructing solutions involves the therapist leading the client with probing solution-focused questions, and further probing to enable the client to develop her own unique solutions. Susan often utilized humor to remove the power of hurtful thoughts and shift her focus to humorous versions of the events of her life, sometimes even to the ridiculous and absurd. Susan always had a good sense of humor, which she often utilized as a way to interrupt patterns of sadness and paralysis. I wanted to maximize Susan's unique sense of humor, since it was a solution that worked well for her. I chose to view this as an inherent strength to be further developed, rather than an unproductive defense. Humor became a tool in therapy to interrupt unhelpful thought patterns. It also joined us together as "teammates" in solution construction.

Susan remained in the lead in constructing solutions, with my remaining in the stance of guide, coach, and partner. The co-construction of solutions in the initial stages of separation and divorce provided Susan with the necessary tools for beginning to feel competent and hopeful that she could survive this life crisis and heal herself. My acting as "co-sponsor" for her enabled her to feel she had an "emotional home base" where she could explore her most painful, distressed feelings, her most embarrassing thoughts, and her worst fears and doubts about herself. Firmly maintaining a solution focus on my part required that I not be drawn into exploration of detailed descriptions of her "complaints," symptoms, and worst feelings.

Rather, focusing on the exceptions to the symptoms/complaints proved to be critical to establishing the seeds of hope that Susan could recover. I maintained a focus on good days, good weeks, and projecting her to a future week in which she was already feeling better. Also, focusing her on looking back from an improved future week was a good way to begin to interrupt her cycle of depression and grief. A focus on constructive language such as "When you are feeling better …," "What have you done that has been most helpful?" and "Which of these solutions would be the easiest for you to do?" implies that the client already knows how to solve her dilemma, that she is already doing things that are useful, and can learn to increase those solutions, rather than need to do anything different.

In addition to concrete solutions that could facilitate Susan's getting out of bed and decrease her depression, it was also important to move into cognitive solutions that helped her to diminish somewhat obsessive thoughts about her divorce and the new life she imagined her ex-husband to be leading. From my own personal experience of divorce recovery, it would have been tempting to prescribe solutions for Susan that I thought might be most useful or that might have worked for me. Keeping within the Ericksonian frame of reference, I chose to encourage and honor the solutions that were unique creations of Susan's own capacity for healing.

LEAVING BEHIND BLAME, SHAME, AND GUILT: WEAVING A NEW LIFE STORY

As Susan began to stabilize and recover from the trauma of her abrupt marital separation and divorce, it became increasingly evident to me that much of Susan's remaining distress was rooted in destructive social constructions that diminished her view of herself as a woman. It was not her actual experiences; rather, it was internalized stories constructed from beliefs of shame, guilt, and self-blame regarding women who "fail" at marriage. Susan's story was in need of revision. As is typical of many women who divorce at midlife, Susan was trapped between beliefs about the "traditional dream" and an "untraditional" lifestyle.

This new lifestyle, divorced at midlife without children, was in direct opposition to what "was meant to be." The life she was socialized to believe was the only worthwhile life for a woman was that of wife and mother. As her daily functioning improved, work in therapy focused on modifying the meaning of her experiences, in effect, re-storying a new version of her life. This version was more palatable to her and diminished feelings of low self-worth and incompetence. As the story was continually rewoven over time, Susan's capacity to focus on herself as an autonomous competent woman grew in leaps and bounds. Early in our work together, Susan's story revolved around feelings of abandonment and her perceived responsibility for the failure of the relationship. In retrospect, Susan reviewed her original version of the story:

S: I remember in the beginning days I thought his leaving was the worst thing that could possibly happen to me. It was devastating. All I could think about was what was wrong with ME. It must have been my fault because HE left ME. I felt so much pain about being abandoned. And then what was wrong with ME that he left. I thought, why didn't he want me anymore? I must not have been good enough at this, or good enough at that. I felt like it was my responsibility to make it work, and I had failed. Then on top of it the fact that he left for another relationship, it was just devastating back then. I thought I was going out of my mind with sadness and blaming myself. That's what made me feel I was "out on the ledge alone." I remember you said when I felt that way, you would come out there with me. It just helped to know I wasn't really going crazy and you understood what was upsetting me.

DC: We've talked a lot over these couple of years about that story being untrue. And we've talked about other explanations for what happened with your marriage.

S: Yes, I remember one of the first things you said to me that totally stuck in my head and helped me when I felt the worst. You said no one person is 100% responsible for any relationship, that it's always at least 50-50. That helped a lot. Actually, you showed me that it couldn't have possibly been all my fault, that was SUCH a ridiculous idea.

DC: How has that original story changed for you now looking back?

S: I realize now I hadn't been happy in the marriage for a long time. I thought about leaving over many years, and I just couldn't do it. On anniversaries and birthdays, I can remember laying in bed and saying, "I don't want this to be forever, it can't be." I knew I wasn't happy, but I wouldn't have left. Maybe I forced the situation, but I couldn't be the one to leave. I think for a long time I knew it was over, I just couldn't do anything about it. Now in retrospect I think it was the best thing that ever happened to me.

DC: That's a much more believable story than you totally blaming yourself. So on some level you had a sense of knowing for a long time that the marriage was not right. Even though you couldn't be the one to leave, you sensed you were going to be out of it at some point?

S: Now I think I did force the issue on some level. I think intellectually I did push him away. I used to imagine someone else being there, or being by myself. I think I made it difficult for him to stay, but it was my way of ending the relationship. It was the only way I could do it.

DC: That was very brave of you to get yourself out of it in that way. Many women never find their way out and stay for many, many years knowing they are unhappy at the core.

S: Before I would have said that it was because there was another woman, but now I see that was just a symptom of a bad marriage. I didn't even know what I was doing when I got together with him. I just did it. And now I think it was a matter of getting up the courage to get him to leave, you know, changing and growing up. I think we changed and grew, and actually grew apart. I started to become much more my own person, and he eventually didn't like that. I think for me it didn't last because I started to see that he didn't have a spine, and he wouldn't stand up for me.

DC: So you are able to see it as maybe a growth process that you started early in your life before you were even grown up enough to know what you wanted?

S: Yes, and you couldn't know what you wanted, that didn't figure into it. It was just this dream that you were supposed to live by. I guess for a long time I always felt stuck between these two different dreams. One was to meet the man, get married, have kids, and live happily ever after. Then when I got separated, it was like oh my god, I have to meet the next man and get married as quickly as possible. And I thought I still was supposed to want the kids. The other dream kept coming back, though. The one where I was seeing myself moving on with my life on my own. I went back and forth, and that's where I felt stuck. I have no sure idea why. I just couldn't shake the old dream off.

DC: That old dream surely was very powerful in its hold on you before you took hold of it.

S: I think I vacillated for a long time, although I couldn't see it. I didn't have a clear idea of what I really wanted to do. I felt paralyzed. There were always these two camps of thought. What my dream was, I had these two different ideas. That was a problem. I just wish I could have said THIS WAY or THAT WAY. I wish I could say I made a decision one way or another about what is okay, but I couldn't, and it was just killing me.

DC: So you finally used your courage to choose the dream you really wanted.

S: I did! (*Smiles*) Now I say I know I made mistakes in the relationship, but that is much different than thinking it was totally my fault, like I did in the beginning. You know you think the woman is the one who is supposed to keep it going. Men look elsewhere, and don't think they need to look within themselves, then they just end up in the same place in the next relationship. I don't even think about it anymore, blaming myself. It doesn't hurt anymore. Now I think too bad for him that he never dealt with himself.

DC: If you could put it in a sentence or two, what would you say?

S: I would say that I have gone from feeling like a complete victim who was abandoned, like poor me, to something totally different. Now I feel like I was courageous to get him to leave so I could move on to a better life. That marriage was destroying me emotionally year by year.

The process of conversation in which linguistics were utilized to change core narratives was an important part of Susan's therapy. Over several years of our work together, many conversations focused on Susan's beliefs about the reasons for her early marriage and subsequent divorce. Eventually Susan was able to look back and connect to a sense of self-knowing that had whispered to her for many years. Although she was unable to act to initiate her separation, reframing her experience to brave acts of "getting her husband to leave" placed her in a position of power and competence, rather than victimization and abandonment. Her husband's entering another relationship was initially a considerable source of distress for Susan. In time, her story was reframed to one in which her ex-husband avoided issues and ran away from the troubles in their marriage. Susan eventually viewed his entering quickly into another relationship as avoidance and dependence. In time Susan learned that that relationship did indeed result in a second divorce for Jim.

The reconstruction of the meaning of loss proved to be a critical intervention in Susan's treatment. In joint conversations, we focused on shifting her story from a narrative of loss, victimization, and abandonment to one of survivorship and courage. Stories that empower women to connect to their sense of knowing, restore control and choice, validate feelings of anger, and shift blame, shame, and guilt are critical to their recovery. Deconstruction of stories based in denigration of women's feelings can change the meaning of their divorce experience from loss to gain. Such an important paradigm shift is often critical to their ability to recover and move forward in their new role as a woman divorced at midlife without children.

SEEN AND HEARD: ON BECOMING AN AUTONOMOUS COMPETENT WOMAN

Exiting the role of wife and potential mother and entering the realm of "woman alone" can often cause considerable emotional distress for women post-divorce. Many times an original marital contract is based upon a woman's tacit agreement to be dependent, silent, and competent at self-care. The necessity to be competent and care for oneself after divorce is often at odds with prescribed role expectations and can result in a state of cognitive dissonance. Exiting marriage and the role of wife often requires that a woman call forward strengths that have been stifled, as well as develop new traits and coping skills that support autonomous competence: the capacity to care for oneself.

In order for a woman to embrace her development as an autonomous competent woman, a major paradigm shift in self-concept is often necessary. Adaptation requires a redefinition of self and restructuring of the self-concept apart from traditional roles. There are many aspects of adaptation to the roles of non-wife, non-mother, dating woman, and midlife woman.

Such was the case with Susan. In addition to modifying the meaning of her experiences of marriage, divorce, and single life, her internalized self-concept was also a critical area requiring meaning modification. Like many other women, Susan had internalized a self-concept that was rooted in patriarchal socialization. The meanings she attached to dependence/independence, incompetence/competence, and silence/voice trapped her in a state of extreme discomfort with her new role. A complex web of expectations regarding being a "good" and successful wife/woman required that Susan be silent, dependent, not too competent, and certainly not angry.

After her divorce, Susan often experienced periods of unexplainable distress and anger. In deconstructing the underlying beliefs of this distress, we unearthed traditional beliefs regarding the devaluation of competence. Also, beliefs were entrenched that she *should* be cared for by a man, financially as well as in all other aspects of her life. Susan was raised in a family of origin in which all of the women were dependent on men for financial well-being as well as many aspects of daily living. The women in her family also did not leave their marriages, even if they were unhappy or emotionally abused. Susan believed the theme she had learned was "any man is better than no man." In her family the role of wife was very much the traditional caretaking role.

Even though on the surface she herself did not believe in this role, she found she had fallen into it in young adulthood. Although Susan was a very bright, creative, humorous person with very strong views, she had stifled many of her strengths to stay in her marriage. Her perception was that as she became her own person and became stronger, the marriage no longer worked. As she was faced with the prospect of living alone and caring for herself, these internal narrative struggles surfaced. A few years into treatment, Susan came in one day feeling distraught, tearful, and angry. Her distress seemed to center around two interconnected themes of self-care and silence. We began:

DC: You look upset today, what's going on?

S: Everything's wrong. I'm having a lot of trouble at work, and I think there is a chance I might lose my job, be laid off. And I've been holding in my feelings about EVERYTHING, and now I'm thinking all these other feelings, angry.

DC: What's the anger about do you think?

S: Well, if I lose my job, I don't know what I'll do. I don't have a backup. And it's making me feel angry about the divorce. You know, almost all my friends, they have a partner, so if one of them loses their job, they can still manage. Now I'm just so panicked and scared, but more angry, like why do I have to do this? And I have been holding it all in and then exploding over little things.

DC: Sounds like we have a couple of things going on here. Let's try to slow down a little bit and take them one at a time. What do you mean why do you have to do this?

S: This, all of this, being alone, paying all the bills, worry about how I will make it, worry about how to fix a lightbulb, worry about who will be there if anything happens to me. I am angry about taking care of myself totally. I never thought that was me. I feel afraid to make decisions about things. Big things. Little things. I have not been comfortable about certain things, you know, about money, buying a car, deciding where to live, deciding what to do with money. You know, totally taking care of myself. It makes me angry. Sometimes I feel paralyzed. I notice indecision about committing to things. Sometimes I get so scared and I think, Oh my god, I don't have a backup. I'm so sick of it. It makes me so angry.

DC: So you mean taking care of yourself since you are single?

S: I guess that's it. I'm so angry about it. It wasn't supposed to happen this way. You know, when I was married he did a lot of things I didn't have to do. I never paid a bill. I didn't even know how to balance the checkbook. And I never had to worry about things like the lightbulb or buying a car by myself.

DC: So the anger is about losing that person who was supposed to take care of you?

S: I can't quite figure it out, I just feel so much anger.

At this point I decided a deconstruction exercise with Susan might be helpful in order to unearth the core beliefs that might be underlying her feelings of anger and distress. Such an exercise is often helpful in partializing destructive beliefs and can provide the basis for reconstructing new core beliefs.

DC: Susan, I'm going to ask you to do an exercise with me. This might help us get to what is making you feel so much anger. It might seem repetitive and annoying while we are doing it, but usually it helps us discover important things. Are you willing to do this with me?

S: Yes, I'll give it a try.

DC: I'm going to keep asking you questions and asking you to continue answering until we don't have anymore new answers. So let's start with you are feeling angry. What do you believe about that?

S: I'm angry because I have to do everything by myself.

DC: Your belief about that is what?

S: I think most other women don't have to do all this stuff that I have to do by myself and I feel jealous of them.

DC: Your belief about that is what?

S: I don't want to do all this stuff by myself. I want it to be back to the way I was when I was married.

DC: Your belief about that is what?

S: That he should still be there taking care of everything, taking care of me, keeping me safe.

DC: Your belief about that is what?

S: That I want to be taken care of. I deserve that.

DC: Your belief about taking care of yourself is what?

S: I think I know I CAN do it. I HAVE been doing it for three years now, but I just don't want it and I feel so angry about it.

DC: And you believe what about that?

S: I want to be taken care of because I never got it really when I was little.

DC: Your belief about that is what?

S: A couple of things. I guess I was raised to see the men in my family taking care of the women, and they were smart but they never did anything for themselves. It was like this unspoken thing, that all you did was be the wife not your own person. Then I feel my parents really weren't there for me emotionally. I got good physical care, but emotional, no.

DC: What do you believe about that?

S: I guess that's where so much anger comes in too, like why didn't they take care of me?

DC: And what do you believe about that, about your parents?

S: I never thought about what I believed the cause of it was, I have just spent so many years being angry at them for what I didn't get. Like why didn't they give me what I needed? I hate them for it.

DC: What's your belief about that?

S: I guess I don't really believe they are bad or mean people. They just had their limits in their own way, and they both had really rough childhoods, broken families, lots of craziness.

DC: What beliefs are there about you when you think of all this?

S: (***Looks down and starts to cry***) I guess with both the divorce and my family, I think it must be something about me, like why didn't they love me, Jim and my parents both? Why didn't they take care of me the way they should?

DC: Is there something else you believe about you?

S: I guess what it always comes back to in my head is that I wasn't wanted, in the marriage, or in my family. I didn't feel wanted. And I think that it is my fault. (*Crying*)

DC: What do you believe about it being your fault?

S: I don't know. Now I am just getting confused. It's more sad than an angry thing. I didn't do anything. I was a good kid. I was always well behaved, and I always did good in school. And in the marriage. I was a good wife. I wasn't lazy, took good care of him, I was always there, never cheated or anything like that.

DC: Does this make any sense to you that this is your fault?

S: No, No. (*Crying*) I guess the anger is a lot of sadness I have been saving up, and it wasn't about me.

DC: No, Susan, it wasn't about you.

Susan continues to weep as we sit silently for awhile.

DC: Susan, I think that you have been stuck blaming yourself for where you are now. And you, like all other women, have grown up being told we SHOULD be taken care of, even if we can do it ourselves. It's not really okay to be the strong woman who takes care of herself. But here you are now. And you have to take care of you, and you HAVE been doing it. Actually, I have been REALLY impressed with how well you have been doing it. You have gotten two promotions, you have taken care of a lot of important things in your life. I know you feel scared, but you are doing it anyway.

S: I feel like I am stuck in some old idea that I should have been like June Cleaver and just stayed home in the apron. And here I had to ruin everything by getting the divorce.

DC: Seems to me like you saved yourself, not ruined anything. We've talked a lot about how you felt the marriage was "killing you emotionally little by little" [her words]. We've also talked about how you couldn't take it anymore, how on some level you had a sense of knowing for many years you wanted out. You never saw yourself REALLY as June Cleaver, did you?

S: (*Laughs*) NO! God forbid! I never really wanted that. It's just you feel like you SHOULD, like June Cleaver should be enough, and it never was for me. I tried to play it, but over the years there was just this nagging sense like this wasn't right. It's just you get stuck with these old ideas. Like I really know in my heart that I am doing good at taking care of me. When I hit a bump in the road all the old feelings come up. The anger, about expecting someone else to do it for me.

DC: So I think this is just a LITTLE bump in the road. You always manage to fly over the bump and keep on going! Pedal to the metal! (*We both laugh.*)

S: You are right. Every time I have come in feeling scared or angry like this, I have found ways to get myself out of it and keep on going. I always get my confidence back. It's just living every day. Getting up and going to work. Making decisions on my own. I also think my sense of humor has helped a lot too.

We continued on in solution-focused conversation facilitating Susan's plan for getting herself to move on from these feelings, and reinforcing practical self-care skills. Susan's fears about self-care were also interwoven with issues of silence that exacerbated her feelings of anger and distress. The issue of silence and inability to speak was also a major area of work in therapy. All of her relationships had been characterized by silence and passivity. We continued on in the session:

DC: We have talked so much about silence and how that is not good for you, and how much a part of all your relationships that has been.

S: I know we kind of came to the conclusion that that was my part in what went wrong with my marriage, that I had all these feelings and things that were upsetting me and I never said a word about it. I didn't say what I needed. I never even knew I could. I just knew you were supposed to accept whatever was going on, that's the way it was.

DC: How do you think you learned that?

S: Well, that's what I saw in the marriages in my family. It kind of went along with any man being better than no man. And as kids we were pretty much told to be quiet, you know, not make any waves.

DC: So speaking up meant making waves? What did that mean in the family?

S: Making waves, making trouble, and mostly getting my parents upset. There wasn't supposed to be any upset in the family.

DC: So you learned pretty early that speaking up about what you needed and what was upsetting you was the same as making trouble. So expressing feelings, anger, and conflict was a bad thing?

S: Oh yes, that was forbidden.

DC: So in our work together we have been talking about how actually staying silent seems to make things much worse for you, with what you feel inside, and then the way you eventually explode.

S: Yes, I want to find a way out of the silence, but it just feels so hard to break the old pattern.

DC: So what used to happen when anybody said anything in the family, what was the price you had to pay?

S: Screaming, dishes flying across the room when you least expected it, or silent treatment because you made trouble.

DC: Wow, must have been pretty scary. And in your marriage what happened when you tried to speak up?

S: Well mostly I didn't, but if I tried there was just this stonewalling kind of silence, kind of like living with the sphinx. Then if we actually did have a discussion it was always defensive and he would turn it around on me, blame me, never admit his part.

DC: So you haven't had such great experiences with speaking up and conversations that lead to positive things.

S: No.

DC: Well let's think about where in your life you have had good experiences with speaking, and who its the easiest to speak with.

S: Probably my best friend, Lynn. It's been different with her.

DC: In what way?

S: I can say anything and I do. It's just easy with her. She never gets defensive, and I'm not afraid I'll lose her, that just wouldn't happen.

DC: You have found words to say things to her?

S: Yes, I never really thought about not having the words with her. They just come. Because I trust her, I am not afraid of making a mistake or being rejected.

DC: So you already do know how to speak and not hold things in, we just have to get you to practice doing more of what you already know how to do. What progress do you feel you've been making with that?

S: I'm still having a lot of trouble. I can't find any words to speak in most situations other than with Lynn when I want to. I just don't even know what to say. I just get so paralyzed. There are things going on with my family that I am not happy with and I don't say anything. And the same thing at work and with my friends. I just don't deal with anything, then it catches up to me and I'm just walking around so angry all the time.

DC: Of the areas you mentioned, which would be the easiest area to practice speaking the way you do with Lynn?

S: Well, I have this issue with Lynn that has been going on for 20 years, that I have been wanting to talk to her about, and I've never brought it up, but it has bothered me for a long time. She's an amazing friend. I trust her. She sometimes gets short with me and hangs up on me too quickly, and I've never told her how much it bothers me. I think if I brought it up she would accept it and it wouldn't jeopardize our friendship. That probably would be easier than any other area. Work would be too risky right now because if I lost it and didn't do it well, I could lose my job.

DC: So what would you think of continuing to practice with Lynn and coming up with some solutions for practicing speaking at work eventually? We can use that issue. Then once you are more successful practicing words you can use the same words for other areas too.

S: Yes, if you can help me with the words. I'll try to practice it with her.

DC: I know you have the words inside you, we just have to get you to bring them out and practice them.

S: You know the other day at work, one of my co-workers was very rude to me, and now that I think about it, I did find what to say. In a nutshell I said, "You will not treat me this way. I am not accepting this." I guess the words are somewhere inside like you said.

DC: That seems like an important thing to say, "You will not treat me this way." I like the respect that you are claiming by feeling that way about yourself now, and for being able to speak it.

For Susan, the issue of becoming an autonomous competent woman and using her voice was initially counterintuitive. A dichotomy of traditional and untraditional beliefs about dependence/independence and silence/voice continued to resurface as core issues for our therapeutic work together over several years. Destructive beliefs were woven through internalized stories of Susan's childhood experience in her family of origin, as well as her marriage. We continued to deconstruct these beliefs and reconstruct narratives that reinforced her capabilities in self-care skills and using her voice. Therapeutic conversation focused on modifying the meanings she attached to becoming competent and able to speak for herself. By combining this with a consistent solution focus, we continued to build coping skills and competence. Susan's ability to "step out of her silence" and speak in all areas of her life was a major goal of treatment. Over time a new story was woven that validated Susan as a successfully autonomous competent self, able to be seen and heard.

INNER RESOLVE: THE CAPACITY TO CONNECT AND BE ALONE

After the initial exit from the role of wife, Susan adapted well to the experience of being single, living alone, and being without children. Susan developed a good capacity to be alone, while still maintaining enough relational connections to meet her emotional needs. Susan's need for relationship differed from Sara's. In comparison, Susan did not have an intense need for one significant other in the way that Sara did. She found living alone quite appealing, and loneliness was not especially an area of distress for her. Her post-divorce adjustment revolved much more around issues of competence, self-care, and silence.

Susan did make efforts to expand her connections shortly after her separation, probably more out of a sense of panic and beliefs regarding finding a boyfriend or second husband as quickly as possible. Originally she began a panicked frenzy of socializing, sometimes with people she really did not have much in common with. Eventually she became more selective with her friendships, enjoyed having a few close, long-term friends, and appreciated her ability to "be a homebody." Susan's distress revolved more around strained relationships with her family. Work focused on improving her family connections and exploring family of origin experiences that seemed to impact her post-divorce adult relationships. Some of her family relationships expanded and improved, others did not. Eventually Susan was able to accept the limitations of her family relationships, as well as to appreciate the benefits of them.

Susan was able to review her progress in moving from her initial fears of exiting the role of wife and being alone:

S: Originally I was freaked out. I was running. I would do anything not to be alone. At some point things changed. I'm not running anymore. I used to be terrified to be alone, especially when my husband had to go away when I was still married. Then when I got separated, it was just unbearable. And now I don't have an issue with it. I like myself, and I never would have thought that I would have liked that as much as I do. When I was first separated I just couldn't go home. I was in every support group there was. And now I truly love going home by myself. I have no problem going out and not seeing anybody. I am absolutely sometimes in my glory. I have this list of lots of things I want to do. Someone asked me if the list was a way of running away. I think it is trying to live a happy life!

I do a lot of different things. I like to try new adventures. People had asked me what my hobbies were when I was married and I had none. I think now people say, "Oh, you are so lucky, you can go wherever you want whenever you want." Now I love having the whole bed to myself, and all the closet space. During the week, there is no difference, my life is pretty much the same as when I was married. On the weekend I either have friends or I don't. In a way it is the same, there is just not another person sitting there watching TV. There's a part of me — well I never lived on my own. I definitely enjoy the fact that I don't HAVE to do anything. I go home and its my space. I can make the bed or not make the bed.

DC: Sounds like you are comfortable with the way your life is now?

S: Now I am. I've learned how to make decisions. Of all the things I think I might have resolved, I think fear of being alone is one. I think I've totally resolved it. There is something very peaceful about it. Now I think I do have an inner strength that comes out when I need it, an inner resolve.

CHAPTER 4

The Developing Midlife Woman

Setting the Stage

> In our culture the development of women has been blocked at the physiological level with, in many cases, no higher need recognized than the need for love and sexual satisfaction. Even the need for self respect, self esteem, and for the esteem of others, the desire for strength, for achievement, for adequacy, for mastery and competence, for confidence in the face of the world, and for independence and freedom, is not clearly recognized for women.
>
> **—Betty Friedan, *The Feminine Mystique* (1997, p. 315)**

In addition to understanding the social context and trends that have contributed to the emergence of women divorced at midlife without children, a theoretical framework is needed to understand the issues, dilemmas, and developmental challenges these women face. Specific clinical approaches are also needed to ground the clinical work and provide guidelines for assessment and treatment strategies.

It is important, however, to consider that theories are also social constructions that are a product of the era in which they develop and reflect the social thinking of those times. Pro-natalist, pro-marriage theories that are restrictive and utilize rigid stages about women's development need to be revisited and viewed in the context of the patriarchal culture in which they were originally constructed. Theories that become reified over time serve to paralyze creativity and rigidify professional thinking. Such reification can minimize the therapist's capacity to search with the client for her own unique solutions.

In general, developmental life cycle theories have stopped short of inclusion of mature single adulthood without children as a normative developmental stage (Dafoe & Popenoe, 2006; Carter & McGoldrick, 1999). Although developmental theories have been somewhat expanded to be more inclusive of women's unique development, there has not been comprehensive consideration of women divorced at midlife without children. Broader criteria for women's development as mature single adults without children need to be included in developmental life cycle theories. Further, theory needs to incorporate recent shifts in women's roles and options.

I do not view either the theoretical framework or the clinical approach presented here as a prescription for assessment and treatment. In the Ericksonian tradition, it is my belief that each client brings her own unique capacities for internal healing and development. The treatment approach needs to remain flexible enough to incorporate the client's individualized revisions of her life story, as well as her own solutions for improved functioning.

In the family therapy tradition, I view my clinical stance within these frameworks as multipositional and nonjudgmental. Although a progressive feminist stance is important as one approaches this work, it is equally important not to judge women who cannot break the powerful emotional ties to traditional role expectations. I view it as my responsibility to be able to accept all possible solutions the client brings that allow me to sponsor her toward health and growth.

Some clients have developed very creative solutions in adapting to the role of divorced woman at midlife without children. These have included part-time relationships, focusing intensely on work relationships and creative achievements, and expanding relationships with friends and extended family members (Casey, 2007). Others have decided to remain alone for extended periods of time in the belief that this challenge will enable them to grow more competent and self-sufficient. Some have viewed periods alone as preparation for a healthier and more fulfilling relationship to come. Still others have made commitments to remaining permanently alone and design fulfilling lives as mature, single adults. Other women have experienced overwhelming discomfort and have been unable to venture into periods of being alone. For those who feel they cannot be without a primary relationship, it is important to be equally supportive to facilitate development of coping skills and solutions that work for them.

An example is Sara, whose case will be described more fully in Part III of the book. Sara came to me for treatment after experiences with a few other therapists that she viewed as frustrating and not helpful. Although Sara's goal was to become more comfortable being alone while hoping for a good relationship, she experienced panic symptoms when actually faced with this circumstance. Sara felt stuck and unable to change her pattern of needing a relationship to be "okay." She viewed this process as temporary and as "practice for the right one." Sara had not really dated much before her early marriage at age 20, had been married throughout young adulthood, and had never lived alone.

Creatively, she had always managed to find a new relationship at the exact moment she most needed one. In the eight years since her midlife divorce, she had not been without some form of relationship for more than a few months. Most were at least several years in duration, one was a long-term friendship. Her relationships were usually at least partially fulfilling to her and, in her view, provided her with some basic emotional needs and a sense of stability. As time progressed, she was increasingly able to avoid or leave relationships she knew were not potentially healthy partnerships. At the very least, she required close, committed friendship.

Sara left her previous therapy when her therapist took a somewhat adversarial position that she must be without a relationship for an extended period of time to improve her capacity to be alone and to prepare herself to attract a "real" relationship. She was also told that these relationships represented a pattern of fear of real intimacy, emotional dysfunction, and weakness. Sara came away from that experience feeling blamed and misunderstood. Sara felt there was an irreparable disconnection between her and her therapist. She felt misunderstood regarding her dilemmas, "stuckness" in her pattern, and feelings of panic about being alone. Although ostensibly the client and therapist had the same outcome for therapy in mind, how to get there was a source of contention between them, rather than a mutual goal. Sara felt her intuition about how and when to get where she wanted to go was misunderstood. In her description, she had experienced the previous therapy as adversarial, rather than collaborative. She had not felt fully "sponsored" and, as a result, chose to search for a different therapist.

Sara tried out periods of aloneness at her own speed. In therapy we explored the positives of the relationships she did have and normalized her need for healthy, intimate connection. As time passed, Sara's need to always be in relationship lessened. She was able to tolerate and enjoy longer periods of being alone, and began to turn down dating possibilities and relationships that did not seem like appropriate potential long-term mates for her. Eventually she reached a place of comfort with a full complement of relationships with a significant other, a close friendship network, and improved relationships with immediate and extended family. Remarkably, panic symptoms eventually disappeared, without ever being a primary focus of the treatment.

My goal in working with Sara was not to fit her into rigid theories that might lead to a focus on dysfunction and viewing her as resistant. Rather, looking at Sara's case from several applicable knowledge bases that enabled me to join with her proved to be very useful. From the social constructionist perspective, I understood Sara's inability to shake the powerful invalidating and devaluing messages she had internalized about her new role. It was also important to explore and understand the complex meaning she attached to being alone. From the feminist perspective, I understood her intense need for attachment, relationship, and connection. Sara had been attached to someone all her life. As she continued to adjust to her role of being divorced at midlife without children, I framed her continuing need for relationship as a strength and attempted solution that was part of her own individualized growth process. In the family context, I also understood that as a woman without a spouse and children, she was struggling to gain a place for herself in her family of origin. In terms of her individual development, Sara was attempting to build strengths and capacities she had never used before to innovate new roles for herself and cope with a very different lifestyle. These perspectives facilitated my ability to sponsor Sara's growth in her own time, with no prescribed solutions. Rather, she was the architect of her own process of growth and development.

From an Ericksonian perspective, I viewed her consistent ability to find a new relationship at critical moments of intolerable loneliness as an ingenious strength and critical survival skill. This solution needed to be accepted at face value as Sara's struggle toward growth. Framing her behavior in therapeutic dialogue as a continual progression toward her healing proved to be a critical intervention. This enabled me to "be with" Sara at the core of her dilemma. It also provided hope and expectation of change and facilitated a trust in our relationship that enabled her to strive toward her eventual goals of increasing her capacity to be alone, conquering her panic symptoms, and hopefully finding a permanent relationship, or being able to accept the absence of one and thrive anyway.

In light of the stereotyping and stigmatizing that have followed women who are not wives and mothers, it is important that theory and treatment break free from these negative traditions, and that client and therapist alike are able to challenge these traditional ideas in creative ways. For me, it is important to remember that I do not walk in clients' shoes, I do not know what is best for them, nor do I know the consequences of change for each one. In light of this, I suggest the knowledge bases presented here not as a rigid prescription, but rather as a useful starting point to be expanded upon and challenged. I view the framework presented here as a guide for understanding the theoretical thinking that has gone before, what is currently useful, and what needs revision to keep pace with changing social issues. For the experienced clinician, this section may serve more as a review. For students, this chapter may be viewed as an introduction to relevant theories needing further study.

RELEVANT THEORIES

Several theories have had an impact on the formulation of my thinking and practice. I view these as critical in thinking about women who are divorced at midlife without children. It is important to note that although I am separating these theories out for the purposes of clarity and presentation, I view them as an intertwined complex system of ideologies. These theories have provided me with a comprehensive knowledge base and overarching framework for approaching this work, as well as my work with women in general. They are social constructionism, feminist developmental theory, role theory, the family developmental life cycle, ego psychology, and Erik Erikson's developmental theory.

Social Constructionism

The theory of social constructionism is a critical concept for understanding how women view their experiences of divorce and potential childlessness. It is a central organizing principle that not only is relevant for work with these women, but also must be considered a powerful core concept that impacts how all women experience and interpret their world. In a society where patriarchy has been deeply rooted for generations, beliefs about women's roles, marriage, divorce, motherhood, delayed childbearing, and childlessness must be viewed as social constructions that are embedded within a complex web of meaning. These meanings have been internalized into women's psyches and, left unchallenged, often drive women's behaviors unconsciously throughout their lifetimes.

Social construction theory is a "postmodern" concept that suggests there is no reality and no universal truth. Rather, individuals create their own reality through mental constructions, perceptions, and beliefs that are institutionalized in society over time (Gergen, 1985, 1991). It emphasizes the location of an individual's perceived reality within a complex social system, in which reality is co-created by human interaction, language, and socially agreed upon meanings. Social interaction generates meaning for people regarding their lives, and suggests that identity is constructed through a process of relationships with others in a continuously changing social context. This meaning is attached to identity and life experiences and is embedded within a dominant social order. It is viewed as subjective, not a universal, objective "truth" that exists outside the person. Meaning is organized and stabilized by the complexity of social processes that are generated over time.

In the social constructionist perspective, meaning is discovered, transmitted, and institutionalized through language and discourse. Language provides order to the world, and in traditional Western thought has been viewed as representing reality. The views, perceptions, and beliefs that individuals construct become evident through the stories and labels they construct about them. A polyocular view suggests that many alternative stories are always possibilities (deShazer, 1985; White & Epston, 1990). deShazer (1994) suggests that stories or narratives are a product of the complex interaction of the individual, outside observers, and the interaction between the two; social processes; and systems. Walter and Peller (2000) suggest that individual stories are shaped and impacted by the dominant cultural scripts that are available at particular points in time, and that the broader sociopolitical context of individuals lives must be considered.

Social constructions that support the preferences for marriage and motherhood are pervasively entrenched in Western society. Women grow up socialized into beliefs that marriage and motherhood are universally desirable conditions that are prerequisites to a fulfilling life (Letherby, 2002; Park, 2002). The roles of wife and mother have been the core symbolic values upon which women's identity has been anchored. Occupying a role and status different from those that are most valued and preferred could be a source of considerable emotional distress for women. Such deviation has traditionally been considered anti-natalist and anti-family.

Sclater's (1999) work on women's experience of divorce suggests that many social constructions about divorce, the meanings attached to it, and women's reactions to it, discount their feelings and experience. Sclater also suggested that women's experience of divorce and the associated range of feelings have been somewhat silent in the professional literature. Some divorce discourses focus on harmonious outcomes, the well-being of children, and condone the suppression of women's feelings of anger, resentment, and rage. Marriage is still preferred, and when one does divorce it should be a "good" divorce (Ahrons, 1994).

Childless women represent a challenge to the prevailing cultural discourses that still elevate motherhood. Even though these premises may have changed over the last few decades, research indicates that discourses that invalidate, exclude, and stigmatize women are still quite pervasive. Socially constructed stigma that arises for potential non-wives and non-mothers has powerful impact and meaning, and often becomes evident in treatment through the narrative stories women tell. These pejorative scripts can be closely bound to symptoms and inability to cope with a life circumstance outside the norm. As women at midlife experience divorce and potential childlessness, exploration of meaning attached to this role becomes a critical area of intervention in therapy. It has been my experience in practice that women's behavior and decision making is often unconsciously driven by these internalized social constructions and meanings. It is critical for effective treatment to give full consideration to the social constructions women have internalized regarding identity, roles, and life experiences. A primary goal of therapy is to bring these internalized meanings into awareness and help women identify what beliefs have driven their behavior and decision making. In effect, a major component of treatment with this group is the facilitation of deconstruction and disengagement from negative meanings attached to less valued roles, and modification and reconstruction of meanings into more positive scripts.

Since therapy is discourse between client and therapist that reflects societal "grand narratives," the language and conversation that occurs in the therapy room can have powerful implications for women's ability to change the narratives of their life stories. In effect, every question, in fact, every statement we make in the role of therapist, is in itself an intervention. Both positive and negative conversation about relationships, marriage, divorce, childbearing, and childlessness serve as direct and indirect suggestions to the conscious and unconscious. Positive stories with reconstructed meanings that facilitate healing and growth can minimize perceived distress and provide a fundamental basis for coping and recovery.

An important tool for the therapist is the self-observing capacity to be vigilant about socially constructed narratives internalized regarding negative biases about women who are not wives or mothers. Self-awareness of transmitting these beliefs to the client in the process of therapeutic discourse is an important skill. The social constructionist perspective in work with these women is a critical starting point, because it is a core organizing principle upon which all else follows.

The Feminist Perspective on Women's Development

Feminist developmental theory informs us regarding the impact of divorce and childlessness on women by providing a context for understanding the importance of attachment, connection, mothering, and responsibility for relationship as central to women's well-being. Miller's classic work (1976) stresses the meaning of loss of relationships to women, as not simply object loss, but rather as loss of identity and core sense of self. Gilligan (1982) also stresses that the end of relationship, especially at midlife, can threaten a woman's sense of worth and lead to melancholia, depression, and despair. Walters et al. (1988) focus on the importance of understanding that relationship loss places women at risk for severe loneliness and meaninglessness, due to the centrality of attachment to their sense of self. In effect, if a woman is unattached, not in relationship, and not caring for others, she may feel a core sense of detachment and estrangement.

Much of the feminist literature of the past several decades has focused attention on normalizing and validating aspects of women's development such as empathy, caring, and a sense of self that develops within relationship and mutual connection to others. Miller (1976) called for a "new psychology" that validated a pattern of development for women centered on the importance of attachment and affiliation with others. She also identified the central concept of women's sense of self-being closely tied to the capacity to develop and maintain relationships.

Developmental theory has evolved to acknowledge that girls develop through connection, differing from a male model of development through separation. Chodorow's classic work (1978) on the reproduction of mothering posited a theory of female intrapsychic and intersubjective development centered on mothering and the mother-daughter relationship. Chodorow placed this relationship at the core of women's sense of self. Her central premise focused on the replication of mothering, as mothers produce daughters with mothering capacities and the desire to mother. Chodorow discussed women's desire to mother and concludes that women's mothering is reproduced on a multiplicity of levels: individually, socially, and culturally. In an updated introduction to her book 20 years after its original publication, Chodorow acknowledged that not all women choose to mother; however, the generalization of her theory still stands, given that most women do mother and gain gratification from it.

Gilligan (1982) also identified significant gaps in developmental theory regarding women. Differences between male and female development, and a focus on the central importance of connection, attachment, and relationships to women as a core aspect of their development and identity have been placed at the center of feminist thought. In this view, identity and intimacy are fused for women, as they define themselves through their ability to care for and protect others. Gilligan identifies prominent discourses in the "voices" of women. These included themes of universal need for compassion and caring, the importance of morality, responsibility for relationships, and reluctance to hurt others at the expense of one's own needs. One can surely anticipate the emotional difficulty that arises for women who decide to step out of relationship and connection by divorcing and not mothering.

The feminist mothering literature places motherhood at the center of women's developmental theory and is somewhat exclusive of women who remain childless, either by delay, design, or default. There has been some criticism that not enough has been done to question the "mother equals woman equation." This literature is also somewhat polarizing, considering mothers' experience as the core of femininity, and in effect "erasing" non-mothers from the developmental equation (Morell, 1993). Women's experience of childlessness remains primarily invisible throughout much of the literature. Even the frequently used terms of *childless*, *childfree*, and *non-mother* define women by what they are not, rather than as women with their own special identity and developmental path. Chodorow did, however, comment on recent societal changes and the increase of women who choose not to mother. Although she did not support a view of "unnaturalness" or deviancy, comprehensive suggestion in her work regarding how these women might be included in developmental theory is lacking. Women who "resist" motherhood challenge us to rethink the prevailing constructions on women's development (Morell, 1993).

Women divorced at midlife without children have grown up psychologically socialized into patriarchal, institutionalized beliefs regarding marriage and mothering. In effect, their status places them out of this expected norm. Understanding the tremendous impact of the absence of relationship for women, as well as the incredible efforts many women will make to attempt to repair this gap, is critical. The attachment, connection, and relationship that most women experience through marriage and motherhood are absent for these women, and may be a considerable source of distress for some. It is equally important to prepare ourselves to accept the experience of women who may not experience such distress, and for whom alternate roles may be ego-syntonic. Framing clinical work through the lens of the feminist perspective provides a guide for therapists for thinking about how women adjust, given overwhelming dominant discourses that still link women's identity closely to marriage and motherhood.

While integrating feminist developmental theory solidly into thinking and practice, it is equally important to "push the theoretical envelope" further to explore views, beliefs, and social constructions that may challenge long-held premises. Given recent dramatic social change, normalizing and validating women who develop in healthy ways outside the roles of wife and mother is a key component of treatment. The "woman equals wife and mother" construction needs to be broken. Alternate roles need to be no longer viewed as alternatives, but rather as valid developmental paths in their own right.

Role Theory

Women divorced at midlife without children are faced with the task of exiting the roles of wife and potential mother, which represents major loss and transition. The exit from these central roles may cause considerable stress for women. A variety of perceptions regarding exiting current roles, transitioning to alternate roles, and creating new roles in the post-divorce period can have an impact on women's capacity to recover and adjust. The ability to successfully adapt to new roles has been considered a hallmark of completed divorce adjustment (Lund, 1990).

Social role theory suggests that individuals are linked to the social environment through the roles they play. Roles represent the joint boundary between the individual and social systems. A role is a set of expectations concerning patterns of behaviors performed as a part of occupying a specific social position (Norlin & Chess, 1988). Several key concepts of social role theory, including role exit and role orientation, have particular relevance for these women due to the centrality of role loss and change in the experiences of both divorce and potential childlessness.

The roles of wife and mother have been the primary social roles traditionally prescribed as central to women's identity and well-being. Adjustment to the loss of these roles is a central task of recovery. The meaning individuals attach to role identities and role loss has implications for their mental health. Meaning attached to role identities and role loss can be associated with considerable symptoms and distress. Exiting the role of wife after divorce has been determined to be a turning point for women and a lengthy, complex process with personal, social, and economic factors (McDaniel, Kusgen, & Coleman, 2003).

Exit from a role that is central to one's identity involves a process of disengagement, distancing, and creation of new identities. The process of divorce involves exiting a primary role identity. For these women, this marks the loss of the socially valued status of wife and mother, and entry into roles of ex-wife/non-spouse and childless/non-mother, which are connected with stigma and devaluation. The stress of the divorce experience may be exacerbated by the fact that there is no culturally defined or acceptable ritual to mark the exit from marriage and the role of wife. Divorce is usually experienced as a major rupture in expected role orientation for women. The meaning and value women attach to their roles affect the ways in which they may adapt to divorce.

Role orientation has also been found to be a factor in women's adaptation to divorce. It has been conceptualized that women whose role orientation is "traditional" desire to maintain pre-divorce roles. Those who are "modifiers" have a traditional orientation, but are more open to change of roles. Those who are "career directed" have a greater ability to develop roles separate from that of wife. Kaufman (2000) also reports that traditional versus nontraditional role orientations regarding the roles of wife and mother impact adaptation to divorce and single life. Nontraditional role orientation is also reported to be a factor in choices regarding career, marriage, and childbearing for women (Reading & Amatea, 1986).

It is also important to note that the roles of "initiator" or "non-initiator" of divorce have an impact on the role exit experience and post-divorce adjustment. Initiators more easily define themselves as single and tend not to carry over aspects of the marital role. Non-initiators are more likely to view themselves as ex-spouses and to maintain this role identity as a core aspect of their self-concept (Duran-Aydintug, 1995).

Social role and role exit theory guide us to consider how women successfully exit prescribed roles and effectively adapt to the social environment through the process of role innovation. Helping women creatively innovate new, fulfilling roles for themselves in the post-divorce, post-childbearing phase is a major component of treatment. Shifting our thinking toward the normalization of alternative roles is equally important.

The Family Developmental Life Cycle

It is especially important to consider the family context for women divorced without children, due to the isolative nature of the role itself. The family developmental life cycle (FDLC) provides a framework for viewing a woman's development from the broader context of her position within an extended family's life over time. It is important to link women to their family of origin, rather than view them as moving forward in isolation (Kaslow & Linzer Schwartz, 1987). This provides a perspective for issues of primary importance to these women, including postponed marriage, delayed childbearing, divorce at midlife, and childlessness.

FDLC is a useful backdrop because it incorporates life cycle measures as summary indicators against which to measure various life events and crises. From a systemic perspective, this helps us to view the woman as a part of a larger, multigenerational system moving through time (Carter & McGoldrick, 1988). A woman's experience can be viewed with a focus on patterns, expansions, contractions, and transitions of an extended family over its life course. The family is also viewed within the larger context of society and its cultural expectations and variations. Expectable transitions and developmental tasks for the family at each transition are central components of the theory. Stages of family development have traditionally centered on marriage, childbearing, and the raising and launching of children. Families are presumed to experience crisis points that are accompanied by complex family role changes.

The family developmental life cycle has traditionally positioned marriage and parenting at the core stages of family development, and the roles of wife and mother have been central organizing principles (Carter & McGoldrick, 1988). In recent years, the FDLC has been restructured to include divorce as a normative life cycle event. Divorce is now more commonly viewed as a normative family crisis that shifts equilibrium and results in interruption of traditional life cycle roles. Postponed marriage and delayed childbearing have also been considered variations that reflect social change.

For midlife women, the divorce crisis requires a transition out of familiar family roles and is further complicated by the life cycle tasks of midlife and aging. While there has been much focus on remarriage, step-parenting, and single parenting, little attention has been paid to women who are divorced at midlife without children. It is important to consider how these women continue on the life cycle course as a part of a complex family system, given that they are "out of sync" with normative stages.

The FDLC also provides a theoretical underpinning for the concept of delayed/postponed childbearing. From the multigenerational family perspective, it is important to consider the stressors and vulnerabilities that exist for women who delay childbearing, as well as those who are eventually permanently childlessness by either choice or default. Poelker and Baldwin (1999) suggest that delayed childbearing impacts a number of life cycle issues and tasks. It places a woman out of sync with her peers and may have extensive ripple effects throughout the family system. Issues such as relationships with and expectations of potential grandparents, aunts and uncles, cousins, and siblings are important issues to keep in mind when working with this group.

There has been little inclusion of childlessness in the FDLC, other than to mention it as a variation in family form. The most recent model of the FDLC failed to include discussion regarding women who do not desire motherhood (Carter & McGoldrick, 1999). Childlessness is discussed from the perspective of unwanted involuntary childlessness. The experience of women with low or ambivalent desire for children is still absent from this literature. Assumptions still remain regarding childless women as bereft, sad, and experiencing intensely painful feelings regarding the absence of children (Carter & McGoldrick, 1999).

Although some expansion and revision of the FDLC has occurred regarding divorce and single adulthood, revision has stopped short of inclusion of mature single adulthood as a normative life cycle stage. It has been suggested that autonomous functioning is equated with disconnection (Carter & McGoldrick, 1999). This theory needs to be updated to normalize and include women who do not desire or have children. It also needs further expansion to include the stage of mature single adulthood for those women who choose not to marry or have children, or who divorce and do not remarry. Generally speaking, inclusion of this stage is also necessary to incorporate the normative life experiences of all mature single adults who reach this stage via various life experiences.

Since these women are part of complex family systems developing and transitioning over time, it is important that treatment include discussion and intervention regarding the impact of their role status on changing family relationships and future family development. As women experience expectable life stages such as loss of older generations, illnesses, and other transitions, it is important to recognize they will journey through these experiences as single adults, without the supports of spouses and children. It is useful to incorporate less rigid stages of family development into clinical thinking, and consider women in the multigenerational growth of the family in a way that also normalizes their development as single women. A broader focus on transition points renders this theory more inclusive of women who do not fit into the traditional time frames and stages. The FDLC concepts of normative stages as societal expectations, crisis points and transitions, developmental tasks, and role changes are all important areas to consider when working with this group.

Ego Psychology and Adaptation to the Social Environment

Assessment of the individual woman from the perspective of ego capacities, strengths, and coping is an important concept to consider, given the life crises of divorce and childlessness these women experience. Ego psychology provides a theoretical framework for the individual's response to crisis through the use of ego capacities and coping mechanisms, and informs our work with women regarding the individual's functioning within the social environment (Goldstein, 1984).

It is important to view women's symptoms from the lens of a "gendered" environment, rather than from the perspective of pathology (Goldstein, 1984; Walters et al., 1988). Individual assessment must incorporate issues that stem from women's socialization in a patriarchal environment. Behaviors that are common to women include passivity, lack of assertiveness, difficulty expressing anger, self-sacrifice, and self-destructiveness. Anxiety, depression, eating disorders, and substance abuse are maladaptive responses to crisis that are also common to women. Special attention needs to be paid to the issues of discrimination, stigmatization, financial deficits, and lack of supports.

Ego psychology focuses on the ego as the component of the personality responsible for mediating between the internal needs of the person and his or her adaptation to the external world (Hartmann, 1939). Ego functions are the essential means by which the individual adapts to the external world and mediates conflicts, trauma, stress, and role transitions. This theory considers the impact of the environment, external events, and crisis on the individual. The ego is critical in helping adults adapt to crises that may overwhelm them and diminish or paralyze normal problem-solving abilities. At intense times of crisis or stress, all adults have the capacity to become vulnerable, and may not possess enough internal and external resources to effectively adapt. Anxiety and fear in these times may signal defense mechanisms into action. This may result in a higher level of functioning as the crisis is mastered. Individuals may also develop maladaptive defenses in order to cope. This perspective is a helpful approach for assessing how an individual is adapting to a life event or crisis within the overarching context of the social environment. It is important to consider if impairments are a function of situational events, ego functioning, current life roles or transitions, lack of environmental resources, or lack of fit between ego capacities and the environment (Goldstein, 1984).

This is a useful theory in providing a framework for the exploration of how women cope with unexpected life crises and the events of midlife divorce and childlessness. It has been well documented that divorce is a traumatic event with profound consequences (Gillespie, 2000; Heatherington, 2003). Subsequent stresses include depression, anxiety, anger, loneliness, bitterness, psychosomatic symptoms, and financial pressures (Wallerstein, 1986). Other authors suggest that the crisis of divorce can lead to increased ego capacities of self-esteem, self-confidence, independence, and mastery and achievement.

However, it is important to be aware of past theoretical discourses that have utilized components of ego psychology to pathologize variances in women's childbearing decision making, voluntary childlessness, and decision for divorce. Popenoe (1936) viewed reasons given for childlessness as rationalizations used as a defense against the anxiety of the childbearing decision-making process. Gutman (1995) suggested that the process of delayed childbearing in couples involves avoidance of intense conflicts and ambivalence and the utilization of denial rationalization, and avoidance to mask these conflicts. Projection is sometimes discussed as a possible defense mechanism regarding childless couples' views regarding negative perceptions about their childless status. Nave-Herz (1989) also suggested that denial and projection are defenses utilized to ward off anxiety and ambivalence regarding childbearing. This historical context of a "deficit perspective" has been incorporated into clinical thinking, and it is important to guard against transmission of these limiting views to the client.

Ego psychology can be a useful concept for assessing a woman's ability to improve functioning, develop ego capacities and strengths, and adapt in a patriarchal social environment. From this perspective, divorce and childfree status can be viewed as growth-enhancing opportunities that can result in increased mastery in key areas of functioning. This theory is a useful guide for inclusion of questions in therapy regarding overall functioning, ego capacities, coping skills, and strengths, and adaptation to the social environment.

Erikson's Individual Life Cycle

Erik Erikson's individual developmental life cycle theory provides a developmental, psychosocial framework that enables one to view women on a trajectory of the individual life cycle with associated developmental tasks. Although it is a theory that views the individual's development in isolation rather than in an intergenerational family context, it is a useful model for understanding women's functioning in relation to normative adult developmental tasks and challenges. Midlife divorce and potential childlessness can be viewed as life cycle crises in need of resolution. This theory also suggests these events can be viewed as opportunities for individual growth and development, in accordance with Erikson's expectable, successive crises of life span.

Erikson identified eight psychosocial stages of the life cycle, and proposed an epigenetic principle in which individuals must resolve specific conflicts in order to cope successfully with later stages (Erikson, 1950, 1968). How an individual copes with the tasks of each stage can effect the course of future development either positively or negatively. Stages of Erikson's model relevant for these women are young adulthood and middle adulthood. Erikson's theory of individual development and expectable stages is based on premises that equate intimacy in young adulthood with partnering, and generativity in middle adulthood with the raising of children. According to Erikson, the central task for young adulthood is resolution of the conflict between intimacy and isolation, via full commitment and connection in an intimate relationship.

The hallmark of Erikson's stage of middle adulthood is completion of the task of generativity. Although Erikson mentioned commitments to society and work in this stage, the primary task involves moving beyond self and partner to the raising of future generations as the route to generativity (Erikson, 1950, 1968). Erikson also viewed generativity as broader than physical production of children, requiring concern and care for the future generations. It is suggested in his model that those who do not complete this task successfully may experience a midlife crisis of stagnation, self-indulgence, personal impoverishment, and lack of intimate commitments. In his view, while altruism, productivity, and creativity are part of generativity, they do not replace it. It is suggested that any event or crisis resulting in isolation and lack of connection can place the individual at risk for emotional difficulty, physical symptoms, or even psychopathology throughout later stages (Erikson, 1950, 1968; Zimbardo & Gerrig, 1996).

Feminist writers have critiqued Erikson's work due to his equation of a theory of human development with a theory of male development to which female development is then compared. This was reflected in his language and frequent use of male examples. Several areas of critique include the importance given to a woman's body as a determinant of identity, personality, and behavior; a double standard of male and female behavior; and the use of the male as the prototype human being to which the female is compared. The specific development of girls and women is sparsely mentioned in his work. The role of women in Erikson's theory is clearly centered on partnering and mothering

(Williams, 1987). As in much of the life span literature, a clearly pro-natalist bias exists in Erikson's schema that excludes women without children.

Erikson suggested that childfree partnerships may result in "an isolation a deux," that is, one that protects both partners from facing the subsequent stage of generativity. The view that procreation is an instinctual drive, and is also women's biological destiny, is supported (Erikson, 1950, 1982). His conceptualization of the "inner space," the womb, supported the idea that women's somatic design predisposed them to identify with motherhood, and uniquely determined women's identity and adaptation to life. It is acknowledged that intimacy and generativity are significantly related to childbearing; however, in Erikson's schema, little acknowledgment of women's development separate from childbearing exists (Erikson, 1950, 1968). Childfree women are viewed as defying the epigenetic law of generativity and at odds with natural psychosocial forces. This theory also suggests that this behavior is a repression of instinctual drive and a denial of the resulting loss.

Although Erikson's model is useful in providing a base from which to view the individual development along a continuum, it is somewhat limiting and exclusive. Lack of professional agreement exists regarding Erikson's belief that adults could be generative in ways other than bearing children. There was some apparent revision by Erikson to include creativity and productivity, and in later texts he allowed for a variety of activities other than parenthood (Erikson, 1975; Shober, 1994).

Overall, in his schema, there has been little attention to the issue of women who divorce and are without an intimate partner at midlife, at a point in the life cycle when the capacity for childbearing is diminishing. In effect, his theory leaves unmarried, childless women out of the model, despite the fact that they still continue on with individual development through their life cycle. Concepts challenging childbearing as an "automatic" instinctual desire, and inclusion of ambivalent or low desire for children also need to be incorporated into life cycle theory. The absence of significant psychological difficulty and symptoms found in women who are not wives and mothers leads to reconsideration of Erikson's theory. Erikson's perspective of these women as developmentally "stagnant" needs revision and reconstruction. Healthy functioning and development outside the roles of wife and mother need to be validated rather than viewed as maladjustment. The concepts of intimacy and generativity need to be broadened to include women who accomplish completion of these life cycle stages in a multiplicity of different and functional ways.

Reification of rigid developmental premises from this perspective is not especially useful when working with women who are divorced, have not remarried, do not have a permanent, intimate relationship, and do not have children. Consideration needs to be given to expanded options for women to achieve connection, intimacy, and generativity. While Erikson's theory does provide a useful individual developmental framework, the absence of focus on women's development apart from the roles of wife and mother clearly represents a gap in this schema. Given recent social change, this gap surely needs revision.

In summary, as one approaches treatment with women divorced at midlife without children, it is important to begin with an overarching contextual framework that captures the complexity of the social and political environment in which they live. Social constructionism provides an understanding of the powerful impact of constructed meaning on women living outside traditionally prescribed social roles. Feminist developmental theory informs our understanding of women's needs for connection, attachment, and relationship, and the impact of absence of these. Social role and role exit theory facilitates an understanding of the complex dilemmas women face who exit the roles of wife and potential mother for less preferred roles. The family developmental life cycle provides a context to view individual women within the system of the family of origin as it moves through time, stages, and transitions. In addition to understanding these contextual issues, it is also important to utilize a knowledge base for understanding the individual developmental challenges for these women. Ego psychology provides a useful frame for assessing a woman's ego functioning, strengths, and ability to adapt to a "gendered" environment. Erik Erikson's developmental model of individual life cycle stages was suggested as a useful theory to frame the individual life cycle tasks and developmental issues along an expectable continuum. From the meta-position of this knowledge base, we can seek to understand and organize the complexity of experience for women divorced at midlife without children.

CHAPTER 5

Midlife Divorce for Women in a Married World

But the mandate survives, if under an assumed name. Today its message is delivered "underground" through the negative images of single women conveyed daily by the media. These images surreptitiously communicate some of our culture's most traditional and destructive myths about women, marriage, and being single.

—Carol Anderson and Susan Stewart, *Flying Solo: Single Women at Midlife* (1994, p. 64)

MIDLIFE DIVORCE ADJUSTMENT FOR WOMEN: OVERVIEW

Although the prevalence of marriage has decreased in recent decades, Western society is still marriage and couple centered. Significant stressors still exist for divorced women who are faced with the task of recovering against an array of social odds. A woman's world can be shaken by divorce at midlife, just when other potentially stressful developmental milestones and tasks come into play. As physical changes, aging parents, loss of family members and friends, the possibility of illness, and awareness of one's mortality come to the foreground, the additional losses inherent in midlife divorce can be challenging at best, and traumatic at worst. Midlife divorce is undoubtedly a complex transition, requiring a major life readjustment. The simultaneous convergence of three major life stressors, divorce, midlife, and childlessness, exacerbate the divorce experience for women (Slater, Banks, & Henderson, 2003).

Given the historically gendered nature of divorce, the dissolution of marriage unquestionably impacts women differently than it does men. Women tend to experience more distress than men in the divorce process, often struggling with not only the emotional impact, but also an array of stressors including major role exit and transition, possible decrease in social activity and relationships, and financial stressors.

The double standards of a patriarchal society in which men's economic and social value often increases and women's perceived value often decreases are evident. Women's experience is further complicated by ageism and the social expectations of a youth-oriented society. The social value of men is also perceived to increase with age, whereas the social value of women clearly is perceived to decrease.

Women who have followed the trend of remaining single throughout young adulthood and delaying marriage may have the opportunity to develop different coping capacities and responses to midlife divorce than women of previous generations. In effect, being single and living alone is currently a much more common experience that provides women with a sense of competence and ability to care for themselves. Belief in these skills and sense of self-competence often is absent in more traditionally oriented women who have not been single for most or all of their early adulthood.

The deeper emotional aspects of women's divorce experience have not been examined fully and are for the most part silent in the divorce literature. Much of the existing literature takes a traditional stance, suggesting a harmonious, friendly divorce is desired, primarily for the sake of children (Ahrons, 1994). Ahrons suggested that divorce should be a "good divorce," in which the goals are ongoing harmonious relationships, remaining a family (although binuclear instead of nuclear), restraining anger, and maintaining healing cordiality. The goal of a good divorce is for all parties to emerge in recovery with a healthy level of functioning. Although the goal of harmonious divorce and cooperation for the well-being of children is a valuable concept, one must wonder where this leaves women in terms of their ability to voice and validate their true emotional experience of divorce. In effect, the process of divorce is not good, and the expectation that it be so keeps us bound to the traditions of denial and the silencing of women's deeper feelings. It diminishes them as full human beings with a range of deep emotions in need of expression. Under the best of circumstances, it represents major loss, trauma, and disappointment. Ahron's view has been contradicted in research that validates the disadvantages women face emotionally and financially in divorce (Wallerstein, 1986).

Sclater (1999) addressed this issue of the suppression of women's divorce experience and concluded that culturally available scripts regarding divorce are limited and tend to silence and pathologize the deeper emotional aspects of the experience for women. Divorce stories of the current era are still embedded with social constructions that intend to deny the meaning of the divorce experience for women. The stifling of emotions is all too universal in women's experience in general. It should not be surprising that women are expected to divorce the same way they are expected to be in the world in general, by maintaining the silence of their true experience. It is important to recognize that stories of anger, victimization, betrayal, and continuous attachment are important to the integration of the experience for women. Research has validated that women's divorce recovery is enhanced by the expression of anger and maintaining a stance that minimizes self-blame. Even narrative stories of villainy and blame of the ex-spouse have been found to improve women's divorce recovery and overall functioning. Narratives of strength, survivorship, and fighting spirit are also important to recovery (Sclater, 1999; Wallerstein, 1986).

Most women view the success of their marriage as their sole responsibility and primary source of connection. Women are socialized early in life to define themselves through relationship. Divorce can catapult a woman into an unanticipated role for which she feels ill prepared. In fact, traits that are beneficial to positive divorce adjustment such as independence, assertiveness, and even healthy aggressiveness are dysphoric for many women (Walters et al., 1988). Due to socialized meanings about the importance of marriage and women's success in relationship, even the most highly functional, educated, accomplished women may react to divorce with fear, anxiety, confusion, and feelings of abandonment and rejection.

Given the increase in midlife divorce for women in the last few decades, and its normalization as a life cycle event, one would think this new cultural acceptance would have resulted in diminished stigma and less distress for women. Even though divorce has become more acceptable, by no means has the stigmatization and denigration of divorced women been eradicated. The trauma women experience is still significant and evident in the narrative stories divorced women relate about their experiences. These stories are undoubtedly reflections of the overarching social context of patriarchy that pervasively colors women's life experiences and perceptions. Devaluation of divorced women has deep cultural roots that have been institutionalized into Western society since Victorian times (Abrams, 2000; Basch, 1999). Although these times may seem distant, in effect, the remnants of these demoralizing ideals are still at the core American culture. In order to understand the modern-day impact of divorce on women, it is important to understand the depth of stigmatization that still persists, with roots in these earlier eras.

The social constructions and morals of the Victorian and Revolutionary eras are the underpinnings of negative societal attitudes toward divorce and divorced women. Victorian ideology espoused the view that the roles of wife and mother were sacred and presumed, and, as such, they were the ultimate in fulfillment for women. Self-sacrifice and innate virtue were glorified, and wives and mothers were the icons of social structure. The tasks of keeping the nuclear family stable and secure clearly were the responsibility of women. A woman's wifely duty also included obedience and responsibility for keeping the man from "straying." In turn, marriage was viewed as providing women with financial and emotional security. Women were also valued as "property" and valued for their childbearing capacities in terms of their ability to produce heirs. In effect, marriage was the route to maintaining patriarchal authority over women (Basch, 1999).

The gendered nature of divorce also was evident in these early times. Divorce was primarily a man's prerogative, and the initiation of divorce by women was almost nonexistent. Divorce was associated with moral decay, corruption, subversiveness, and shame. Conservatives feared divorce would shake the foundations of social order. Remarriage was also viewed with disdain as a mark of impurity. In this era, divorce and remarriage were often deleted from family histories due to the extreme shame and embarrassment they evoked. These cultural norms of previous eras have not simply disappeared, and undoubtedly have left an emotional legacy in the psyche of society, despite much progress and social change. The concept of single woman is still primarily defined as "woman without a man," and carries with it socially mandated shame, stigma, and devaluation.

It is important for clinicians to keep these socially constructed underpinnings in view as a frame for the divorce experience of women. One must go beyond a rigid view of the stages of divorce and adjustment and incorporate underlying structural and societal issues that have a major impact on not only on women's perceptions of themselves as they divorce, but also their capacity to recover. Divorce is entrenched in a patriarchal culture embedded with meaning regarding marriage, childbearing, and divorce. Prevailing patriarchal assumptions are an essential part of women's social upbringing. These assumptions shape a woman's conscious and unconscious views of self and have a pervasive impact on many important life decisions. Many women find it difficult to "loosen" themselves from these assumptions, and this in turn can be a stumbling block to divorce recovery. Walters et al. (1988) suggested that clinicians need to be aware of gendered messages and social constructs that frame and limit women's behaviors. These include the real limitations of women's access to social and economic resources, sexist constructs that restrict women in directing and developing their own lives, and the belief that women alone are responsible for the success of relationships.

Adjustment can be severely impeded by entrenched beliefs regarding a woman's value in relation to her attachment to a man through marriage. Many women find it difficult to disconnect from the belief that they should be taken care of on multiple levels by a man, and that they cannot be successful or happy without such support. This belief seems unrelated to a woman's actual competence, and seems to exist on a core level, even when a woman's real functioning belies this belief.

Adaptation to divorce also seems to bear a relationship to traditional versus nontraditional beliefs. "Traditional belief" women seem to have the most difficulty shifting their focus away from the marital relationship and role of wife, have difficulty reorganizing, and report more emotional conflict and depression. In effect, the more traditional and conservative a woman is in her views, the more emotionally difficult it can be to break away from traditional role expectations. A more feminine (traditional) orientation seems to be related to more passive, conventional reasons for divorce. "Feminine orientation women" marry earlier, stay married longer, are older at the time of divorce, less educated, economically more dependent on husbands, and experience more depression. More traditional oriented women also tend to hold on to dysfunctional marriages longer.

In effect, the less traditional and conservative a woman's views, the less trauma she experiences throughout the divorce process. Less traditional expectations of marriage and child rearing and more interest in education and career can affect women's initial expectation of marriage, as well as expectation of divorce and subsequent adjustment (Hansson et al., 1984). Women who have more progressive views about their own ability to modify their roles adapted more rapidly and are able to develop new roles more quickly after divorce. "Career-directed" women seem to adapt most rapidly, as they already have experience functioning effectively in different roles prior to divorce. In effect, the major shift in roles brought about by divorce is not as much of a trauma or challenge for these less traditional women (Wijnberg & Holmes, 1992). In their work on divorce adjustment, Hansson et al. (1984) found that "less traditional women" experience less depression, have a lower sense of dependency, and greater sense of accomplishment and confidence.

In therapy, women often reveal these biases in descriptions of their everyday experiences. Many women report assumptions by others that surface in conversation and validate the ongoing stigmatization of divorced women. Consistent comments and questioning from family and friends can be quite distressing. Questions such as "Have you found anyone yet?" "How are you handling being alone?" and "How do you manage?" all reveal biases that presume divorced women must be unhappy without a spouse and children, and must undoubtedly be in search of a man. Many of the women in the research study reported that although they themselves were quite content with their lives, the perceptions and comments of others were sometimes more distressing than how they actually felt.

One client poignantly stated:

> You know some people, friends, acquaintances, and even an aunt of mine, the first thing they always ask me is if I have met anyone yet. It's like they don't care about the rest of the things I am doing in my life, and like I don't exist as a whole person if I haven't found anyone yet. I am so much more than that. There are so many advantages to living alone and having complete independence and freedom. Sure I get lonely at times and there is the need for closeness and caring, but it doesn't devastate me. Mostly I feel contented, and at moments I think, Gee my life is great just as it is. My happiness no longer depends on "getting" a man. Why can't they see that?

In the long term, divorce can be growth producing and development enhancing for many women, who often learn to develop new skills and coping capacities that increase their post-divorce functioning. The well-being and functioning of divorced women sometimes surpasses the well-being of women who are either newly married or in long-term marriages (Bursik, 1991). In fact, many women express relief regarding exiting the role of wife, stating they do not miss the role of caretaker or the emotional responsibility for the relationship. Three areas of consideration regarding midlife divorce adjustment follow here: the precipitating factors of midlife divorce, impact of midlife divorce on women, and clinical issues.

THE PRECIPITATING FACTORS OF MIDLIFE DIVORCE FOR WOMEN

The precipitating factors that contribute to midlife divorce for women have undoubtedly changed over the last half of the 20th century. In earlier decades, it was primarily acceptable for women to divorce only for concrete reasons such as abuse and neglect, financial nonsupport, or alcoholism. Rarely, if ever, did women choose divorce to meet unfulfilled emotional needs and pursue a desire for happiness. In keeping pace with the cultural changes of the present era, precipitating reasons for divorce for women have shifted dramatically. Women have become much more able to express their needs and expectations of marriage as more emotionally fulfilling and intimate than in previous eras. They have also become more able to voice desire for emotional connection, intimacy, appreciation, personal freedom and independence, and support for career and life goals. Women are more frequently leaving marriages at midlife that are characterized by disconnection, lack of emotional fulfillment, and lack of support for their life and career goals. Women's ability to actually leave unsatisfactory marriages has been greatly enhanced by the increase in higher education for women, improvement in career opportunities, and real capacity to earn more money and financially support themselves (Enright, 2004).

TAKING STOCK: THE PROCESS OF MIDLIFE REVIEW

Though there are a complexity of multiple determining factors for midlife divorce, the midlife developmental crisis or transition is a primary factor that has often been cited. The occurrence of midlife divorce has been found to be related to developmental issues and transitions that frequently occur in the stage of midlife. Developmentally, the stage of midlife and the associated "midlife crisis" are typically characterized by processes of life review, reassessment of life goals, increased awareness of mortality, and associated role transitions. The midlife crisis often results in a period of personal disorganization and reorganization that impacts relationships and role expectations. A sense that "time is running out" often drives individuals to take risks not taken at earlier stages in life. Issues that were somehow manageable before midlife can become critical factors that cause a major shift in the marital relationship.

A variety of reasons exist for the deterioration of marriage in midlife. These include affairs, abuse, diminishing companionship, lack of communication, lack of affection, lack of validation from spouse, and desire for more independence. Other reasons given for midlife divorce include the disappearance of love, lack of verbal and physical affection, lack of attraction to spouse over time, and general dissatisfaction with marriage (Enright, 2004).

It should be noted that many midlife divorces occur after marriages of 20 years or more. Multiple causes come into play for these long-term marriages. Divorce often follows a decrease in marital stability and satisfaction, and a long period of decision making, sometimes over a decade or more (Langelier & Deckert, 1978). Divorce after a long marriage tends to bring high amounts of stress as well as high amounts of relief for these longer-term couples. Consideration also needs to be given to precipitating factors for midlife divorce for shorter-duration marriages, given the current trends toward delayed marriage. In effect, what shifts occur for couples who marry in their 30s and 40s after extended single status in young adulthood, and subsequently divorce at midlife?

In relation to longer-term marriages, younger age at first marriage seems to have a negative effect on marital stability at midlife, in that lack of maturity seems to contribute to marital disruption (Wu & Penning, 1997). In effect, those who marry in early adulthood usually marry after a shorter "search period," increasing the likelihood of a mismatch. Although these longer-term marriages seem to start well, the quality of many of these relationships seems to deteriorate over time. These longer-term couples report a decrease in pleasurable time spent together, with some stating their marriages were never right to begin with, nor were they prepared to deal with marriage at such a young age (Hayes, Stinnet, & Defrain, 1980).

Several precipitating factors are specifically associated with women's decisions to divorce at midlife. Women who maintain less traditional viewpoints about women's roles are more willing to act on needs for self-actualization and independence. Women with higher education and the absence of children have also been found to be more likely to divorce at midlife (Wu & Penning, 1997). Many women in the process of midlife divorce reveal an increasing desire for freedom and happiness. Many also discuss increasing perceptions that their spouse never contributed to their self-esteem, and they disliked the way they had come to feel about themselves in the course of the marriage.

This process of life review, changes in an individual's goals and desires, and a taking stock of one's life can result in couples moving away from each other emotionally at this stage. In their work on midlife divorce, Arnold and McKenry (1986) found that individual midlife transitions for men included an increased focus on expressiveness, nurturing, and being good providers. Women were found to focus more on independence, assertiveness, and achievement. The change in individual needs can cause a rift in the marital contract that previously worked for both members of the couple. These issues can surface in therapy as increasing marital dissatisfaction and a critical need to renegotiate the original marital contract.

These developmental shifts of the individual at midlife can result in couples evaluating the benefits and costs of remaining in marriage. In their work on the determinants of midlife divorce, Lloyd and Zick (1989) found that the perceived benefits of remaining married include companionship, affection, sexual expression, social approval, shared religious beliefs, children, shared memories, and financial security. The costs of remaining married include unfulfilled goals, low interaction, long-term disenchantment, sexual problems, infidelity, physical disability, and other midlife problems. The perceived barriers to divorcing include overall investment in the marriage, dependent children, and lack of social support. Benefits of divorce for men were perceived to be availability of a more appealing spouse. For women, benefits of divorce appear to be perceived availability of a more rewarding lifestyle, more self-actualization, and assertiveness. If a couple perceives that the costs outweigh the benefits of marriage and are unable to formulate a new agreement for their relationship, divorce may become an option.

The increase in economic independence of women over the last several decades has had a positive relationship to the likelihood of their choice for midlife divorce. Women with higher education status are more likely to divorce, given their capacity to earn higher wages. The risk of midlife divorce is associated not only with women's individual economic status, but also with a couple's joint economic status, that is, the higher the economic status, the less the risk of divorce since the consequences are greater economically for the couple. In effect, the accumulation of economic wealth and emotional investment inhibits midlife divorce, and longer marriages are not easily dissolved due to "reservoirs of jointly held economic and emotional capital based on long term investments that are not easily abandoned" (Heidemann, Suhomolinova, & O'Rand, 1998, p. 221).

Let us return once again to Sara, who is a case in point regarding these precipitating factors of midlife divorce. As previously mentioned, Sara's marriage was her first and only adult relationship, having married her first boyfriend in early adulthood. In effect, Sara had a very short search period, with little experience in dating. Sara acknowledged she had not thought through what she wanted in a relationship and felt she had been automatically driven toward marriage. She presumed that was what most women did and said yes to the first guy that showed up with a ring. At the time of this first relationship, tremendous prestige and status was associated with becoming engaged and seemed to be the goal of most young women's experience, although rarely consciously acknowledged or verbalized.

Sara began a process of considering separation and divorce at least five to eight years before her actual separation. In these years of contemplation, Sara seemed to unconsciously prepare for the possibility of divorce. She completed a college degree and was able to improve her financial earning power and ability to take care of herself. This was a major factor in her perceived ability to eventually leave her marriage. She recalled chronic unhappiness and detachment that increased throughout the first decade of her marriage. When she reached the age of 38, Sara felt "something just clicked." In an apparent process of midlife review, she began to imagine herself remaining in her marriage until the end of her life and became increasingly distressed about the thought of staying. There was an increasing urgency about changing her life. She stated, "I thought if I stayed in that marriage and looked back when I was 80 and saw that I never experienced a good relationship or true intimacy, I wouldn't have been able to live with myself." This is a viewpoint that is often echoed in stories of midlife women. Relationships that seem tolerable throughout early adulthood become viewed as mistakes that become intolerable as women begin the process of midlife review and arrive at the midlife transition.

Sara related that the chronic unhappiness and dissatisfaction in her marriage had never been confronted. She maintained the behavior of a good woman, that is, remaining silent about her emotional distress and needs. For a number of years, Sara never entertained the possibility of an open, real conversation with her husband about the lack of intimacy and deterioration of their marriage. In retrospect, she recalled powerful messages from the women in her family of origin regarding the value of remaining silent and not making trouble in marriage. For the majority of the years she was married, she continued to assume sole responsibility for making it work. In her view, intimacy and connection in the marriage deteriorated over the years to the point where it was nonexistent. As Sara began to voice her dissatisfaction with the original marital contract, her husband became more disconnected and silent and was unwilling to work toward improving the marriage. Sara entered therapy on her own due to her increasing distress and desire to leave the marriage. Her husband refused to attend couples therapy, and thus the marital contract was unable to be renegotiated. Over a period of several years in therapy, Sara weighed the benefits and costs of remaining married. When she eventually perceived the costs of remaining were too great, she initiated separation and eventually divorce, finally feeling she had to take the chance to explore what else life held for her.

As women enter into therapy at various stages of the divorce process, it is important to understand and explore the "Why now?"—the precipitators that influence the decision to divorce at midlife, as well as the decision to enter therapy. Exploration of precipitating factors is a critical area to address in therapy in order to help women understand the decisions that have led to their midlife divorce. This exploration should include a review of decisions made in young adulthood, as well as assessment of the woman's response to the stage of midlife. Family of origin relationship patterns and gendered messages to women are important areas of understanding that need to be explored. It is important to facilitate a woman's ability to reconstruct the meaning of her past experience in a useful way that helps her move forward into a healthy adaptation to midlife and beyond.

THE EMOTIONAL IMPACT OF MIDLIFE DIVORCE ON WOMEN

Due to the combined stressors of divorce adjustment and midlife developmental tasks, midlife divorce can be viewed as a crisis with traumatic emotional consequences and serious financial and social repercussions for many women. Divorce recovery at any stage is a multifaceted, complex process with multiple endings and beginnings, and is often viewed as an evolutionary process, rather than as complete at some point in time (McDaniel, Kusgen, & Coleman, 2003). The impact of midlife divorce can be more devastating than in young adulthood due to the multiple stressors and developmental issues that are unique to this life cycle stage. The midlife issues of physical aging, reassessment of life goals and values, coming to terms with the loss of childbearing capacity, and acknowledgment of one's own mortality are exacerbated by the tasks of divorce recovery. These include adjusting to single status, loneliness, reworking identity and roles apart from marriage, loss of in-law family, forming new relationships, and adjusting to financial needs. Issues such as depression, loneliness, anger, poor self-esteem, and anxiety can be significant. Recovery can also be affected by difficulty finding an appropriate partner or remarrying (Marks & Lambert, 1998; Wallerstein, 1986).

In the short term there are undoubtedly major areas of distress that can be anticipated for women. In addition to the emotional impact of divorce, areas of functioning requiring adaptation include formulation of new identity and roles, expansion of family and social relationships, and financial adjustment. Throughout the divorce process, high stress should be considered normative, not pathological. In the initial stages of the divorce crisis, regression and disorganization are common, even for highly functioning women.

In general divorce has been found to be stressful even in the presence of family support, social support, work satisfaction, good child care, and an amicable relationship with ex-spouse. Clinically significant depression is often reported and associated with lingering effects of an emotionally unfulfilling marriage and ongoing consequences of the divorce, such as lack of social support, lower income, lack of social activity, and lack of a romantic partner. Social isolation and lack of a support network seem to be significant factors in lack of adjustment (Thabes, 1997). However, distress does diminish after this initial crisis and many women return to reorganized, normal functioning as time progresses. More recent research indicates that women's functioning can be improved post-divorce, as they gain new skills and coping capacities.

Wallerstein's landmark work on divorce adjustment provided valuable information on the impact of divorce on women at midlife. Her original study examined the impact of divorce on white, middle-class families in northern California. The 1986 follow-up study of her initial work indicated significant age-related differences regarding divorce recovery for women. As Wallerstein stated, "Women in this study who were forty or over at the time of the marital rupture appear to be socially and perhaps psychologically disadvantaged in this rebuilding task" (Wallerstein, 1986, p. 76).

Overall, the persistence of anger, bitterness, and loneliness were still prevalent for women. Despite the passage of a decade or more, feelings of distress and perceived failure had not significantly diminished for this group. Women in the "over 40" group reported ongoing anxiety about living alone, exacerbated by the reality that none had remarried or had a stable relationship at the 10-year mark. One hundred percent reported moderate to severe loneliness. Many of the women over 40 who had been married a significant portion of their adult lives had suffered grave financial difficulties since divorce. Over 50% of the over 40 group also displayed more psychosomatic symptoms and clinical depression. The older group tended to have withdrawn emotional investment in the world and had narrowed their interests and expectations about the possibilities for their lives. It was also evident that the support of friends and family had not alleviated the ongoing emotional strain of divorce. Wallerstein, however, identified positive themes for the older women of increased self-confidence and good self-care.

Wallerstein concluded that the ability to rebuild after divorce was age related. Women in their 40s fared the worst in all age categories. The follow-up group of women divorced in their mid-30s fared much better than the older group. Although loneliness was also prevalent, they were significantly happier overall, had less financial difficulties, reported more career success, and were overall more resilient.

It should be noted that Wallerstein's study is now 20 years old, and ongoing social shifts of the past few decades may now result in outcomes that differ from her original study as well as her 10-year follow-up. Wallerstein's outcomes have been somewhat refuted by more current research. Twelve years later the work of Marks and Lambert (1998) did reconfirm evidence that divorce was more difficult for women in general, with a significant negative effect on psychological well-being associated with remaining single for five or more years. However, Marks and Lambert found that midlife adults had more psychological resilience and capacity to recover from divorce than younger adults. These authors concluded that by midlife, adults had developed increased coping capacities that had an impact on divorce adjustment in positive ways. In effect, midlife adults have had more opportunity to practice coping capacities and responses to various life crises. In some cases, those who remained unmarried reported better well-being in personal growth and autonomy than those who were remarried. This information contradicted previous perspectives of marriage being universally beneficial and midlife divorce being exacerbated by stresses of aging, depression, and struggling with transition (Gander, 1991; Kitson, 1988).

In a more recent study of divorce impact and adjustment, Heatherington (2003) examined the patterns and differences of divorce adjustment of men and women. Her work indicated that although the divorce experience encompasses unhappiness and despair, most women were quite resilient and were able to adapt successfully in two to three years. A substantial number of women in this study described feelings of enhancement and fulfillment post-divorce, having formed substantial positive social relationships, increased supports, and gained new coping skills. In many cases women reported that their emotional functioning and sense of self were improved.

Another factor that impacts a woman's divorce adjustment is the type of support she receives. In therapy it is important to explore topics of sources of support, social networks, and family of origin and kinship support. Questioning and exploration in therapy regarding the nature of social support and its impact are especially important for this group, as women without children may have more difficulty establishing adequate support networks. Women who have a large social network of friends tend to fare better than those who have limited social support. Divorce often results in a loss of an in-law family, something that is often overlooked as a significant loss. Women have described losses of not only parent in-laws, but also sibling in-laws as significant relationship losses. In some cases long-term relationships of 20 years or more with in-laws are cut off abruptly with the initiation of the separation and divorce process, often with no closure. This surely has implications for clinical work with these women. The need for increased connection to extended family of origin and friendship networks is an important focus for therapy, and one aspect of the work is facilitating a woman's ability to expand these networks and relationships in both the pre- and post-divorce stages.

It is also important to explore the type of support an individual woman finds most helpful, as this is not universal. For some women, listening by friends seems to be the most helpful type of support. Emotional support tends to decrease depression and anxiety and to overall boost morale and improve mood. Divorced women seem to benefit most from listening, socialization, and emotional support, rather than provision of material support. In fact, in some research studies on divorce adjustment, it has been found that material and economic support is actually associated with increased long-term stress.

It was concluded that those who receive material support have fewer resources and therefore may experience feelings of inadequacy, incompetence, and loss of autonomy (Miller et al., 1998). In effect, listening, social support, and improved relationships with family tend to buffer the impact of divorce more so than money.

It is important that an approach to therapy for women be individualized and take into consideration variant responses and coping abilities based on age. Although many adjustment issues are generic to all age groups, the reactions of women at 35, over 40, and over 50 usually encompass differences specific to each age group. For example, issues regarding completion of childbearing, menopause, aging, and retirement become more noteworthy in the older subgroups. This was evident in my own research project, in which women revealed nuances in their concerns about adjustment. Women over 45 tended to be much more resolute regarding the completion of childbearing potential and much more concerned about aspects of aging and family losses. Concerns about plans for retirement and the older years came to the forefront for this group as they faced the possibility of entering the next life stage as a single woman without children.

THE ECONOMIC IMPACT OF MIDLIFE DIVORCE

Income adequacy and financial well-being appear to be critical factors in overall divorce adjustment for women. The economic consequences of midlife divorce for women can be pervasive and devastating and can place some at high risk for financial strain or poverty. In many cases women's standard of living decreases dramatically after divorce, and these economic shifts can create tremendous stress that can make recovery difficult. Morgan's (1991) work on the economic impact of divorce for midlife women found that divorce was associated with a loss of economic protection. This is not simply due to divorce alone, but rather a composite of initial choices made before, during, and after marriage and gender inequity in the labor marketplace.

Women tend to be economically more vulnerable than men. There are more concerns for older women who face the retirement phase as a divorced woman. Financial adjustment can have a major impact on a woman's ability to socialize and create a fulfilling lifestyle that enables her to experience a variety of new socialization opportunities. Positive socioeconomic status and work success seem to increase positive self-identity and feelings of competence in divorced women. In effect, positive self-identity is more likely to develop when a women copes on her own and is able to provide successfully for herself financially, rather than depending upon another. Increased economic status is associated with reduced stress and feelings of independence, control, and freedom from hardship and anxiety (Rahav, 2002).

Work identity separate from marriage is essential for good divorce adjustment, and work role is an important buffer of stress for divorced women, and is positively related to self-esteem and inversely related to distress. Employment is often experienced as meaningful and provides social interaction, support, a sense of productivity, and positive distraction that can contribute to psychological well-being (Bisagni & Eckenrode, 1995).

The economic risk of midlife divorce for women is an important area of exploration in therapy, especially in the contemplation and pre-divorce stages. The therapist's role should encompass facilitation of exploration of all the financial consequences of midlife divorce for the client, both short and long term. Financial status is important due to the impact it may have on overall well-being, recovery, and coping capacity. In fact, a woman's economic dependence or independence is a primary factor in her ability to even consider separation and divorce at all.

Women's distress over finances can be exacerbated by loss of friendship networks, neighborhood supports, and drastic changes in the quality and quantity of social activity. In effect, stressful economic circumstances can impact a woman's ability to afford to socialize and create an interesting, fulfilling lifestyle, an important facet of recovery (Heidemann et al., 1998).

The case of Sara illustrates this point. In retrospect, Sara believed she began preparing herself for the possibility of divorce at least a decade before. She returned to college to complete her degree in nursing, with goals of increasing her income and improving her job opportunities and her ability to take care of herself financially. She believed she unconsciously knew this was a critical first step in increasing her ability to actually leave her marriage.

Over the years I have worked with women who have decided to remain in unhappy marriages due to the reality that the economic impact of leaving would be too great to cope with at midlife and beyond. For women who have never supported themselves financially, the prospect of doing so seems daunting. From an Ericksonian perspective, I have viewed it as my responsibility to support their growth and development within whatever lifestyle they choose, whether that be staying married or divorcing. I recall one client who poignantly discussed her feelings of being "trapped" in an emotionally disconnected marriage with an alcoholic husband. She stated:

> I am trying to live my own life and make it as happy as I can, knowing that I don't want to be there, but I have to be financially. I considered leaving and actually stayed away a few times overnight. But I have never supported myself, and I don't feel I could make it on my own now at this stage of life. I live my own life, I make new friends, do fun things I like to do. I just have to pretend in some ways that I am single and living alone, there just happens to be someone there. It works for me. It's the only option I can manage right now.

As a therapist it is sometimes a natural temptation to become entrenched in pursuing a goal of convincing a woman to leave an unfulfilling marriage. From the Ericksonian perspective, her solution can be viewed as the only one that worked for her at that point in her development and growth process. In her view, she created a win-win situation, that is, being able to maintain a financially stable life while at the same time creating a separate life within the confines of marriage. She viewed this as survival. I would not presume to predict if this client would ever be able to improve her situation in a different way. As long as this solution was workable for her, as her "sponsor," my role was to help minimize her distress and understand the pace and timing of her individual growth process. If she could not comprehend being able to survive financially as a divorced woman, it was not in my role to favor a goal that she could not perceive of as within her coping capacity. Exploring the financial dimension of divorce for midlife women is a critical area of investigation in therapy. In a holistic approach to treatment, it is important to recognize and include the practical financial issues that bear a strong relationship to women's capacity to cope emotionally with divorce.

THE CLINICAL ISSUES OF MIDLIFE DIVORCE

Women divorced at midlife are faced with the unique challenges of simultaneous stressors of divorce recovery, midlife, and aging. The clinical issues for women divorced at midlife can be categorized into a two general components. These components encompass issues of loss and grieving and the adjustment issues of midlife. In effect, women are vulnerable to this "double whammy" associated with the combination of divorce and midlife and aging. Treatment needs to encompass the interplay between mental health issues, social structure, and the socialization of women. The emotional, physical, and socioeconomic impact needs full exploration in therapy at all stages: pre-, during, and post-divorce. In addition to facilitating women's adjustment to the immediate crisis of divorce, it is also important to consider the bigger picture of the complex, ongoing adjustment issues women face once the initial crisis is past. If these ongoing aspects are left unattended to, women may be further at risk for significant depression, increased anxiety and panic, social isolation, and financial decline.

Counseling needs to encompass a full range of life areas that can be potential stressors for women. These areas include the emotional aspects of divorce, loss and grieving, role exit and transition, adjustment to major lifestyle changes, identity issues, changes in family and social relationships, midlife and aging issues, and financial adjustment. Walters et al. (1988) suggest that interventions need to include helping women develop new social skills, broaden relationship networks, focus on occupational skills and goals, identify new role choices, develop strategies for a fulfilling and rich life without a man, and take charge of their lives by challenging beliefs regarding helplessness and failure.

From a developmental perspective, tasks may be required that have not been accomplished previously. These tasks may also require substantial assertiveness and even aggression as women need to advocate for themselves in the divorce process and beyond. These tasks may be perceived as antithetical to traditional women's roles of nurturer and caretaker. These may include financial decisions, developing roles and socialization outside the constraints of marriage, and making other important decisions alone. Although these tasks represent the possibility of ego growth for women, the stress of these issues can be overwhelming and may result in depression, confusion, and immobilization.

It is important to view clinical issues from a holistic perspective within the context of cultural socialization processes and broader societal issues. It is equally important to normalize divorced women's presenting problems and symptoms, rather than locating them within a framework of individual psychopathology. A feminist-informed perspective views gender issues as intertwined with components of divorce, not as separate issues (Lund, 1990; Walters et al., 1988). Women's symptoms and post-divorce behavior reflect the messages received throughout a lifetime of gendered socialization. The therapist's ability to affirm and validate the importance of connection, nurturing, and emotionality for women is critical to the success of treatment. The meanings attached to loss of connection can contribute to paralyzing symptoms usually centered around anxiety and depression. These symptoms need to be viewed in the context of gendered messages that place attachment and relationship at the core of women's well-being. Therapists should keep in mind societal biases that sometimes contribute to framing women's reactions as crazy, hysterical, or selfish. Validation of normal reactions is an important clinical tool to enhance ego functioning in a time of crisis.

The reconstruction of narrative stories and the meaning of loss is a critical area of exploration in therapy. It is important to explore not only meanings and stories attached to the divorce experience, but also beliefs about relationships, marriage, divorce, and childbearing that had an impact on decisions made in young adulthood. Helping a woman to review these narratives retrospectively in context and construct a new understanding of her behaviors and decisions can minimize feelings of self-blame, low self-worth, and distress. This review and reconstruction process also can be critical to a woman's ability to move forward and adapt in a healthy way to her new status.

Divorce not only presents the emotional loss of a spouse, but often entails the losses of in-law extended family, friendship networks, social position, and status. Serious economic consequences and decline in standard of living can also be experienced as significant losses. Major loss issues often result in tremendous grief and sadness and feelings of failure, anger, guilt, loneliness, and regret. One should also be alert to the possibilities of clinical depression and anxiety.

In addition to initial grief and bereavement issues, major role transitions and identity reformulation are major tasks. Identity disruption and internal conflict over new roles also are pertinent issues. Women can have a difficult time adjusting to alternative roles, given that there are few roles as highly valued as the primary roles of wife and mother. A woman living alone without children is a role that still lacks underlying societal support and acceptance. Many women struggle to stay within the norm, utilizing tremendous amounts of emotional energy to find a man, a process that can increase distress.

Considering the importance of relationship and connection to women, loneliness can be a significant clinical issue in the post-divorce experience, and more prevalent for women than men. The greater impact of loneliness for women has roots in the socialization of women into roles of dependency and connection to others. Women can sometimes have difficulty establishing new relationships that may help buffer loneliness. Divorce still is associated with stigma that can contribute to isolation and loneliness. Loneliness can be exacerbated by feelings of rejection, feeling "out of sync" at specific places and events, completing daily tasks of living without assistance, and making decisions alone (Woodward, Zabel, & DeCosta, 1980). In many cases, the time since divorce does not diminish loneliness.

Guilt is another clinical issue that has its roots in patriarchal social constructions. Internalized values of responsibility for relationship can surface as intense feelings of guilt, regret, anxiety, and selfishness that can contribute to role strain and depression. In effect, women are "at war" psychologically, battling prescribed messages and expectations that make the lack of relationship an unbearable anomaly for many women. The redefinition of self in light of these messages makes recovery a more complex and difficult task. Guilt is related to distress, depression, continuing attachment, and poor adjustment. Adjusting to divorce requires dealing with a sense of inadequacy and shame and the capacity to develop a new sense of self. Even with the acceptability and normalization of divorce, internal guilt regarding the breakup of a relationship is a significant factor for women who have been socialized to be the caretakers of relationships. Initiation of separation and divorce proceedings is still intolerable for many women (Chapman, Price, & Serovich, 1995; Walters, 1988).

Spiritual and religious beliefs may exacerbate guilt and stress for divorcing women. Many women report their spirituality is stronger as a result, others report spirituality is damaged. It is important that women's spirituality be considered as a clinical issue in need of exploration in the post-divorce adjustment phase. Divorce is a crisis point that may enhance or diminish spirituality, and in turn, spirituality can either enhance or diminish a woman's capacity for recovery and adjustment. Women report depressed and anxious feelings, anguish, pain, feeling frozen, perception of being in a black hole, and discontent, as well as personal growth, affirmation, and perception of spirituality as a powerful tool (Nathanson, 1995).

For these women, the stressors are further exacerbated by the occurrence of divorce at the stage of midlife. Another complication is the pressure of "time marching on" and less available time to correct previous life decisions and reorganize. Midlife is a time of physiological change and psychological life review. The physical changes of aging are denigrated in our society, especially for women. Many women in this stage are also facing the physical and emotional implications of the advent of menopause. This too may add to the stress of this traumatic event and subsequent adjustment.

Stress for women divorcing at midlife may also be exacerbated by sexual issues normally confronted at this developmental stage. The difficulties of maintaining an active sexual life after divorce and coping with the prospect of finding a new partner at this stage may be daunting for some. Women who have had dysfunctional marriages with inadequate sexuality as a component may be at risk of acting out rebelliously to validate their sexuality and desirability. Options include sex with ex-spouse, short-term partners, long-term partners, and masturbation. They may attempt to revitalize themselves through short-term relationships. These relationships often become unfulfilling after some time, and loneliness may ensue. Cleveland (1979) identifies five basic motivations that may impact behavior: counteracting perceived marital failure; acting out and rebelliousness; validating one's femininity; seeking companionship, affection, and intimacy; and maintaining an ongoing connection through relationship. Clinicians need to be prepared to assist divorced women without partners in considering all their options to maintain their sexuality and sense of connection.

Let us return briefly to the case of Sara. Sara felt that her experience of therapy prior to her midlife divorce prepared her for very little of the challenges she would experience in the post-divorce stage. Although Sara felt therapy facilitated her decision to divorce, the immediate grief process, and recovery after the initial crisis, little attention was paid to the ongoing and future areas of adjustment to midlife and aging Sara would eventually face. Issues regarding physical and emotional changes of aging and menopause, the difficulties of returning to dating after many years of marriage, finding an appropriate partner at midlife, changing family relationships and losses, and socioeconomic issues were not explored in therapy before Sara divorced. She also felt there was not enough preparation for the actual daily tasks of living alone, and how she might prepare to deal with loneliness. Her spiritual beliefs also were not a focus of her original therapy, and this would have also been an important resource to utilize in her adjustment. She felt it would have been helpful to think through these aspects in preparation for her midlife divorce and a possible future alone. Although Sara felt her decision to divorce would not have changed, she felt she would have benefited from a better sense of the challenges that lay ahead in her post-divorce years, as well as taking stock of her strengths ahead of time.

Midlife divorce for women in a primarily married world is undoubtedly a complex, time-consuming process involving major role exit and disruption, as a woman moves from "married couple" to "single woman." A holistic perspective for treatment is useful in preparing a woman for adjustment to divorce in all emotional and practical areas of her life. Therapists need to be knowledgeable of issues of loss and grief, change in role and status, identity issues, changes in extended family and friendship relationships, financial adjustment, and midlife changes. These all need to be framed within the larger perspective of socially constructed societal beliefs that place women at a disadvantage to begin with.

CHAPTER 6

Childless in a Mothering World

> You are born, you grow, you are impregnated, you have a child, it grows; this is true of all cultures, recorded and unrecorded, the ones we know from life, and the recondite ones which only the far-traveled anthropologist knows. But is this all there is to life for a woman today?
>
> **—Betty Friedan, *The Feminine Mystique* (1997, p. 143)**

OUT OF SYNC IN A MOTHERING WORLD: THE STIGMA OF CHILDLESSNESS

In a world where most women achieve a sense of connection and belonging through marriage and mothering, being childless places a woman "out of sync" with the majority of her peers, at risk for stigmatization, emotional vulnerability, and needing to adapt to an unsupportive social environment. In approaching therapeutic work with women without children, it is important to understand the depth of stigmatization they continue to face, its effect on women's internal self-perception, the impact of external pressure from others, and the coping skills required to adapt (Dever and Saugeres, 2004).

Almost three decades ago, Russo (1979) defined the "motherhood mandate" as a societal norm that requires that all women bear children, and upholds motherhood as the definitive role for women. Anderson and Stewart (1994) further validated that, although Russo's concept is several decades old, the mandate by no means has disappeared as a social construct. It is still a core premise that impacts women greatly, although nowadays some of the message is "hidden underground." It has been reported that even the younger generations still validate that having a child is an experience that every woman should have (Longman, 2004).

This positioning of motherhood as the preferred social status, often referred to as pro-natalism, has been institutionalized throughout the 20th century through religious teachings, literature, and psychological theories, all of which have promoted a value-laden ideology that idealizes motherhood and pathologizes non-motherhood (Dever & Saugeres, 2004; Davis, 1982). Even though Western society as a whole is becoming less child centered, childlessness is still interpreted as an act of selfishness (McManus, 2006).

Even though recent societal change has allowed for the voicing of women's ambivalence about childbearing, a motherless identity is still stigmatized in Western culture. Voicing feelings of ambivalence, lack of desire, or even dislike of children primarily remains taboo. Throughout history, the roles of wife and biological mother have traditionally been closely linked to the value of women and, in fact, to the very core of their identity. These roles are still viewed as the only real acceptable roles for women, with other roles being second rate and not as good as "the real thing." These socially constructed roles are ascribed with meanings and role expectations that have powerfully defined women's lives and choices for generations. The centrality of motherhood has not only been built into the entire fabric of society, but has also been internalized into individual and collective psyches. This polarizing ideology about women's roles, in effect, results in not only stigmatization of women by others, but also positions that women devalue and compete with each other.

Women without children represent the "other" or "stranger" in Western society. In effect, the role of outsider and deviant helps to define the role of insider and preferred (Letherby, 1999). Weedon (1987) suggested that the maintenance of an ideology requires the discrediting and marginalizing of the experience that it seeks to redefine. The diametrically opposed concepts of stranger and other, belonging and not belonging, commonality and difference, acceptance and exclusion, contribute to the marginalization of women who differ from a prescribed norm. Women who either choose non-motherhood or find themselves outside the norm by default are often scapegoated and devalued in pervasive ways.

Societal biases are reflected in the very terms that are used to describe women without children: ***childless***, ***childfree***, and ***non-mother***. These define a woman by what she is not in relation to her connection with children, and not by what she is as an adult of value in her own right. It is significant that these terms are rarely, if ever, applied to men without children. For lack of a better term, I will use these terms interchangeably, although my preference would be not to describe women at all by their mothering or non-mothering status.

The stigma attached to childlessness has been evident in Western society for all of the 20th century, and can clearly be traced back to the early 1900s. The social constructions of earlier times have undoubtedly left a powerful legacy for childless women. Childlessness is still discredited and met with a multiplicity of negative reactions and attitudes in the current day. In the early 20th century, it was noted that voluntarily childless women were viewed as dangerous, melancholy, degrading, and indicative of social decay (Hollingsworth, 1916). Women who chose to remain childless were historically viewed as selfish, narcissistic, and child haters with dysfunctional family backgrounds and difficulty with intimacy. These myths and stereotypes have left an emotional legacy that has been difficult to debunk (Casey, 2007).

In his early work in 1936, Popenoe studied the motivation of childless couples. Even his description of his work, reasons for voluntary refusal to bear children, demonstrated the negative bias evident in that era. His use of the term *refusal to bear children* would imply that an expectation or demand was placed upon women with which they refused to comply. This perspective victimized women by expecting that they conform to mandated expectations, rather than supporting a woman's childbearing decision as a conscious choice, free of bias. In Popenoe's research, the most frequent perceptions of women without children were related to self-centeredness, wife's career, economic pressure, health, dislike of children, and marital discord. Popenoe's interpretations of these reasons reflected the negative connotations of the times, including the following descriptions about childless women: self-centered, social climbers, wanting to be free to travel, too busy making money, never satisfied, would be disturbed by a child, would have their looks and figures spoiled by pregnancy, not wanting to make the sacrifice, not wanting to stay home, and preferring work instead. Popenoe also stated that economic and health concerns were both defensive rationalizations, and viewed most motivations as implausible or unacceptable. In his later work in 1943, negative constructions continued to be evident in questions such as: How many women are childless against their will? Why do married persons avoid having children? These two early studies demonstrate the pervasive stigmatization of childless women that was evident in the early 1900s.

This stigma remained evident in literature throughout the first half of the century, as childless women were continually viewed as self-involved, neurotic, and in poor health (Houseknecht, 1977). This view is still present in more current literature that documents the continuing presence of negative biases and stigmatization over the last several decades (Dever & Saugeres, 2004; Park, 2002).

Although one might assume that significant social change would have allowed for deconstruction of these negative narratives, in the late 1990s, the biased "deviance and dysfunction" perspective of women who delay childbearing or chose childlessness continued to be reflected in the experiences of childless women and throughout literature and research (Thornton and Young-DeMarco, 2001). In several research studies in the late 1990s (Lampman & Dowling-Guyer, 1995; Mueller & Yoder, 1999), it was reported that childless women are still viewed by others as less caring, more career driven, less committed to family life, lazy, insensitive, lonely, and unhappy. They are also perceived as greedy, non-nurturing, child hating, and lacking knowledge about children. Postponement and permanent childlessness continue to be connected to poor parental nurturing, dysfunctional family dynamics, rigid discipline, narcissistic tendencies, or feminist biases. These descriptions directly echo the descriptions and words utilized by early researchers in the field a half century before.

Stigmatization also tends to be stratified, with voluntarily childless women the least preferred, and mothers presumed to be the most emotionally healthy. Perceptions about "involuntarily" childless women include viewing them as anxious, stressed, and more committed to family life than women who are childless by choice (Mueller & Yoder, 1999).

Women also report experiencing considerable pressure from others regarding childbearing after they have been married a few years. Pressure from family members as well as friends and acquaintances increases after several years of marriage, and peaks around the seventh year of marriage. In effect, if a couple has not borne children or expressed interest in doing so, others begin to verbalize expectations in the form of intrusive questions, biased comments, lecturing, and unsolicited medical advice (Mueller & Yoder, 1999). Women often describe facing intrusive comments and questions from others regarding their plans to have children, whether or not they are "trying" (if not, why not?), and assumptions that life and a future without children would undoubtedly be emotionally distressing and intolerable. It is remarkable that men do not usually report being on the receiving end of such interrogation and examination of their motives.

THE EFFECTS OF STIGMATIZATION ON CHILDLESS WOMEN'S INTERNALIZED VIEW OF SELF

Given the pervasiveness of stigma and denigration of childless women, an important area of consideration in therapeutic work is the exploration of women's view of self and the meanings connected to a childless role. Whether a woman is childless by her own choosing or through divorce or infertility, it is important to explore the internal narrative stories she tells about her life circumstance and non-mother role, as these stories can have a critical impact on her ability to cope with stigmatization and denigration by others. Narratives that minimize self-blame, fracture the "woman is only valuable as mother" formula, and increase a woman's perceived value within other roles can decrease distress and foster coping and adaptation.

In the research study, it was significant that most of the women felt comfortable with their childfree status and were able validate their low desire for children by tracing narrative stories to their childhood histories and experiences. For most, the state of non-motherhood seemed ego-syntonic, as evidenced by lack of significant psychological symptoms or distress. Most related a lack of significant grief and sadness about their childfree status. Many of the women related they did not necessarily feel negative about themselves; however, they still were often affected by perceived negative reactions from others.

Although most of the women in the research study felt positively about themselves, other studies report that many women are greatly impacted by negative perceptions of others about them as women without children, and internalize these denigrating views. However, much of this literature is now several decades old, and more current information about childless women's experiences and perceptions of self in the current era would be useful.

An example is Judy, a 50-year-old woman who, in a therapy session, poignantly recalled the following:

> I can remember when I was a little girl, I never was the one that played with dolls and the house thing. I was always the one out riding around on my bicycle with the wind in my hair, wondering what adventures I would have when I grew up, and thinking of all the places I would travel to. I always had this "wanderlust" kind of thing. I never felt this deep need to be a mother. My sisters always knew that was what they would do, and I never did. I love what I do now. My life has been more adventurous and fascinating than I could have imagined. That's why I just don't get it when people express sorrow when they hear I don't have children. They assume my life just can't be as good as theirs, and I never understood that. One time I overheard someone say I must have an unfulfilled life. What is their need to judge my happiness because I don't have children? It's just another way of keeping women in their place.

Another area of important inquiry in therapy is the exploration of the differentiation between voluntary and involuntary childlessness, as these two experiences do carry with them different meanings. A woman who chooses childlessness often feels empowered in designing her own life choices. Women who have a strong desire for children and are unable to bear them due to infertility often feel a grave sense of inadequacy, shame, and loss.

Miall (1986) explored the perceptions of involuntarily childless women to determine if they perceived this status as denigrating and stigmatizing. Almost all the women regarded their infertility as negative, damaging, and an indication that they were a failure. They reported feelings of anxiety, isolation, conflict, inadequacy, and shame. Many women are hesitant to tell others about their status, and secretiveness, deception, and "preventive disclosure" are often utilized as coping strategies. The author concluded: "The personal possession or secret sharing of infertility has profound consequences for the social identity and behavior of actors" (Miall, 1986, p. 279).

THE IMPACT OF THE STIGMATIZED REACTION OF OTHERS

In addition to coping with internalized feelings about self as non-mothers, women also are required to deal with the reactions, perceptions, and narrative stories of others in reaction to their non-mothering status. Social discourses that degrade and marginalize childless women still persist, despite social change that would imply increased acceptability of this status. A body of work in the late 1990s and early 2000s indicates that women continue to feel stigmatized and perceived as deviant, desperate, and dysfunctional, even though they may not feel that way about themselves (Letherby, 1999; Gillespie, 2000). One-dimensional stereotyping and rigid expectations of women's roles in general, whether childless, pregnant, or mothers, minimize the complexity of their feelings and experiences. Assumptions that each of these roles are free of conflict and that women are unconditionally and consistently happy in their specific roles are naïve at best. Childless women are often viewed from opposing extremes: as one whose life is always exciting and carefree, or always lonely and self-absorbed. Assumptions abound regarding pregnant women as equally happy all the time and "superwomen" mothers as able to handle several roles without conflict or stress (Shields & Cooper, 1983). Another prevalent assumption is that all psychologically healthy women must want children. In turn, this can lead to incorrect assumptions that women who do not have children must always be in emotional distress.

Gillespie (2000) identified three common reactions of others to childless women: disbelief, disregard, and perceptions of deviance. Disbelief takes the form of those who do not believe women's feelings and choices are valid, and insist that all women who are voluntarily childless are "future mothers who will undoubtedly change their minds," thus disregarding and discounting women's feelings and desires. Others deny a woman's childless status by disregarding her decisions as valid, stating the belief that most women will eventually regret their decision.

As an example, I once overheard a group of midlife, highly educated professional women discussing the childless status of Oprah Winfrey. One colleague stated: "What is wrong with Oprah that she doesn't want children? That she doesn't have children? Of COURSE all women want children, that's for sure. There must be something wrong with her relationship, and you know she's not married either. That's just not natural." This is just one small example, and surely is validation that the legacy of rigid beliefs about motherhood is still entrenched in the current culture.

Women report experiencing both silent, implied disapproval and overt criticism. The perception of childless women as deviant takes the form of assumptions that they must be depressed, anxiety ridden, and, in fact, come from dysfunctional family backgrounds. Since women frequently internalize these messages of disapproval, it is important to understand the powerful impact of others' reactions, and to explore their experiences within their social context, extended family, and social network.

FROM UNCONSCIOUS TO CONSCIOUS: THE COMPLEX PROCESS OF CHILDBEARING DECISION MAKING

The social changes of the last century have resulted in a shift in childbearing decision making from an unconscious to a conscious process. More frequently, women of all social backgrounds are evaluating childbearing decisions, and such a process is no longer an option only reserved for an elite class of women. Women of the baby boom generation have grown up in a changing time when the options of higher education and careers have increased dramatically. With more emphasis on the value of education and paid work outside the home, these opportunities have become sources of valued identity, self-respect, social relationships, and networking. Over the last few decades, women's interests have expanded to include a variety separate from childbearing, including education, career, financial stability, improved marriage, personal freedom, and control of one's life.

Baby boomer women are faced with the demands of competing roles and complex options for their lives. As the possibilities of these roles have increased, social institutions have not kept pace with these demands, resulting in a cultural lag that places increased stress on women struggling to sort out complex role choices and being expected to "have it all." Many women have been unable to sort out how to balance self-development, education, and career with the demanding responsibilities of family life and raising children (Moen, 1998). Although men's roles in the home and family have shifted somewhat, it is well known that most women are still primarily responsible for the well-being of children, family, and relationships.

These shifting norms have resulted in childbearing intentions becoming less stable than in previous generations; they may shift significantly over the course of a woman's childbearing years, and are often reversed as time progresses. Though a minority of women make an early and permanent decision to remain childless, many women who verbalize a plan for childlessness in early adulthood often reverse that decision and do become mothers. Many others postpone having children until age, career, and established lifestyle significantly reduce the possibility of having children. As "postponers" age and begin to view midlife, desire for children often changes when faced with the possibility of decreasing fertility and the "last chance" phenomenon (Heaton, Jacobsen, & Holland, 1999).

The childbearing decision-making process tends to be highly changeable as a woman progresses through the life cycle stage of her childbearing years. This stage can be characterized by the contemplation of various competing lifestyles, options, roles, and opportunities. As conflict increases over the traditional mother role and other options, women often feel at a loss as to how to combine these demands of competing roles. A normative developmental period of personal freedom and growth for women in young adulthood has emerged as a shift in the life cycle, and women are now faced with the difficulty of weighing the benefits of personal freedom, autonomy, and a childfree lifestyle against the long-term responsibility and commitment of mothering (Daniluk & Herman, 1984). Younger generations of women are increasingly considering childbearing an option, rather than a mandate, and are becoming much more aware of the difficulties of balancing the desires for education, careers, and other lifestyle pursuits with motherhood (Yogev & Vierra, 1983). This has resulted in a higher rate of childlessness in women in young adulthood, as compared to women approaching midlife. In effect, as opportunities have increased for women, values have shifted to reflect these possibilities. Current-generation women are more focused on values differing from those of previous generations. These values include achievement, individualism, professional and career interests, and personal freedom. As women achieve higher education and more labor force participation, it has been found that childlessness increases.

Women have also been more able to voice complex feelings about their choices and childbearing. A combination of positive and negative factors contribute to childbearing decision making. Women often relate a variety of factors involved in their decision making, including enjoyment of current lifestyle, interest in education and career, disinterest in children, desire for privacy and serenity, dislike of maternal role, population and environmental concerns, desire for personal freedom and spontaneity, unpleasant childhood, concern regarding husband's ability to father, perceptions that friends with children seem unhappy, perception that children detract from marriage, and concern regarding intrusive in-laws. Control of one's life and independence also are important factors. Women often perceive these options as growth enhancing and freedom giving.

In her 1993 research study Morell provided some important information about women's childbearing decision making. She explored the life stories of intentionally childless women with a focus on identifying psychosocial factors. Her work described women who were striving for full and meaningful lives apart from motherhood. Many stories demonstrated women must constantly engage in acts of subversion in pursuit of roles not viewed as traditionally feminine. Morell's work normalized a host of psychosocial factors that are growth oriented rather than pathology based. The women's stories revealed such factors as desire for self-expression, self-reliance, independence, education, culture, economic self-sufficiency, achievement, interest in a 10-year career plan, and wanting "more and different." Themes of very early resistance to the restraints of expected feminine roles were also included. Some felt they never desired children at all, and not all of the women experienced conflict in response to their decision. These women did marry, but had very definite ideas about their lives separate from children.

It is important to understand childbearing decision making as a complex process that has become to involve sorting out a variety of choices and life goals, rather than a mandated expectation for women's lives. The dilemma of competing roles and demands has not been met with societal supports that would enable women to freely choose between all options. Decisions for postponed childbearing or permanent childlessness seem more related to conflict regarding role choices and concerns about a period of self-development, rather than deviant or pathological functioning.

COPING STRATEGIES FOR ADAPTATION IN A MOTHERING WORLD

Socially constructed pejorative beliefs about childless women have undoubtedly left a legacy of stigma that challenges women not only to develop self-acceptance, but also to adapt to a disapproving and unsupportive social environment. If living with an identity that differs from the majority of one's peers is met with consistent disapproval, a considerable amount of emotional energy may need to be channeled into coping and self-management. Women must often deal with not only their own self-doubt, fears, and sense of a lack of connection and belonging, but also the negative reactions and denigrating perceptions of others. Childless women often feel they are required to explain and account for themselves and their decisions in ways that other women are not. Women also are victimized by stigma that, for the most part, does not apply to men. We do not refer to men as childless, nor do we seek to examine their motivations or experiences of not having children in the same way we label women and examine their motivations.

Several coping strategies and defenses seem to be beneficial to women attempting to adapt this circumstance. Many women report that the telling of their story of childlessness is in effect a "coming out" of sorts and is as difficult as it is for gays and lesbians who come out. Others report that defensive strategies such as silence and secret keeping must be utilized in order to fit in to a world that does not accept them.

Park (2002) identified defensive strategies women use to adapt such as passing as postponers, identity substitution, condemning the condemners, asserting the right to self-fulfillment, claiming biological deficiency, and redefining the situation. In effect, it has primarily been unacceptable for women to clearly verbalize that they are not mothers, do not desire children, or cannot have children biologically. As a result, women are forced to use subversive means such as changing the stories they present to the outside world in order to minimize stigma and negative reactions.

A coping strategy that has been found to be beneficial to women without children has been the development of social and friendship networks with others who do not have children. This reference group support is an influential factor for those who do not have children and do not plan or expect to have them at any point in the future. As childless women deviate from the prevailing social norm, reference group support is important in terms of providing a sense of belonging and connection to a group that can provide an alternate norm and decrease feelings of abnormality and not fitting in (Houseknecht, 1977). In my experience as both a therapist *and* a researcher, I have found that women who have strong and dense networks and reference group support feel the least distress and the most acceptance about their childfree role.

POSTPONED CHILDBEARING: STRATEGY FOR COPING WITH CONFLICTING ROLES

Postponed childbearing is sometimes viewed as a possible solution to an internal conflict modern-day women face regarding competing traditional and modern roles and alternatives previously not available to women. A woman's inability to sort out options and desires for her life can result in conflict that requires the development of acceptable solutions to this intrapsychic dilemma. Postponement can be a temporary solution to the stress of sorting out these various conflicts. It has sometimes been considered a radical trend that has increased over the last few decades, the longest historical period in which childbearing delay has remained constant (Welles-Nystrom, 1997).

While many women do eventually bear children, postponing tends to take the form of a series of decisions over time that often lead to eventual permanent childlessness. The number of childless women had increased to 1 in every 5 by 2004, as opposed to the 1 in every 10 reported in 1976 (Lawler Dye, 2004). Many couples find themselves childless by default after a long period of postponement (Dafoe & Popenoe, 2006). For many couples there is never an explicit decision or moment in time when they declare: "We have decided we don't want children." These couples often relate a history of somewhat unconscious decision points along the way, and in retrospect cannot describe how they progressed from postponement to permanent childlessness. Gutman (1995) suggests that couples may be ambivalent, neutral, passive, avoidant, defensive, and in denial, masking intense conflicts, that result in drifting into voluntary childlessness. These issues and decisions run through the relationship and life cycle of couples like a common thread, with many postponements at various life cycle transitions along the way. However, this strategy can be problematic if fertility diminishes or time runs out via midlife divorce. If a woman has postponed childbearing for a number of years without a definite decision, these events can upset the apple cart. A midlife woman can find herself facing childlessness by default due to divorce in the critical childbearing years.

Delaying parenthood into the 30s provides women with a period of personal development in young adulthood and the freedom to pursue other goals such as obtaining an education, developing a career, solidifying a marital relationship, and obtaining financial stability before embarking on childbearing. Postponing tends to be related to multiple factors rather than just career development per se.

Previous tradition dictated that women left home to enter directly into a marital relationship and childbearing. In contrast, many women are now leaving home and embarking on a period of independent young adulthood and living on their own (Dion, 1995; Carter & McGoldrick, 1988). It is suggested that postponed childbearing is an adaptive response to current social patterns and dilemmas, and that developmental milestones of the life cycle should be expanded to include a broader range of possibilities, rather than measured by rigid milestones and age stratification.

THE LINK BETWEEN POSTPONED CHILDBEARING AND PERMANENT CHILDLESSNESS

While initially utilized as a coping strategy for sorting out conflicting and competing demands, postponed childbearing is often a route to permanent childlessness. Stating a woman's plan is for postponement can be a self-protective strategy and is often perceived as a more acceptable route to childlessness. Women relate they are not exposed to as much stigma, criticism, harsh reactions, or questions if they verbalize a desire and plan to possibly bear children at some point in the future. Voicing a definite decision not to bear children is more often met with negative reactions and intrusive questions (Heaton et al., 1999). Rarely is this process ever a one-time decision at an early point in young adulthood. Many couples use the strategy of passive non-decision-making, postponing for many years, sometimes for the entirety of their childbearing years.

Women's childbearing intentions have become more changeable over time, in that women who postpone may or may not end up wanting children at any point in the future. In fact, most women do not actively decide to have no children. Rather, a series of postponements eventually can lead to voluntary childlessness. Callan (1983, p. 262) states, "For many who postpone, the series of deferments in time represents an implicit decision not to have children." It is suggested that early in their marriages, postponing couples are indistinguishable from other couples. However, given some time to enjoy the advantages of a childfree lifestyle and experience the benefits of continued postponement, childlessness can become a permanent state. Traditionally there have been some assumptions that the postponement of childbearing is an indication of lack of marital dissatisfaction and possible marital disruption. Over the last several decades, a central question in some of the professional literature has focused on whether delayed childbearing promotes or hinders marital stability. One paradigm suggests postponed childbearing may enhance marital stability by allowing couples time to strengthen their bond and enjoy the freedom and independence of the childless state. The opposing perspective suggested couples might delay first births due to tension and instability in the marriage. It has also been hypothesized that women who delay childbearing may be more independent, less traditional, and more likely to seek divorce. It has become clear that postponed childbearing is more commonly about seeking a period of adaptation, self-development, and relationship stabilization, rather than about narcissistic tendencies or pathology within the marital relationship.

There has been some consideration of the impact of the women's movement and feminist thought on women's postponement of childbearing. Many women describe the impact of feminist ideology and the resulting cultural shifts on their lives. Most describe awareness of the women's movement during late adolescence and felt it had significant impact on their decision to postpone childbirth and pursue a broad range of personal development in young adulthood, not just careers (Dion, 1995). Women who are postponers often have a greater focus on nonfamily work, educational attainment, financial security, personal freedom, a secure personal life, leisure activities, and personal goals. These factors constituted an overall developmental period of personal growth (Dion, 1995). Women's experience of postponed childbearing indicates that a new life cycle stage has developed in which women are concerned about a broad range of personal growth factors.

Given the immense social change that has had a major impact on the way women live their lives and the decisions they make, the life cycle needs to be expanded to normalize a period of marriage without children for women. A woman's life course that includes postponed childbearing or permanent childlessness is not necessarily related to marital dissatisfaction (Heaton et al., 1999). We also might not exclude this as a possible assumption. A period of young adult development without children can be normalized, rather than viewed as a reflection of dysfunctional individual and family functioning.

DISRUPTING A LIFE COURSE: POSTPONED CHILDBEARING AND MIDLIFE DIVORCE

Given that many women are now delaying both marriage and childbearing in order to solidify developmental achievements and gains in early adulthood, the event of a midlife divorce may force the childbearing decision to an untimely conclusion, in effect, prematurely disrupting an undecided life course in the planning stages. Although couples may unconsciously be on a course toward permanent childlessness, a premature disruption may cause considerable stress, vulnerability, and unexpected feelings of loss. This may occur either through a voluntary decision or by default due to the event of a midlife divorce. Marital disruption at midlife can result in reduced time available for childbearing, since this can render a woman single at a critical point in her childbearing years. This experience may also result in hesitancy to bear children in a subsequent relationship, due to the real possibilities that it, too, may fail (Mosher & Bachrach, 1982).

The disruption of marriage at midlife, and the subsequent possibility of permanent childlessness, may cause internal stress and conflict. Women can be at risk for anxiety, panic attacks, depression, loneliness, feelings of inadequacy, suicidal feelings, and feelings of being out of sync with peers. These events may also initiate a grief process regarding the realization of moving from postponing childbearing to possible permanent childlessness.

However, for women who were solidifying a decision for permanent childlessness through postponement, this disruption may help them arrive at a decision point they were unconsciously moving towards in any case. As therapists, it is important to be aware of assumptions that all women will experience grief regarding childlessness, as this is not necessarily the case. I, myself, was guilty of holding this bias in formulating the questions of my own research study. I anticipated that the women of the study would be highly likely to experience depression and anxiety due to their childless state, midlife divorce, and absence of remarriage.

As you will learn in Part II, the majority of the women in the research study displayed an absence of symptoms of anxiety or depression and were highly functioning, describing feelings of comfort and happiness with their lifestyle, and little to no regret about their previous choices to postpone child-bearing. It is important for therapists to check for assumptions that the process of postponement is related to an individual pathological process, narcissism, or dysfunctional family dynamics. Broader explanations of the nuances of childlessness are needed (Dever & Saugeres, 2004). It is also important to keep in mind that childbearing decisions are sometimes influenced by child-hood experiences of loss and dysfunctional family life. (Mejumder, 2004).

An example is Alissa, who, in retrospect, was able to trace her postpone-ment and lack of desire for children over two decades. Alissa related that as her views changed over time, she recognized there was always a reason not to pursue childbearing, as she always felt that "other things were in the way." Having grown up in the 1960s and 70s, in her late adolescence and early adulthood she was very concerned with social issues and beliefs about bring-ing children into a dangerous or difficult world. As time progressed, Alissa pursued her education and surprised herself with a meaningful career filled with many achievements and recognition. The timing never seemed right, and so Alissa continued to postpone both marriage and childbearing. Alissa did marry in her mid-30s; however, her desire to postpone childbearing con-tinued. Alissa recalled the impact of caring for a newborn during the loss of her best friend's family member shortly after she had given birth. She recalled feeling the responsibility of caring for a newborn as being daunting and seri-ous. This further solidified her position of postponing.

As many women in the research study related, on some unconscious level, Alissa believed she knew her marriage was "not right," and childbearing was not a path she wanted to follow. Concerns were also expressed about the fathering capacity of her husband, as well as her own overall happiness should she stay in the marriage. Alissa finally realized in retrospect that the wish for children and the desire to stay married were never as strong as the desire to do other things. By the time of her midlife divorce, Alissa had con-structed a fulfilling life that included the responsibilities of volunteer work with children's foundations in underprivileged countries, as well as a senior executive position in an altruistic profession.

Returning to the case of Sara, like Alissa, she also described a long process of delay over two decades of her young adult life. Sara also never recalled one decision point or any period of time in which she felt a strong desire or need to bear children. Rather, she viewed herself as having drifted into childlessness with many unconscious decision points along the way. She described contentment with her life in the early years of her marriage in young adulthood. At the points in time when her married friends were having children, the desire did not increase for Sara. She was happy with her work life, and friendships and married life provided her with a certain level of contentment and emotional security and belonging. She pursued her education and a teaching career working with children that she continued to enhance throughout the years with various promotions and interesting professional pursuits. Sara's period of self-development seemed to suit her emotionally. In retrospect, Sara also realized that during a 20-year period of young adulthood, the desire for children was never strong enough for her to do anything about it, and she never actively pursued getting pregnant during her married years. Sara also recalled the absence of distress regarding lack of children. She stated:

> I just never had many thoughts about wanting children. And then year after year, well, other things just became more important to me for my life. I always liked working and going to school. I enjoyed traveling and my hobbies and my friendships. I guess you could say there was a certain level of comfort in the way things were. I never felt like this desperate need to have a baby like some of my friends. It was like their whole life revolved around it, and mine never did.

CHAPTER 7

Summary of Part I

In Part I, the meaning of divorce at midlife and potential childlessness for women in a pro-marriage, pro-natalist world has been explored. Recent social change and a subsequent cultural lag in response to that change has "trapped" many women between conflicting role demands and a dichotomy of traditional and untraditional beliefs regarding women's roles and choices. The process of adjustment to this role has undoubtedly been facilitated by a changing social context. Significant cultural shifts have allowed women to express interest in and choose a variety of lifestyles and role choices. These shifts include postponement of marriage and childbearing, changing expectations of marriage and desire for children, and increased acceptability and availability of divorce. In effect, women have been more able to question and challenge the "woman *must* equal wife and mother" equation. The voicing of ambivalence regarding marriage and motherhood has become more acceptable. Choosing marriage, motherhood, or divorce has now become a conscious process of option review, rather than an "automatic" life course.

THE IMPACT OF SHIFTING SOCIAL CONSTRUCTIONS

As cultural norms have shifted, women are now finding themselves caught between traditional and untraditional beliefs about role choices for their lives and the course they desire their life to take. In effect, women have become trapped between two eras in which women's roles have differed markedly. Cultural values and institutionally embedded social constructions regarding women's identity and preferred roles have traditionally made it difficult for women to adapt and thrive emotionally and psychologically outside the norms of marriage and motherhood.

Many women describe internalized beliefs about the centrality of the roles of wife and mother that have a pervasive impact on their decisions and behaviors in early adulthood. These decisions also bear a connection to the occurrence of divorce at midlife. Women's original expectations that they *should* marry and mother mirror overarching, organizing societal constructs firmly embedded in definitions of women's identity. According to many women, marriage and motherhood are perceived as prescribed or mandated roles, often unconsciously so.

As a result of these beliefs, many women marry in early adulthood, even when desire is low, and even when they perceive it is a mistake. Midlife often results in a transitional "crisis" in which life choices and goals are reviewed. An increased awareness of mortality sometimes pushes women forward toward divorce. At this life cycle stage, midlife women sometimes describe realizations that they had made poor choices for marriage, or that they had not desired to marry at all. This leaves women with the task of deconstructing and reconstructing traditional beliefs to be more congruent with their midlife role expectations, choices, and desires. The process of "re-storying" life narratives is a critical coping skill for women in this marginalized role.

POSTPONEMENT OF MARRIAGE AND CHILDBEARING

As a result of growing opportunities for women, shifting social norms, and conflicting role demands, many women have been faced with confusing dilemmas about whether they can balance marriage, mothering, education, career goals, and other life pursuits. It can be difficult to sort out these role choices. Postponement of marriage and motherhood has become a temporary solution to this dilemma. Postponing can provide valuable time for women to sort out their feelings about role choices. This period of delay can also result in development of emotional and relational maturity, important self-care and coping skills, financial independence, and the capacity to be alone. These are skills that become critical for many women later in life, whether they have been married or not.

While postponement has its advantages, it has also become a contributor to the increase in women divorced at midlife without children. As women postpone these decisions, their life path can be short-circuited by a midlife divorce. Should they divorce at midlife after postponing childbearing, the result may be eventual permanent childlessness. This disrupted life plan, one that most women do not consciously plan for in early adulthood, may cause considerable distress.

CHANGING EXPECTATIONS OF MARRIAGE

Another contributing factor to midlife divorce for women without children is the contemporary changes in expectations of marriage. Marriage has traditionally been viewed as a mandated role and preferred status for women, and as a lifelong commitment not to be broken. Many women who express distress, extreme unhappiness, and lack of fulfillment in their marriages still believe divorce is unacceptable and the commitment to marriage must be honored, no matter what. Having made an "early mistake," at midlife many women come to realizations that they desire more from marriage than a "mandated arrangement." Expectations of marriage have now changed to incorporate women's desires for more emotionally fulfilling and highly compatible partnerships. Cultural shifts also reflect changes in reasons for divorce, from concrete factors to factors such as increased desire for emotional fulfillment, better communication, higher levels of compatibility, need for self-actualization, and desire for independence.

CHANGES IN DESIRE FOR CHILDREN

Changes in women's desire for children is also a contributing factor in the increase of divorce at midlife for women without children. Childbearing decision making has now become a much more conscious, complex process of option review, rather than an unconsciously decided life course. The ability to sort out the costs and benefits of having children and to voice varying levels of interest has also become much more acceptable. In their life stories, women often reveal a dichotomy of traditional and untraditional beliefs regarding motherhood. Many women's life narratives in early adulthood include romanticized expectations about mothering. At the stage of midlife, women relate more realistic views and a desire to review options regarding childbearing. This is a change from earlier generations in which childbearing was just what one did.

Competing role demands have led to an increase in postponed childbearing. In effect, postponing as a temporary solution to this conflict often helps to minimize the stigma of an early permanent decision for childlessness. However, although much progress has been made in the acceptance of a variety of choices for women, the status of being childless or childfree still represents an experience of stigmatization and devaluation for women. A negative internalized view of self is often validated by the negative perceptions and reactions of others.

Women who believe they had high desire for children in young adulthood also sometimes come to the realization that their feelings have changed and recognize ambivalence at midlife. Ambivalence can surface as a passive stance of inactivity in pursuing childbearing throughout young adulthood. Many women in the research study drifted into continual postponement of decisions regarding childbearing, processing their desires over time, and reviewing their feelings at various points in early adulthood. Many connect this underlying factor to reasons for their midlife divorce. At midlife, some women also relate reasons for postponed childbearing as concerns about the continuing viability of their marriages and concerns about their husbands as potential fathers. Some women describe feelings of low desire for children that remains a firm conviction into midlife. Others recognize that traumatic family and life events may exacerbate an already low desire for children. Issues expressed include: overall dislike for the responsibility of raising children, the impact of significant losses, and difficult life experiences.

Other themes for divorced women include concerns about dealing with the responsibility of child rearing alone, financial impact, the absence of a father figure, and beliefs regarding mothering alone as second rate.

THE INCREASE IN ACCEPTABILITY AND AVAILABILITY OF DIVORCE

The availability of divorce as an acceptable choice for women has also increased the occurrence of midlife divorce. However, despite increased acceptability, the legacy of stigma with roots in earlier times still remains. Even when a woman is the initiator of divorce, it still shakes her world and is counterintuitive to the visions many women have for their lives. It is important to consider not only the obvious emotional impact of divorce, but also the meaning of the loss of connection, intimacy, attachment, and value. The economic impact of midlife divorce is also a core area of consideration in working with these women. In effect, money often defines a woman's choices and her ability to expand her experiences, socially, educationally, and professionally.

Most women state they have no regrets about divorce. However, some do express significant regret about original decisions to marry in early adulthood. Divorce is often perceived as providing women with an opportunity for personal growth and an ability to consciously review feelings about relationships, marriage, and childbearing. Many voice interest in another relationship in the future; however, they express the desire for an improved relationship in which they could retain their "voice" and independence.

From many women's perspectives, independence seems to be a significant advantage of midlife divorce. Women who are able to cultivate independence and focus on its advantages, rather than focusing on loneliness, tend to fare better in the post-divorce stage. This is an important shift that enhances women's coping ability. This lack of loneliness can be related to a woman's capacity to expand connection, intimacy, and attachment by developing increased family connection and support, dense social networks, good capacity to be alone, and financial ability to pursue stimulating lifestyles and activities that minimize stress.

Although, in general, many women report a lack of significant overt stigma regarding divorce and childlessness, they do report that openly supportive comments of family and friends often conceal subtle, underlying assumptions questioning women's ability to be happy and fulfilled in the absence of marriage and motherhood. Even though women do not particularly have negative perceptions about themselves, the discrediting narratives and negative assumptions of others are often internalized. Women who occupy this stigmatized role in a social context that is still centered around marriage and motherhood are faced with three significant developmental challenges: divorce recovery, potential childlessness, and role exit and transition. This "triple whammy" requires adaptation to a potentially stressful lifestyle "out of sync" with the majority of one's peers.

PART II

Telling Life Stories: Constructions, Narratives, and Beliefs

OVERVIEW

The stories and experiences of women divorced at midlife without children are as varied as they are interesting. Chapters 8 and 9 of Part II will provide the reader with a cross section of the clinical themes of women adapting to this role. The themes are demonstrated via narratives in the women's own words. Chapter 10 will follow with the stories of four women who speak of their life experiences from different perspectives. In these four life stories, desire for marriage and motherhood ranged from low to ambivalent to high. These diverse stories capture several major themes that run throughout the narratives of many women's lives, and will provide a backdrop for the clinical approach and case examples to follow in Part III, the remainder of the book.

It should be noted that most of the women discussed here were from a highly educated group with minimal financial stressors and more than adequate income. Geographically, the group primarily represented metropolitan areas and was not as racially or culturally diverse as was hoped for. Given these limitations, the information gleaned from the work still provides important clinical information that, to my knowledge, has not been discussed in a comprehensive manner in the literature previously. It is hoped that broader exploration of these issues will be studied in the future among women who are more racially, culturally, and financially diverse. I view the work I completed as a starting point, and it is hoped that others will carry this work forward by further study of diverse groups of women adjusting to this life circumstance in the coming decades.

CHAPTER 8

Paralyzing or Empowering

The Power of Socially Constructed Beliefs

> The loss of women's voice, the inability to find a language and system of logic to represent our experience, the "dis-ease" of feeling and living in incongruity has profound implications. These inconsistencies become raised as personal doubts that invade women's sense of themselves, compromising their ability to act on their perceptions.
>
> **—J. V. Jordan et al., *Women's Growth in Connection* (1991, p. 169)**

The experiences of women's lives are intricately intertwined with socially constructed expectations that are translated into beliefs, mandates, and stories, and are transmitted from generation to generation. Women divorced at midlife without children are out of sync with a number of prescribed expectations by the very nature of their life circumstance. Beliefs about marriage and motherhood, as well as the absence of these, undoubtedly can create an internal disconnect that can be very difficult for women to adapt to. These entrenched expectations and resulting beliefs surface in therapy as clinical themes as women relate the stories of their lives and role choices. The following two chapters demonstrate the major themes that have surfaced with women in both therapy practice and the research study. These themes are critical areas of exploration in therapy, as they are often rooted at the core of women's distress, decision making, ability to adapt, and coping capacities. The themes that have been identified provide clues to clinicians regarding areas of investigation in therapy with women who are considering decisions about marriage, childbearing, and divorce. The following guide may be useful in considering exploration of relevant themes:

- Beliefs about marriage and motherhood:
    - Beliefs in early adulthood

Beliefs after midlife divorce
- Desire for children:
  - Desire for children in early adulthood
  - Desire for children in midlife
- Feelings about the divorce process:
  - Reasons for midlife divorce
  - Realization of early adulthood mistake
  - Lack of emotional connection in marriage
  - Increasing differences/decreasing compatibility
  - Stressors of possible infertility
- Initiation of the divorce process
- Retrospective feelings about divorce

BELIEFS ABOUT MARRIAGE AND MOTHERHOOD

The Pressure to Marry in Young Adulthood

Despite the plethora of roles, choices, and opportunities now available to women, the "prescription" to marry and mother still seems pervasive and is often still an unconscious, internalized stressor that compels many women to marry in early adulthood. In some cases there is a sense of knowing it is a mistake, and in other cases women proceed while really not desiring to marry at all. Despite the trend of delayed first marriage, beliefs still exists regarding marriage and motherhood as the most valuable and worthy choices a woman can make. For many, choices of alternate roles and lifestyles are not consciously in women's decision-making repertoire in early adulthood. At midlife, some women describe an awareness of the learned "messages" that had an impact on their behavior and decisions earlier in their lives. Many women describe an unconscious expectation and assumption they will marry and have kids. Many midlife women were still raised in the era when this was primarily an unconscious thought process, as opposed to a conscious decision-making process. In adolescence and early adulthood, many women view themselves primarily as potential wives and mothers. As a result of these embedded beliefs, many women marry their first boyfriends in their early 20s.

An example is Becky, who dated her first boyfriend from the age of 16 and married him at age 21. She reflected that she always assumed they would marry:

> It was what you were SUPPOSED to do [marrying and having children]. I mean it wasn't quite as shallow as that, but it was as basic as you were going to get married and have a baby and that was what you DID. I mean, even with going to school it was like what was the point of going to school anyway if you were going to be home with kids? That was the mentality of the times.

Bonnie, who met her ex-husband at age 18 in college and married at age 23, also recalled the unspoken assumption between the couple while dating that they would marry and have children when they finished college. She recalled her plan:

> We just assumed all along that we would get married. I always assumed that I would work for awhile and then have a family. Yeah, I would work for awhile and then get pregnant, and then they would go to school and I would go back to work part-time. I think I just always assumed I would get married and have children. I always assumed I would have children. Yeah, I think I had assumed moving along, I had a good family life, and so there was no thought of not having kids.

Some women were exceptions to this prescription and related stories of a lack of focus on marriage or childbearing in adolescence or young adulthood. Even with a lack of desire for these roles, many women still found themselves gravitating toward them as life goals, if only unconsciously. Lynn was such an exception. She stated:

> I never had a compelling desire to get married, and in fact it was something that I was not sure I ever really wanted to do. I don't know exactly why. I could speculate. It seemed like women had to struggle so much with children, you became a non-entity almost, and women were never respected.

Assumptions regarding marrying by a certain age were often present in many women's stories. There is an unspoken time frame by which society expects marriage to occur, and this standard is surely entrenched in women's psyches. This standard is often internalized and, if not met, can become the source of distress and feelings of difference, inadequacy, low self-esteem, and grief. Perceived pressure can be exacerbated when women observe their friends marrying and having babies in young adulthood.

Marcia met her ex-husband at age 21 when she was in college. She married at age 23 as she had expected. She recalled "pushing it" because she felt time was wasting and "it was time" to get married. The couple actually postponed their wedding once due to the groom's reluctance; however, Marcia continued to push for marriage. She stated:

> Mostly what had happened was that I had graduated from college and he had gotten a job and we were living in two different states. I was the one who seemed to push it. I was 23 and all my friends were getting married and it was time to do something. It was a pressure that I put on myself.

Janice also recalled that even though she didn't think she was looking to get married, when the opportunity presented itself in her late 20s, she felt that it was something she should do. She described a hypothetical plan she always had regarding expectations of marrying and having children by a certain age. She subsequently felt this contributed to her entering a marriage she knew on some level beforehand was not right and might not work out:

> We thought we were at the right age to go ahead and get married. We were 27 and 28, and it was a fine time to get married. Yeah. Sure, why not? Let's do this. I loved him, or so I thought. I think it felt like the logical next step to get engaged and married at that age. I wanted children my whole life. When I was 12 I wanted to be a nurse and get married and have children by the time I was 25. That was the plan.

In addition to assumptions regarding marrying and having children by a certain age, some women also expressed the realization that role choices other than marriage and motherhood had never been perceived as available for them. This is not to say that these roles were exclusive, as many women also had interest in pursuing education and careers. However, the most valued roles were usually perceived to be wife and mother. The impact of messages received from society that women *should* get married and have children seems to have a critical effect on decisions to marry. Lynn, who never felt compelled to marry or have children, believed that she had acquiesced out of a perceived societal obligation.

She expressed her awareness of societal messages toward women:

> I'll never forget when I was about 25 and I was out with my mother and she said, "You are never going to be anything without a man," and I was like WHAT? But that's the kind of stuff you had to deal with. That I wanted to be something else was probably more societal and culturally based than anything else.

Janice, who married in her late 20s, thought she was happy with how her life was going and didn't particularly think she was looking for marriage at that time. She described her reasons for proceeding to marry and associated them to perceived societal beliefs:

> Marriage is important to me. I believe the purpose of marriage is to be completely monogamous, to not have anything open. From what I understand, that is why the foundation of marriage was established, so that there are no other parties involved, also family and religious beliefs. I think that is what society has told our generation.

Beliefs About Marriage After Midlife Divorce

Beliefs about marriage shift for most women after a midlife divorce, ostensibly as a result of their divorce experience and the opportunity for reflection, self-examination, and life review. The divorce experience can result in increased cautiousness and hesitancy to remarry. At midlife there is often greater interest in being more selective about choice of a partner and desire not to repeat mistakes made in young adulthood. This cautiousness can take the form of ambivalence about dating and remarriage. Concern can also surface that the newly found "self" could be lost, including expression of voice and control over their lives, should they remarry.

Kim, who had high desire to marry in her early 20s, following in the example of all her friends, expressed ambivalence about remarrying at midlife:

> I don't care if I ever get married again. He would have to be the right guy. He's got to be good in bed. I'd rather not be with somebody if he's not right. Why waste my time? I see a lot of people stuck in relationships. A lot of people are miserable. So why do it? Why be miserable? I could join a dating service but I don't want to.

Pat also expressed fear of settling for a relationship the second time around. She related:

> My biggest fear is like maybe settling for a relationship that isn't really what I want, that's my biggest fear. I miss being in a couple, yeah, I just miss having a partner. I have mixed feelings about being alone or being with someone. I was in this relationship and it wasn't perfect. We had a really good time together. There was nothing really wrong, it just wasn't great. I sort of promised myself that, and I hate this word, but I just didn't want to settle for something that wasn't great.

Women also expressed the fear of making another mistake, and the fact that they have become much more thoughtful about the qualities they were looking for in a partner post-divorce.

Janice related her cautiousness and the qualities she wanted in a partner at midlife:

> I've gotten a lot more critical over these three years. I think I would be more selective of the qualities and make sure they were a better match with my family and friends, beliefs, morals and ethics. I need someone who has more of the foundation that I have in my values. Good family values. I want someone with a good family background. Someone that is well adjusted to society and sociable, someone that wants to expand their interests. Someone that wants to share, someone that wants to know about my interests. Someone that wants to accept me and my family in their life.

Peggy, who married twice, similarly related her amended expectations at midlife:

> In terms of a relationship right now, I'd be looking for someone who is more mature than my ex-husband is, someone who is not a partier. I don't want someone who drinks a lot or travels. I don't want to be

> with a drinker, nope. I'd rather be alone than with a drinker. Well I know I won't put up with any crap from anyone as much, men. You know I won't put up with anyone drinking or treating me bad. Been there done that before, can't be bothered.

FEELINGS ABOUT THE DIVORCE PROCESS

The success of marriage is still perceived to be primarily a woman's responsibility, and divorce is still a stigmatized experience for many women. It often evokes complex feelings, reactions, and perceptions. The legacy of unacceptability, shame, and guilt for women has not loosened its hold on women emotionally. The reasons for midlife divorce, the initiation process, and retrospective feelings about divorce are important clinical themes to explore in therapy. Several key themes include emotional needs not being met, increasing differences and incompatibility, communication breakdown, and marital strain due to possible infertility.

REASONS FOR MIDLIFE DIVORCE

Realization of Early Adulthood Mistake

Many women expressed the belief that marriage in early adulthood was a mistake, and that they had some awareness of this prior to marrying. However, the pressure to marry superseded this sense of knowing. The power of dominant cultural scripts is still a critical factor in many women's decisions to marry in early adulthood. Some women described a sense of knowing they were entering marriages that were most likely not going to meet their emotional needs.

Lynn recalled her awareness of warning signs prior to her marriage. She also connected the lapse of three wedding licenses as a sign of her ambivalence and hesitation regarding the marriage. She stated:

> I think it was a troubled relationship from the beginning. There were times from the very beginning where he was a control freak and had a lot of emotional issues that he was projecting onto me. We were together about six years and he wanted to get married, and I was ambivalent, very ambivalent. I think we got three licenses that lapsed. He finally gave me an ultimatum and said, "Either we get married or I'm leaving." I guess there was something about him leaving, that I agreed to get married and we were married in a civil ceremony at city hall.

Janice remembered being quite happy planning goals for her life when she met her ex-husband. She felt that she was not looking for marriage at that time. She found herself somehow going ahead with marriage plans anyway, even though there were warning signs that the relationship might not work out. When asked why she proceeded with the marriage, she described a feeling of pressure, embarrassment, and anxiety regarding her perception that friends and family would be disappointed if she canceled her plans. Janice had a sense of shame about her thoughts the night before her wedding that she was not doing the right thing, but felt she could not get herself out of the pending marriage at that point.

Lack of Emotional Connection in Marriage

At midlife, some women described no longer being able to tolerate a relationship that was not meeting their emotional needs. This has been found to be a frequent reason for divorce at midlife (Enright, 2004). After years of unfulfilling marriage, distress can become intolerable at midlife as women begin a process of midlife review. Several women related that at midlife they became aware of greater expectations of marriage as a source of emotional nurturance with a partner. Early marriage is a common occurrence, with many women never consciously considering the qualities that they desire in a spouse.

Lynn felt that her relationship had been emotionally unfulfilling and, in fact, abusive for most of the marriage. Her husband's lack of emotional nurturing and caring for her worsened when a close friend of Lynn's became terminally ill. Her husband asked for a divorce while her friend was in her dying days. Lynn felt this timing was a narcissistic act by her ex-husband and was emotionally abusive to her. She painfully recalled:

> My ex-husband was basically very distant, aloof, disconnected, and he was verbally abusive. Nothing I could do was right. I was too fat, too skinny, my hair was too short, my hair was too long, my friends were this or that. Eventually my marriage began to look like any other abusive relationship. I wasn't having the shit beaten out of me or anything, but my friends began to isolate. I became this nuclear person. Around two weeks before my best friend's death, my husband asked me for a divorce. We were going into my friend's last days. At that point I knew I couldn't be with someone who would be that cold and uncaring.

Increasing Differences/Decreasing Compatibility

Decreasing compatibility and increasing differences often come into play in midlife divorce. After a period of at least several years of marriage, differences can be perceived as too great to reconcile, with diminishing compatibility. After "automatically" being driven to marry and choosing partners without a period of "search," women often described realization in midlife that the gap in compatibility was too great to bridge. Communication breakdown also can be a main contributor to midlife divorce. In the post-divorce state at midlife, women often seek a deeper level of compatibility than in their early adulthood marriage.

Becky described the gap in emotional connectedness as a gradual drift over time:

> I'd say that we just drifted, we were not soul mates. He was there. He would be there. I just think we were different, and sometimes you just can't go back, you can't reinvent it.
>
> He just wasn't the love of my life, he wasn't my best friend. Sometimes I wondered how we got together. I mean there wasn't a dislike, it wasn't bitter or angry.

Peggy also described her sense of growing difference and incompatibility after embarking on an early adult marriage to "keep up" with peer pressure:

> At first we got along really well, we kind of have the same personality, but I think we didn't have things in common. Little things, like music. I know that is little, but mainly he wasn't home and he was more of a drinker than me. Like we would go to a party and he would drink a lot with his friends, and I'm not into that. I'm more of a homebody, I'm not a partier. He was immature, he was always running around all over the place. I like someone to be home. So I think that is where we didn't have something in common.

The Stressors of Possible Infertility

Possible infertility is also a factor that can increase to intolerable proportions by midlife as childbearing capacity is waning. In cases where women are attempting to follow prescribed time frames for childbearing, being unable to complete those plans "on time" can cause considerable distress in marital relationships. Some women related tales of distancing, acting out, and lack of communication when faced with possible infertility.

Janice recalled the deterioration of her marriage after an early miscarriage:

> I had a miscarriage, and he was great through that, but he was very insensitive after it. After that I had a very hard time. A lot of issues were coming out after the miscarriage. When I lost the baby it was really devastating for me. He would even say things to me like, "Let's just have a kid and it will be fine." I had a hard time with Mother's Day because it would have been my first Mother's Day. He was kind of insensitive to me. It took me awhile to get over it. You'll never get over it. I started going to a counselor because I thought I was depressed because of the baby. Then we decided to go to therapy together and it was the end.

Pat also had difficulty conceiving and described how, just as the couple was beginning to pursue adoption, they began to isolate themselves from each other and build separate lives:

> I think the fertility problems were certainly a contributing factor. Not being home at night, developing separate social lives, it was probably just too painful. We were pursuing adoption, we had a home study done. We were just about to do it. We were going our separate ways, and then we never quite finished the adoption process. Then the relationship started to get bitter and fighting. We were not spending enough time together. Half of it was my fault, half of it was his fault. We basically built separate lives.

Lynn also felt that infertility issues were a contributing factor in her divorce. She related:

> He decided we should have children and he felt that was the issue. I was 42 and we had to deal with secondary infertility, so we dealt with all the medications and everything. I think I went ahead with it more because of him. Boy did I put myself through hell. At one point I said, "I'm not doing this anymore," and I stopped it. One night he came home and he blew up and he told me he was seeing somebody else.

THE INITIATION OF THE DIVORCE PROCESS

Pervasive beliefs about commitment to marriage, perceived responsibility for the success of relationships, and fear of failure, in many cases, affect women's emotional ability to initiate divorce. Although having serious concerns regarding remaining in their marriages, many women do not consider initiating the divorce themselves as an option. High value on the commitment to marriage often leads to beliefs of permanent bonds to marriage, sometimes even in the face of emotional or physical abuse. Women also voiced concerns about being perceived as a failure, should they divorce. Given the perceived societal prohibition against divorce, women sometimes utilize an affair outside the marriage as an indirect route to exit an unsatisfactory marriage. Divorce is still viewed as an unacceptable option, even in the face of a deteriorating marriage. Even the experience of increasing abuse sometimes is not enough to trigger the exit from a marriage. Despite significant social change that has made divorce more acceptable, it remains extremely difficult for many women to clearly state they desire to divorce, and to initiate it without hesitancy. Marcia recalled that when she began graduate school psychology courses, she realized that her husband had a potentially serious problem with alcohol. Despite the seriousness of this issue for her, she felt initiating a divorce was in no way an option, as it would symbolize her failure as a wife. She stated:

> There was alcohol involved but I never felt that leaving him was an option for me. Oh it crossed my mind all the time and I would use it. I would say it, but no, I would never leave. I gave him an ultimatum. I said, "Either you stop drinking or I'm going to do something." I never

> had any intention of leaving. He left. There was no me leaving him. I'm Catholic and was feeling like God would disapprove, you know. The big thing was feeling like I failed, and no one in my family gets divorced.

Lynn also believed her marriage had become emotionally abusive with physical abuse an increasing threat. However, due to the perceived meaning of her marital commitment, she did not view extricating herself via divorce as an option. She explained:

> No, I never thought of divorce. Once I made the commitment, I was a committed partner, a faithful partner. I was very supportive. My husband was very complicated. He kept secrets. I'll never forget this little book saved my life. It was about verbal abuse and it was describing me. It talked about how you are diminished and I was the exact character in there. One time he physically attacked me and that's when I thought, Oh boy am I screwed.

Some women experienced feelings of being "pushed into divorce," attached to feelings of inability to initiate the divorce themselves, being bound to beliefs about lifelong commitment to their marriages. After waiting and hoping for reconciliation for several years, they eventually initiate divorce proceedings due to inactivity on their husband's part.

After hoping for reconciliation for two years, Marcia finally acknowledged that her marriage was over and initiated the divorce:

> I did everything to initiate the divorce. I did even his part too. The first year I thought he would get it out of his system and come back. The second year he wasn't getting it out of his system and he moved an hour and a half away, and at that point I realized this was stupid. I realized there was no reconciliation and I was just going to do it. It just happened.

Sara recalled similar feelings:

> I waited as long as I could. I kept secretly hoping that he would come forward and say he really wanted the marriage. That never happened. He just kept acting out isolation and refusal to communicate. At a certain point, I think it was after three years of hoping, I finally said, "I can't do this anymore." It was the end of the line, and the dream was over.

The initiation of an affair can be an indirect route to exiting an unsatisfactory marriage for some women. Directly acting upon a divorce is viewed as an unacceptable choice associated with guilt and shame. An affair seems to be a more acceptable alternative.

In her view, when Peggy's marriage began to deteriorate due to fertility problems, she began to gravitate toward a married man she had known before her marriage. She stated:

> I think I had a problem with somebody else in the background. I had feelings about this other person before I got married, someone that I never got over from before, but I felt okay to get married. But then when we had problems, I started thinking about the other person. I started thinking about getting divorced, and at that point I started talking to him, and I felt like I wanted to be free to go with him. We started talking again when I was separating, and I started focusing on him, which I think was wrong.

Janice also recalled feeling that her emotional needs were not being met in her marriage and gravitating toward another man with whom she quickly entered into a relationship:

> After two years I pretty much knew I wasn't happy with the whole situation, and by then I met this other guy, who I ended up getting married to, and that was really the whole thing behind the divorce. Again that was very stupid, but nevertheless it got me out of the situation. It gave me enough strength to get out of the situation. I think I would have eventually gotten out of it anyway, but it would have taken me longer.

Pat also recalled her involvement with a married man during the time that her marriage was deteriorating due to possible fertility problems:

> There was an extramarital affair during the separation period. I was involved with a married man. I think when you meet somebody new they are larger than life, and the old person doesn't measure up in any way. It sort of took the focus off. He was older than I was and he was really complimentary. He was a mentor, like this guru sort of that opened me up to a whole other world. We didn't deal with it so not to hurt each other. I went through like a wild period, but nobody connected the dots. I've just done it now through therapy.

RETROSPECTIVE FEELINGS ABOUT DIVORCE

After midlife divorce, regret about original choice for marriage can be common. These feelings are also often tied to feelings of regret, shame, and guilt about divorce. Although women often feel they made mistakes with earlier choices, midlife divorce seems to provide an opportunity to rectify those mistakes, in effect, a second chance. Marcia believed she would not have chosen her partner and expressed regret that she had not made an appropriate choice in her 20s. She stated:

> I would have liked to do it differently. I wouldn't have married my ex-husband. I wouldn't have done it. I knew it wasn't right. I have this thing about those lost years. That I can't go back and be 20 again

> and start differently with somebody else and produce a child and a happy marriage.

Despite having adjusted well emotionally to divorced status, some women expressed regret about midlife divorce and viewed themselves as responsible for the failure of their relationships. Pat, although not unhappy with her current lifestyle, did express regrets, significant guilt, and responsibility for the perceived failure of her marriage:

> I have all these regrets that I can't say. Like I should have been, I should have given it another chance. I should have stayed with it. I would have gotten out of the relationship and given it a real shot without that. I think that there are so many waves in relationships, you know highs and lows. I think if we could have ridden out the low we would have been fine because I sort of got a voice and I think that I could have communicated differently, but that's hindsight. He's remarried now. There's a lot of remorse and guilt that I ruined it.

Becky, although continuing to feel her husband was not the right choice for her initially, also expressed regret and self-blame:

> I wonder what it would have been like to stay together and have children. You know when you look at relationships, he wasn't a horrible person. He was very good. It was not somebody that was creepy. So I really feel that it was a foreign type marriage. It wasn't bad, it wasn't hostile, but it wasn't like "lovey dovey." If I looked at a relationship, I would be so different now in a relationship than I was. I think I know that if you really want to be with somebody, you really have to support them. It doesn't mean that what they say is gospel. But you have to support them and I don't think I did that when I was younger.

DESIRE FOR CHILDREN

Desire for Children in Early Adulthood

In therapy, it is important to explore the possibilities of low desire or ambivalent desire for children. This subject is often taboo and is not generally an issue that women feel comfortable speaking about openly. Lack of desire can be manifested by a woman's lack of effort to become pregnant or pursue childbearing by alternative means during young adult/childbearing years. Childbearing desires are often re-evaluated over time. Hidden concerns can surface about husbands as potential fathers. Of the women I worked with in both therapy and the research study, only a small number expressed high desire for children in early adulthood. Those women who reported lack of strong desire for children, in retrospect, recalled an absence of focus on the mothering role in adolescence and early adulthood. For these women, there was often never really a clear-cut decision point. Rather, feelings became clarified and were revisited over time. Women also sometimes become aware that they always had some internal sense that childbearing was not right for them, sometimes consciously, sometimes unconsciously. It can be common for women to voice a long-standing belief that they desired children in young adulthood. However, in actuality, they recognized their behavior contradicted that belief. In effect, ambivalence was manifested by inactivity in pursuing pregnancy.

Bonnie always assumed that she wanted to be a mother; however, in retrospect, she recognized her lack of activity in pursuing pregnancy and lack of communication about the issue with her husband:

> I feel weird looking back because I think I really wanted to be a mother, but I wasn't preoccupied with it, and my husband was not. We didn't talk about it. We never had the talk. I do remember thinking, I guess I should have kids before his brothers do, but it was just a fleeting thought. I never really put it on the table, and I guess I really wasn't that driven, and he wasn't. I don't know why I didn't act on it. I was prepared to be a mother. I think I would have been a good mother, a hands-on mother.

Becky, who married her high school sweetheart at age 21, was married six years without attempting to get pregnant. She also recalled ambivalent feelings while first married:

> I always wanted children, but I also didn't want them right away. I had no problem waiting when we were first married. I loved being able to go away with other couples. As much as I wanted children, I didn't want them right away. I was starting to get ready for that when things started falling apart. I was 27.

Kim described a conscious desire for children; however, she recognized that, in her 20s and 30s, dating a man for 10 years who did not want children diminished her childbearing chances.

> I always wanted children. I always wanted one. I didn't want to ruin my figure. I'm very family oriented and grew up in an Italian neighborhood with a lot of kids. I dated a guy for 10 years who didn't want to have kids. I wanted children with him, but I never pushed him. I said I could do without the kids. I would have married him but he wouldn't commit.

Ambivalence is sometimes related to perceived concerns about marriage and about the husband's ability to father adequately. Marcia connected her ambivalence and weak desire to concerns she had throughout the 10 years of her marriage that she had made a mistake and did not want to exacerbate it with a child. It was notable that Marcia was unable to voice her concerns to anyone and remained in the marriage, forgoing an opportunity for children. Marcia expressed her concerns:

> After the fifth year of marriage, the drinking was really bad. I knew he wouldn't be a good father. I knew he wouldn't be there for me. I knew I'd have to raise the child by myself. It came up in my mind, "He's not going to be a good dad." He had a hard time caring for himself, and for somebody with zilch life skills, would I be able to care for a child by myself? I had no confidence that he could care for a child. It was okay if we screwed up our lives, but don't screw up a kid's life.

Janice, who also always voiced a strong desire for children in early adolescence and young adulthood, also described her reasons for not pursuing pregnancy as related to concerns about her marriage and her husband as a potential father. She stated:

> I thought I didn't want children anymore. I realized I didn't want children with him because I realized he wouldn't be a suitable father. The things he would say and do, I never could have lived with. I never could have handed over my children to his friends and family. I think it was the marriage—that I didn't want the marriage anymore, and I didn't want children with him.

For women for whom the desire for children had seemed high from adolescence on, the role of mother seemed of utmost importance. Janice, who married at age 28 and subsequently suffered a miscarriage several years into her marriage, discussed that one of her primary dreams in adolescence and young adulthood was to have children. She recalled:

> Oh GOD yes! ABSOLUTELY, ALWAYS! I always wanted children. Oh yeah, absolutely we both wanted children. I wanted children my whole life. I wanted it. I always wanted children, even before I was married. I always had a lot of desire. We started trying as soon as we got married. I always wanted like 10 kids NOW. I wanted a huge family, the traditional life. We DEFINITELY wanted children.

Desire for Children in Midlife

In many cases, low or ambivalent desire for children in adolescence and early adulthood still seemed to remain a consistent belief at midlife. Several women who described low desire and low interest in children since adolescence retrospectively recognized that as life progressed, traumatic life events and significant losses had probably exacerbated their initial low desire.

Lynn felt that her desire not to have children had remained fairly constant into midlife. She believed her family history of early abandonment by her parents, and their emotional difficulties and poor marital relationship colored her desire for both marriage and children. She commented on her feelings of fearfulness regarding mothering:

> Sometimes I look back on my life and I think having children is a real act of hope and you have to be courageous and have lots of guts, and I don't think I had it. The reality is, when I look at it, the devil is in the details. So I go, "Okay Lynn, let's say you could do this with children," and I always say no. And when I am really gut honest with myself, I realize that's who I was.

High desire for children in young adulthood can be transformed to ambivalence or low desire after a midlife divorce. Peggy, who seemed sure she wanted children and began trying to get pregnant as soon as she was married, expressed ambivalent feelings regarding childbearing at midlife. This seemed to symbolize a loss of independence to her:

> Sometimes I go back and forth, I have different feelings. I guess everybody does. Sometimes I don't want a child, but then if I don't have one, you feel like you are missing out on something. I think most people feel that way. There is a teeny part of me that says I can sleep late on Saturdays. I don't have to worry about the responsibility. It is a big responsibility. I like being independent right now. I have different feelings, but I mostly do want a child. I would like a little girl of my own. I really do want a child. I know it's a lot of work.

Peg, who also initially believed she wanted a very traditional family life with at least several children, described a decision-making process that had surfaced since her midlife divorce. She also expressed concern about loss of freedom now at age 43:

> At this stage in my life without knowing who I am going to do it with, it's a decision. It's not just a no-brainer. I'm in a decision-making process—Can I do it alone? Do I want to do it alone—that kind of thing. I'm undecided. Some days I wake up and say yes and there are days when I say no. I mean I have a nice life. And there is definitely room for a man and a child, but I don't know.
>
> There is this other side of it, where I could see having a career, traveling. But when I'm 70, I want to have an adult child. I'm not sure I'm into the baby and all that stuff that goes along with it. The cute baby stuff, yeah, but all that other stuff, I have my doubts. But I think I would do it anyway. Now it is a real choice, a conscious choice. Before it was never really a conscious choice, it was just what I was going to do. It was a natural process and it was what was desirable. Now it's like okay, let me really, really think about this. There are two paths I can go on. It's a tough decision at this age.

Becky, at age 50, also questioned the strength of her drive initially and expressed her concerns about giving up the freedom to be in control of her life, should she have a child. She stated:

> I guess the drive wasn't that strong, that plus not having a partner there. But I think if you really want to do something you can find the money, so I think it was the partner. Maybe, in fact, not even the desire, but I never thought about it that way, like why don't you pursue something, because I would love to have a child. I think it would be a wonderful thing. I have always been surrounded by children, so I do like them, love them, whatever, but maybe I didn't want the responsibility. I've always been able to come and go as I please.

Even Janice, whose desire was always high in young adulthood, believed her desire for children had changed from a somewhat dreamy vision to a more realistic expectation at midlife after her divorce. She stated:

> I guess I'm so much more realistic now as to what it takes to have a family. I mean the work involved, the juggling, the fighting. I'm looking at the reality of having children right now, not the vision and the dream, like more realistic. I'd love being with them. It's not the dreamy kind of thing anymore. It's really the reality of what is entailed. And now it really doesn't bother me as much, it's not as bad as it used to be.

Beliefs regarding the unacceptability of mothering via alternate means, regardless of low, ambivalent, or high desire for children, often surface for divorced women. These beliefs can be associated with traditional social constructions regarding the meaning and implications of parenting outside the norms of traditional family life. Most of the women also revealed practical concerns regarding the responsibility of child rearing alone. Many expressed the belief that mothering alone through alternate means was not an acceptable choice for them. Several expressed a traditional belief that parenting should be within the context of marriage. Marcia, who had not made any attempt to become pregnant during 10 years of marriage, expressed concerns about both the responsibility and financial pressure of mothering alone:

> If I adopt I don't want to do it myself because I just know that I wouldn't have the ability to do it by myself. I'm worried about patience. I'm worried about a child who would come from a broken home and would I be able to deal with all the ups and downs by myself. And there is the feeling of not wanting to do it by myself. Definitely finances figure in. I don't feel like I make enough money, you know, like for college, clothes, and stuff. I think it is just because I don't want to do it by myself.

Lynn also felt the work involved in parenting alone would be too difficult to consider it an option. She explained:

> It's a lot of work. It's too much work. I've taken care of children and supported people in my family and friends of mine who are single parents and definitely it's not something I want to do. It's not the responsibility, it's the work, it takes work to raise children. You know I'm 50 and in good health, but you need an energy level. For me, I have a very small family and I think, Okay, what if you adopt a kid and something happens to you? Should I die or something, what would happen? I have to think about that.

Several women echoed similar feelings about not wanting to parent alone, considering this as a second-rate choice to doing it with a spouse. Several had considered the option of adoption, but felt they had concerns about managing the logistics of caretaking and the financial pressures alone. For several women, traditional beliefs that mothering should be done in the context of marriage and an intact family seemed to be a barrier to consideration of alternate means of mothering, and several expressed beliefs about the importance of mothering in a traditional way. Janice related her thoughts regarding alternate means of parenting:

> I couldn't do any of those things, adoption or artificial insemination. I really wanted to do it with a partner. I couldn't do that; it wouldn't be right for me. I would rather open myself up to someone who had children, who was divorced or widowed. Absolutely I'd have to have a solid relationship to do the children piece. I feel to have children I would want to bring them up in a solid foundation. Why make it any weirder on them? I don't want to have some stranger's child. No, that doesn't appeal to me.

Becky also had internalized beliefs about the preference for parenting in the context of marriage:

> I guess I have ruled out adoption. I still hope if I meet someone with kids I could have them in my life. That's how I look towards having a child more so than adopting. I think certain things you just want to do with somebody else, a shared thing. Logically, I think that as women we are more than capable, but I just think that it was subconscious with myself. Even like buying a house, I couldn't imagine buying a house, it just didn't seem right for myself. I mean now I would. I think that played a big part in it, it was just something that should be shared. I wanted there to be someone else that was going to share it with me, the responsibility and the joy.

Socially constructed beliefs have a powerful impact not only on women's decision making, but also on their capacity to cope with changes in their life circumstance through the process of divorce. Women divorced at midlife without children are often "trapped" between two sets of beliefs: those internalized unconsciously in early adulthood and those formulated as a result of the process of midlife divorce, life review, and an increased sense of self-knowing.

The beliefs presented in this chapter provide clinical information regarding important areas of investigation for therapy when working with women divorced at midlife without children. It is important to facilitate identification of beliefs in different stages of the life cycle and explore how those beliefs may have changed over time. It is also important to facilitate transformation of unhelpful beliefs into constructive narratives of coping, survivorship, and growth in the post-divorce phase. The exploration of these themes can also be useful when working with young adult women who are considering marriage, childbearing, and divorce.

CHAPTER 9

Out on a Limb

Beliefs About Role Exit and Transition

> The glorification of women's role, then, seems to be in proportion to society's reluctance to treat women as complete human beings, for the less real function that role has, the more it is decorated with meaningless details to conceal its emptiness.
>
> **—Betty Friedan, *The Feminine Mystique* (1997, p. 239)**

As a result of being divorced at midlife without children, the exit from the roles of wife and potential mother become a major challenge for most women. Adaptation to the role of single, dating woman is also a challenging developmental task, an experience that can seem quite foreign to women who have been married all of their young adult lives. Although the initial stage of role exit via divorce is commonly characterized by significant grief reactions, anxiety, and depression, many women prove to be very resilient in their construction of fulfilling roles and evolution to a new lifestyle.

The process of role exit and transition involves detachment from traditional role expectations and redefinition of self. This can be a challenging task for women divorced at midlife without children. In therapy it is important to explore a woman's adaptation to role exit and transition to role innovation. The following issues should be considered for exploration:

- Initial exit from the role of wife
- Mobilization and recovery: adaptation to role exit
- Development of narratives of survivorship
- Independence and loneliness
- Adjustment to the absence of a partner
- The role of dating woman at midlife
- Concerns about midlife and aging

- Coping and adaptation to role transition:
  - Perceptions of reactions of others
  - Family relationships
  - Development of supportive friendship networks
  - Work and career
  - Financial adjustment
  - Use of psychotherapy as support

INITIAL EXIT FROM THE ROLE OF WIFE

The initial exit from the roles of wife and potential mother is a potential crisis point in a woman's life that can have a significant impact on her emotional and psychological well-being. Initial reactions can include significant grief reactions such as shock and numbing. Anxiety, depression, physical illnesses, and exhaustion are also common. In some cases, initial adjustment is also affected by significant feelings of shame, guilt, and perceived failure. Symptoms are commonplace during the first one to two years of the separation and divorce process, regardless of which spouse had initiated the divorce. Attempts to hide the perceived shame of their status by keeping it secret from immediate family members confirm the shame still attached to divorce.

Women commonly described a period of numbness during which the emotional impact of separation and divorce seemed blocked from awareness. Becky recognized a numbness that ensued after her separation:

> I never really went through the emotions. I think I pushed it out of the way. I really didn't mourn. I think I kind of kidded myself like because it wasn't hostile, okay this was fine and this was no problem, not realizing the effects it has on you.

Keeping separations secret from immediate families for as long as a year can be an attempt to cover over feelings of guilt, shame, and responsibility for the failure of the marriage.

Marcia stated:

> I didn't tell my family. It was almost three months before I told my mother he left. I told my sister after a month and a half. I did not to tell anyone because I thought he would come back. And I thought nobody needed to know. The reality of it, if I tell somebody, then it is true. I didn't tell anybody at work. I guess I thought he'll come back. After telling people then I would have to deal with the fact that he really left me and he really treated me as bad as … Also, I'd think I failed that my husband didn't love me.

Bonnie kept her separation secret from family and friends for one year. She related:

> I didn't tell my parents. They came down at Thanksgiving and I didn't tell them, and I think the reason was, you know, feeling like a failure, and I was still feeling that he would come back. If he had come back in those six weeks I never would have told them. I was just thinking he would come back. I didn't tell people in the first year of Christmas cards. I said very general things which were true.

Ten of the 12 women in the study related experiencing significant anxiety and depression during the initial period of separation from their marital partner. Marcia recalled anxiety, fears, and depression that manifested as a psychosomatic symptom of abdominal pains and a subsequent hospitalization:

> The first year I didn't sleep. I lived in a ranch-style house and I was scared. I would think, How am I going to make it? How am I going to make it without him? How am I going to pay the bills without him? I didn't eat. I was so depressed. It was a difficult time. I was grieving for what I thought was going to be a lifelong relationship. I was in shock. It was a crazy time. I can't even begin to describe how crazy it was. I was anxious, though I functioned. I never missed a day of work. At one time I became so depressed that I admitted myself into a psych hospital because I felt like I was going to crash. I told them I think I am going to have a psychotic break. I admitted myself for 72 hours. They slept me with IV medications, and then I did much better after that. I went on Zoloft for about a year.

MOBILIZATION AND RECOVERY: ADAPTATION TO ROLE EXIT

Surprisingly, after the distress and grief of initial role exit subsides, most women seem to make a significant emotional recovery and adjustment subsequent to the initial exit from the role of wife and potential mother. The absence of anxiety and depression experienced upon the initial period of separation and divorced was noteworthy in both clinical practice and the research study. Significant coping skills such as self-soothing and calming, self-care, internal strength and determination, and increased capacity to be alone seem to enhance recovery. The phrase "I don't have to" was often mentioned by women in the study and related to feelings regarding the role of wife as associated with overwhelming caretaking responsibilities.

Post-divorce, many women enjoy aspects of single life and living alone that contribute to feelings of self-sufficiency, control, and "having a voice." Many women construct fulfilling social lives and are rarely lonely. Some women experienced occasional loneliness that they felt they learned to manage well. A disadvantage described by some women was missing the experience of sharing life with a partner. Mobilizing oneself to reorganize life after a midlife divorce helps women in their ability to move forward with a new lifestyle. Mobilizing, focusing on new roles, reorganizing lifestyles, and developing new interests and friends are coping skills that enhance divorce recovery.

After suffering severe anxiety and depression in the initial stages of divorce, Lynn mobilized and reorganized. She described:

> I started being more physically active. That really helped. Over time I really started doing a lot of reading on Eastern philosophy and Buddhism, and doing breathing and meditation. That coupled with cognitive therapy, that's really what got me through it. Somehow little by little I began to let things go. I don't mean to say I got up and I was a different person. It takes time. It must have been showing in my face that I was a lot happier. People used to say, "Oh, you look a lot happier."

Peggy, who felt initially paralyzed and unable to mobilize herself, reviewed her reorganization:

> I am trying to do a little more and get out more. I am trying to get hobbies. I do gymnastics every week, which I love. I took that up again after I got divorced. I read now. I watch Lifetime channel. That got me through it. It gets your mind off of it. I'm doing a little better. I feel like I want to be living my life and out doing things. A new friend has helped me a lot. She knows a lot of people and we go out.

Many of the women perceived that their emotional state was greatly improved subsequent to the initiation of their separation and divorce. Of note was the absence of descriptions of ongoing depression and anxiety. Lynn commented:

> I'm probably in the best place I've ever been in. I'm very much at peace with myself. I was working through a lot of stuff. I was tapered off the medication after a year, and I never went back on it. My mood was fine and I felt like I could handle things through therapy.

June related:

> Emotionally I'm good. I definitely think things through with a much clearer head. I tried so hard to get myself back up from the divorce. It was so hard to get myself up from that point. I don't ever want my life to sink that low again. I would say that it took me about a year, and that was just the beginning of my comeback! It's still a process, it's always a process. Maybe it was a progression over two years. Each day felt better and better. I was coming out of it. All the bad stuff was starting to melt away little by little. It was all baby steps. I started to feel something. I had no feelings. I was emotionally void. It was a turning point where I felt I was starting to dig myself out of the black hole. I'm doing really well now!

In retrospect, Pat was surprised at her diminished anxiety and good emotional state:

> I'm doing remarkably better than I thought. I am totally focused on my career and being with my friends. I am not having any trouble sleeping or being home at night. It is remarkably okay. I'm actually pretty happy at the moment, but I'm surprised! I thought I would have a lot of anxiety, but I don't, and frankly I'm shocked about it! That period of nothing, I was extremely anxiety filled, a lot of anxiety, a lot of obsessive thoughts—What is he doing? Why doesn't he love me—extremely anxiety filled. And now I'm not. I'm kind of happy. It sounds strange!

LEMONS OR LEMONADE: THE DICHOTOMY OF INDEPENDENCE AND LONELINESS

The advantages of living single life can often be perceived as a sense of gaining control over oneself, lifestyle choices, and decisions. In the study, many women commented on how greatly they enjoy the independence and freedom of being single and living alone. Although they had worried about loneliness prior to their divorce, in actuality they found that loneliness was rare, and contentment about living alone increased feelings of well-being. Many women described enjoyment of the full lives they had constructed for themselves post-divorce.

Succeeding in developing the capacity to be alone can translate into a sense of self-efficacy and independence that promotes self-esteem and emotional growth. Bonnie related positive feelings about having control and independence:

> I think the independence is a big thing. Just independence and that would be traveling, working, how late I stay up, what I make for meals, whether I clean up the kitchen, whether the house is a disaster. (*Laughs*) It just doesn't matter! Even if the house is a mess I don't have to clean it up for Sunday, stuff like that! I pretty much like being able to set my own schedule and not answer to anybody. I'm a little selfish but I am enjoying it.

Pat also associated being single with gaining control over herself and feeling that she had "regained her voice" in her post-divorce adjustment. She stated:

> I can make decisions on where I go and what I do. I'd like to think that my husband was somewhat controlling. I really didn't have that much of a voice. I have a voice now in my own life. I like to think I would have it in a relationship again, and I did because I did have it in my last one. I might be a little too independent at this point. I spend a lot of time with friends and on my own. I'm remarkably better than I thought.

Marcia related her enjoyment of decreased caretaking responsibilities:

> I love living by myself. I have my own set ways, and the stereo and the TV are on at the same time and there's nobody to tell me to turn it off. I don't answer to anybody. I don't have any pets and I barely care for my plants. Sometimes I like it. I don't have to worry about messing up my kitchen. No one to pick up after, it's nice and quiet, do what I want. (*Laughs*) There are a lot of advantages. You don't have to worry about anyone else. I don't have to cook.

ADJUSTING TO THE ABSENCE OF A PARTNER

Although living single life can be enjoyable, the feeling of missing the sharing of the ups and downs of life with someone often surfaces after divorce. This was perceived as one of the disadvantages of not being married. Some women describe this as one of the most difficult aspects of adjusting to exiting the role of wife. Lynn described her skills in managing fleeting feelings of loneliness:

> I'm not one of these people that feels uncomfortable living alone. I don't feel I have to have a man in my life to feel complete. I have a lot of interests. I'm an avid reader. I started writing poetry recently. I'm also interested in textile arts. I've been dancing, and really working on some of those things. I'm an avid Buddhist philosophy reader and I'm thinking of trying to find a Buddhist community that fits me.

THE ROLE OF DATING WOMAN AT MIDLIFE

The need to adapt to the role of dating and socializing at midlife after at least several or many years of marriage can prove to be challenging, frustrating, and humiliating for many women. Some described feeling devalued as mature women. Many expressed concerns regarding the ability to meet appropriate potential partners. Feelings of frustration, discomfort, and humiliation regarding dating experiences were somewhat common. Marcia, who had been single and dating for 13 years, expressed her frustration regarding the necessity to attend singles events in order to meet someone. She stated:

> Right now I have been struggling. It has been 13 years of dances and the new thing was the speed dating thing. It's almost like, I've done all this shit and I never liked doing any of it. It was boring, it was monotonous. It was the same old thing. If I stand in a corner one more GOD DAMN time waiting for a guy to ask me to dance I swear I'm going to kill myself! (*Laughs*)

Peggy similarly expressed frustration regarding being in the dating scene at midlife. Her feelings included a sense of discomfort of going to bars and frustration regarding not finding acceptable ways to meet someone appropriate. She related:

> Dating and trying to meet someone has been terrible! I go to work, I go home. There are not really any places to go. I don't like to go to bars. I don't think there is really much out there. I don't see a light at the end of the tunnel. And when you go out, everyone is younger, 20s. My friends used to go out and don't anymore. People get a boyfriend and get settled. We used to all be single. I tried the Internet. Everyone on there looks like an ax murderer! (*Laughs*) I just don't feel comfortable doing it.

Bonnie also recounted difficulty discovering acceptable ways to meet an appropriate partner:

> I haven't decided where would be a good place to go to meet somebody. I'm just not into that at this moment. Nothing changes over the years. It's the same stuff. What am I wearing? What am I saying? What's he saying? Am I boring? Am I this? Am I that? On the one hand, I look forward to meeting people. I like meeting people and learning about them. I haven't decided if I would try the Internet or a dating service. I just don't know. I don't feel time's a wasting. I don't feel I have to rush.

Frustration can increase over time regarding inability to find an appropriate partner, and many women found that it is more difficult than they had anticipated, despite making substantial efforts to do so. Some also expressed needs to find a different-quality partner than the first time around, seeking more emotional connection.

Janice, who perceived of herself as having done a great deal of dating, expressed her frustration regarding not having yet met the "right" person:

> I've gotten so much harder on the dating thing, for good reason. It really has come down to a business plan here! It's not about who can make my heart skip a beat. You know, you have to find out if they are jerks or not. I've really made an effort at meeting somebody. I've tried online dating. You have to be very wary of that, that's where the trust level comes in. I think you have to market yourself to get the right people, and at this point in the game you kind of get particular. You say, "Don't get me anyone who is plastic, who doesn't have a decent job, who is figuring out who they want to be." You say, "Get me someone who is worthwhile."

ROLE ADAPTATION TO NON-MOTHER

Surprisingly, for most women, the adjustment to the loss of the role of potential mother was described as good, with minimal grief reactions. The lack of descriptions of intense mourning was significant in the research study. Descriptions surfaced regarding brief, fleeting periods of mild sadness over time, sometimes exacerbated by the presence of children.

Bonnie, who felt she had always wanted children, came to realize that she had never actively pursued any options for motherhood. She described contentment with her current life and lack of sad feelings regarding the absence of children:

> I still like children, but it doesn't make me sad. Now I don't feel sadness for me. I guess because it is less of an option. Maybe if I were 25 and not dating anybody, and if I were more hopeless, it might be different and I guess I just feel this is what is chosen for me. I think I just came to terms with not having children over time. I never thought the marriage would break up. I guess part of me always assumed I could always get pregnant. I have no depression, no anxiety. Things are good at work. I always have things to do. I don't come home and say, "Gosh what am I going to do?"

Marcia, who was married for 10 years and never attempted to get pregnant during that time, seemed surprised by the lack of sadness she experienced:

> I feel adjusted. I've worked on it a lot in therapy. I thought that I should get more sad and spend more months grieving it. I really didn't spend that much time grieving it. There's just something about it, that I had the opportunity for those 10 years and I never did it. I think there was a weak desire. I had hoped I would meet somebody. I thought about it in my early 30s—if I don't get married, I'll never have kids. At that point I said if I didn't meet somebody by the age of 40, I'm never having kids. I told people. I was a little sad, I'm never going to see a little me. It was just a little sad. It's just a part of life. I had so many kids around I never cried. I never went through a big depression or sadness.

Pat, who thought she had high desire for children in early adulthood, felt she had made significant adjustment to life without children and, similarly to the others, felt there was little sadness manifested in her daily life. Fleeting feelings of mild sadness were sometimes experienced when in the presence of others with children. Janice described such feelings:

> I think I am mostly sad when I am around little babies. When I am going about my life I am fine. It's only with that new baby smell around you or playing with your friends' kids. It's at different times. I went to one of my friend's kid's soccer games, and I'll never forget this, seeing one of the kids do something great. There was such a huge amount of happiness in their eyes. It really depends on the day. There was a time when if someone were to tell me they were preg-

> nant I would cry and maybe the next day I would be happy for them. My emotions were all over the place. Now it is like sort of okay. I'm used to it. It doesn't bite as hard. But it is sad. There is a void.

CONCERNS ABOUT MIDLIFE AND AGING

Issues about being divorced at midlife include concerns about physical signs of aging and its effects on women's ability to find a suitable partner. Several women commented on the societal double standard that devalues women and elevates men as they age. Several also expressed concerns about their well-being in old age should they remain without a spouse and children. Also, worry was expressed about physical aging and its effect on limiting chances for attracting a potential partner, remarriage, and the possibility of bearing children. Lynn eloquently captured a core social construction regarding the double standards of aging:

> The irony and paradox of male versus female is that there is a fundamental lack of justice in evolution. Let's say that a 50-year-old man can start out brand new and will ultimately marry someone younger and have that family. But because of biology I can't do the same thing. I mean I'm 50 and I think I'm the perfect specimen! (*Laughs*) I'm hot to trot and have all kinds of things to offer, but a man I would be interested in his 40s and 50s is looking for like 25-, 30-, and 40-year-old babes, and I'm not that babe.

Pat described her concerns about physical changes in her 40s and the impact of aging on her ability to attract a partner. She related:

> My therapist has actually encouraged me to focus on aging because I am clearly peri-menopausal. My body has changed. I have mood swings. I have gained weight. I stopped smoking. We always laugh about "You don't get fat in your 40s, you get thick." I've never been one to obsess about food and I don't want to. But it's hard. My clothes aren't fitting and I don't feel attractive. Then I start to get in a bad mood and I think I will meet a man and he will see a 33-year-old who will look much more attractive. You know I worry about health issues.

COPING AND ADAPTATION TO ROLE TRANSITION

Adaptation to the roles of non-spouse and non-mother in a social environment that does not provide significant support for women out of the norm proves to be a complex developmental task. Coping requires dealing with reactions of others as well as internalized stigma, shifting family relationships and friendship networks, mastery of work, and financial adjustment.

PERCEPTIONS OF REACTIONS OF OTHERS

Many women differentiated between overt, supportive reactions by others, and internalized beliefs regarding others' perceptions about the women's status. These include beliefs that women must be and desire to be with a man, and perceived devaluation of women without children. Several women described beliefs that exacerbated feelings of difference and inadequacy. The women felt at times others did not react negatively about either divorce or childlessness because it is not so uncommon anymore. Several related that they had not experienced significant negativity or stigma regarding their circumstances. Bonnie stated:

> I think it is more commonplace than it used to be, so theoretically it should be easier. There are a lot more career women and a lot more lifestyles in general. I have not, that I recall, had anybody say to me it must be hard not to have children. No. No, or just to make me feel less of a person because I don't, and really nobody has made me feel that way.

Peggy also felt that the commonality of divorce as well as different lifestyles contributed to others accepting her circumstances as well. She stated:

> They don't really ask anything about children. I don't think it's like it used to be. I think women are independent and people probably just say she really hasn't met anybody, the right one. I think they used to think, Oh my god I can't believe you are not married. I don't think anybody sees me differently. I don't get any reactions about that. People are pretty accepting.

In the women's experience, the assumption was often expressed by others that women can't be happy alone and without a man. Several women related experiences regarding others' reactions in which the underlying message implied happiness could only be obtained for women in the context of marriage and motherhood. Janice related a story regarding a visit to her gynecologist, at which time he commented on her status of being single without children:

> Of course my family wants me to find someone. Some people say, "Oh yeah, you need a man! You're such a catch." My gynecologist asked me what I am doing for birth control and I said nothing because I'm not having sex. He put down the paper and said, "What do you mean? You are 38, you are alone, and you should meet somebody, and I wouldn't be telling you this if you were ugly." He said if I don't have a boyfriend next time I come back he won't see me. But they are just looking out for you. They don't want to see you alone.

Marcia related her perception that others assume she needs a man in order to be happy:

> It seems like there is a comfort level to ask me any questions about my life. I see it as intriguing because they would not ask a married person. They probably think they have a right to ask me because I'm different. I think there is a curiosity because, like, how are you living your life if you are not married? My nephew asked if he could pray for Aunt Marcia to get a boyfriend. So they look at me as Aunt Marcia who was never married, because they didn't know my ex. We never talk about when Aunt Marcia was married. What we talk about is that Aunt Marcia lights candles to get a guy.

Lynn also related her experience of others' reactions to her single status:

> I've been asked a million times, people ask, "When are you going to get remarried?" Especially here at work, people have known me for years and they sort of see me as this vibrant, modern kind of person, which is how I see myself. And it's like people always say, "Why aren't you hooked up with somebody?" I don't think people accept that too much, that it is okay to be without somebody.

Women often perceived that other people viewed them as anomalies because they are without children. Several described underlying perceptions and feelings of stigmatization by others, whom they believed perceived them as "weird" for not having or desiring to have children. Lynn stated:

> Oh yeah, I get that all the time, they say, "How many children do you have?" and I say, "None," and they say, "OH MY GOD, that's so interesting because your personality is like you are a mother." But that doesn't mean I have to be a mother. I get that a lot. Sometimes there are certain people who I think I am selfish or how could I live without children, or say, "Are you going to adopt?" And I say, "No, I am not going to adopt."

Family Relationships

The women in the study almost unanimously felt that their families, although saddened by their divorces, reacted with support and empathy. This was perceived as a critical support throughout the divorce process. Women expressed a difference in the type of support received from mothers and fathers, with mothers being more emotionally empathic listeners and fathers offering concrete help. The support of siblings was also valued by some women.

Mothers' ability to listen in a nonjudgmental and empathetic way was also found to be an important support. Bonnie recalled that even though her mother's style was not usually one of verbalization of feelings, her ability to listen on a consistent basis was extremely helpful. She stated:

> As I recall, I did a lot of talking and they did a lot of listening. My mom isn't one who verbalizes support. We got in the pattern of talk-

> ing every Sunday. I would tell her things. I was more providing the information and she was listening. She doesn't initiate. I always felt I had their support. They were always concerned about safety and money. I didn't get the feeling that they thought I messed up.

Similarly, Peggy noted the support she felt through her mother's listening and the increased closeness that followed in the post-divorce period:

> My mother was helpful. She just talked to me and she saw my ex-husband was very immature. It helped when people listened. Now I see my mother a couple of times a week and talk to her on the phone every day or every other day. It was helpful for what I went through.

Fathers' support can also be extremely helpful to midlife women. However, their support often differs from mothers in that it is more concrete. Fathers tended to offer financial support and practical help around the home. Marcia, who had kept her separation secret from her parents for a year, related the support she received from her father once she revealed her circumstances:

> My parents were really supportive. My dad was wonderful because at that point we knew my husband wasn't coming back, it was going on the second year. My father took us on a family trip to Alaska, all my aunts and uncles and people from church. They helped me get ready for the sale of the house. My dad painted all the rooms and my mother helped me with yard work and washed all the floors and all that kind of stuff. I had kind of just let go.

Becky, who also kept her separation secret from her parents for many months and feared her father's reaction, recalled the emotions she felt when she learned of her father's support:

> Once I told my father, he was helpful. It was Thanksgiving and we had separated the previous January. I finally just told my father that this was the case and he was, "Well, this is your house and you can always come." I always cry when I think about it.

Sibling relationships can also provide critical support and emotional security during the divorce process. The importance of family support for the women's adjustment was also further exemplified by the exceptional cases of several women who felt their families did not meet their needs for emotional support throughout the divorce process. Several described their unhappiness with the lack of emotional support they perceived from their immediate families.

Pat's perception was one of lack of support from both parents. She stated:

> There was estrangement. I had a wall up. My parents weren't helpful, they thought they were but they weren't, and I challenged them on it. I took them to family counseling and it was an ugly period. My

> mother to this day feels I unfairly accused her of not being supportive and maybe that's right.

Becky shared her resentment regarding her family's requirement that she hide her divorce from others. Although her parents "were there" and offered her financial support, she felt more acceptance and emotional support would have been more beneficial to her. She recalled:

> To be honest, I didn't get a lot of support. They would always be there. The hiding of it was of course a subtle thing. I guess not so subtle. But at the same time they were there if I needed anything. They weren't hostile. It's hard to explain. They were embarrassed that they made me hide it, but I didn't feel that on a day-to-day basis. They were just there. They didn't really give me financial help. I was always able to manage on my own, but I always knew it was there if I needed it and that made me feel secure.

Developing Supportive Friendship Networks

The presence of strong friendship networks is a critical factor that can have substantial impact on diminishing loneliness and can increase a woman's contentment with her single lifestyle. The women I have worked with who have had limited relationships with friends tend to fare much worse overall than those with close and dense friendship networks. Friends seem to be extremely important in divorce adjustment. Most of the women had successfully developed and maintained strong friendship networks that provided them with frequent socialization opportunities as well as emotional support. Bonnie described how her network developed as a result of attending various activities for separated and divorced people:

> My social network now is GREAT! I've got a lot of friends and keep busy. I think of all the friends I have as a result of the divorce. It's kind of a mixed blessing. I went to a workshop that was more spiritual based. I just happened to make good friends. I wasn't looking to meet them and now they are eight-year relationships that I didn't expect.

Becky described the importance of her friends' ability to listen and the importance of both single and married friends. She stated:

> I also have a lot of friends, people that go way back many years, that we grew up together and we are still friends to this day. I had a lot of help. People that would just listen to me. I had a lot of friends to spend time with. Most of my friends were married and some of that shifted, but I still stayed close to them. You know, I'm not the kind of person who's afraid to be the third person, I never thought like I can't be the third person. I maintained the relationships, but there were always enough single friends that you started to change what you did, so I never lacked for being able to get out and be social. I

> have many acquaintances, a really tight group of women friends who have really carried me through thick and thin, and without them I would probably be dead. I can honestly say that.

Socializing with other peers of similar status for reference group support can also assist in facilitation of recovery. Pat, who felt uncomfortable in the suburbs surrounded by married friends and families after her divorce, moved to a large metropolitan city and developed a new network of more diverse friends that provided her with comfort and less of a feeling of difference. She recalled:

> I feel comfortable in my friendship circles. I made friends with different people and I am setting up my life in a way that is better. So I think that's part of it. I think it's like survival.
>
> I've put together a group of friends that are much more eclectic and not conventional. I think there is a reason why I am very close with a single mother, friends who lead a nonconventional life. There are all generations of people, single people, babies out of wedlock. It's just different. I am much more comfortable there than in conventional circles.

Bonnie's development of a new network through support group activities provided her with a consistent group of divorced friends who provided emotional and social support. She stated:

> I was in a women's support group that was like a six-week session. We had all different types of backgrounds and different lengths of divorce. We would talk for two hours and then we would get together afterwards and talk for another two hours. It was about coping with divorce. There were eight of us. For about a year four of us would get together and just do different things. Then I went to a group for separated and divorced Catholics where I met a wonderful friend. It was great! Since then I have met many other women and men and we have done a lot of activities together.

Career and Financial Adjustment

Experiences of competence at work and focus on career can be critical to role adaptation and post-divorce adjustment. Many women felt during the most difficult times of their divorce that focusing on their job saved them. Surprisingly, none of the women reported experiencing significant financial stress subsequent to divorce. Several actually reported significant career advances and salary increases in the post-divorce period. Many felt a great sense of pride in their ability to care for themselves financially since divorce.

Judy revealed her belief in financial independence, resourcefulness in earning money, and caring for herself financially:

> I always believed I should take care of myself. I always had two or three jobs to support myself. I'm not worried. I make $135,000. I

> always said to myself that I will always be very independent. You know, when your husband drops dead and you are on your own raising two kids as my mother was, she always drummed it into my head that you have to be financially independent.

Importance of Psychotherapy

The utilization of therapeutic support groups as well as individual therapy is also a critical component that can be helpful in recovery and adjustment. Nonjudgmental listening and a therapist's ability to facilitate decision making and choices were viewed as the most helpful components of therapy. Support groups were especially helpful to the women, as they found it comforting to be around women of similar circumstances. Bonnie related that support groups not only assisted her with her feelings, but also were a source for socialization with others in similar circumstances:

> The support group was most helpful. I did a couple of different things, sharing my feelings with other people. We were all anxious to talk about it and we were all in the same boat, then the socializing and doing things together. The groups also had lots of one-night workshops on the aspects of dealing with divorce, the anger, the whole range. I went to almost everything. I went to some twice. It was probably a combination of the subject and meeting people. It was very helpful putting things into perspective and being able to talk. I learned a lot from talking to each other and going to meetings. I wouldn't be where I am without that. I felt like I wasn't alone.

Several women also described that their therapist's ability to listen nonjudgmentally was critical to their recovery. Judy described how the supportive approach of her therapist helped her to explore and validate her decisions and feelings about getting divorced. She stated:

> I think going to therapy was very helpful. Being in therapy you have somebody you could trust and talk to and kind of figure stuff out, that was very helpful. I felt kind of at a loss and felt like I needed to work it through. I changed therapists and I found somebody that was good. We had seen someone as a couple and I felt I needed someone else. What was helpful was whenever I felt I was having second thoughts, I would talk it through with her and I would realize that I really wasn't having second thoughts. I was in therapy as I separated and she helped me clarify my thoughts about what I wanted, and helped me not feel afraid of it.

Becky also related that nonjudgmental listening and her therapist's ability to propose different perspectives was helpful to her:

> I continued for about a year after. I think it was helpful just to have somebody to talk to, not that I had anything horrible. But it was kind of like a freedom where you could say anything because you think they probably have heard much worse. Obviously, they can show you another perspective. He used to say with men you can't complicate it, it is just black and white, and there is no gray in between and it is just black and white. I think it was helpful.

Lynn eloquently summarized her conviction that therapists should be supportive of a woman's desire to exit marriage and make alternative choices as she reviewed her own growth:

> Therapists need to support that it can be a liberating experience and a growing experience. I don't think therapists realize enough when women are being verbally abused. But it is not an absolutely negative experience. It takes some time to get to the other side, but there is light post-divorce and hope springs eternal. I guess it also depends on your particular constitution. I can look at it and go, "WOW! Who would have thunk?"

CHAPTER 10

The Women Speak

> In describing their lives, women commonly talk about voice and silence: "speaking up," "speaking out," "being silenced," "not being heard," "really listening," "really talking," "words as weapons," "feeling deaf and dumb," "having no words," "saying what you mean," "listening to be heard," and so on in an endless variety of connotations all having to do with sense of mind, self-worth, and feelings of isolation from or connection to others.
>
> **—Mary Belenky et al., *Women's Ways of Knowing* (1986, p. 18)**

A woman's desire for marriage and children encompasses many complex facets of beliefs, meaning, and life experiences. Desire can range from low to high, and can also include ambivalent feelings that may wax and wane over the course of a woman's young adult and midlife developmental stages. Until recent generations, women's silence about lack of desire and ambivalence has been the norm. In effect, "speaking the unspeakable" has been a difficult challenge for many women. Open exploration of a woman's desire for the roles of wife and mother is an important area of investigation in therapy.

The life stories that follow represent four differing perspectives on the role of divorced woman at midlife. The women discuss their desire for marriage and children in early adulthood and midlife, as well as aspects of post-divorce adjustment. Although levels of desire for marriage and children differ among them, common themes and beliefs are evident regarding the experience of divorce at midlife without children. The following perspectives are represented in the stories of four women:

June: Low desire for marriage and children
Judy: Ambivalent desire for marriage and children
Alissa: High desire for marriage, low desire for children
Peggy: High desire for marriage and children

THE ARTIST WHO NEVER WAS: THE STORY OF JUNE

June was an artist in the making. As an adolescent and young adult, June had dreams of studying the fine arts and earning a living as an arts professor and professional artist. Those dreams were never fulfilled since June followed the expected path of marrying her first boyfriend at the age of 20. June felt she always had low desire for marriage and children, but had been unable to act on her true internal "voice." At the time, she viewed her real desires as unacceptable choices, and as most women did, she too followed the prescription to marry.

As a teen in a small town in the Midwest, June met her first boyfriend, whom she married after less than one year of dating. June felt pressured to marry and saw no other option for herself at that time. June believed she never really wanted to marry or have children at all. At age 20, the idea of not marrying was not in June's repertoire of thoughts. Not marrying was never perceived as a conscious option in her young adulthood. In retrospect, she believed that a role choice "out of the norm" of marriage would have been too risky emotionally. Thus, she was compelled to "go with the flow" of societal expectation. To make any other decision would have taken an amount of courage that she believed at that time she did not have. She was unable to act on a sense of knowing of another lifestyle she desired. She recalled feeling her life was predetermined, and that marriage and motherhood were universal givens not to be questioned.

In retrospect, June discussed her thoughts about marriage as an unconscious decision:

> He [ex-husband] was kind of aggressive about wanting to get married, and you know, I was going to get married and have kids like everybody else in the universe, and so he looked pretty good, and so there you go. It was sort of like choosing a career, you should be a teacher or you should be a nurse, which would you like? It wasn't as if you had all the alternatives. Other options other than getting married were just never on the table. I never thought about other options, a choice. Which is what I think is one of the problems with our whole social structure. People should be able to say, "Well, I could not have kids, or I could not get married, or I could do this," and it's just not there.
>
> It was like a lot of my life. I don't know, was it the times or the small town, whatever. You know your life is pretty much laid out there and you got married and you had kids. I didn't think about it. I got married at that time because it was like I had to get married to SOMEBODY and he wanted to get married, and so there you go. You know I was going to get married and have kids like everybody else in the universe and so this looks pretty good. I thought I was ready to have kids, I mean what else did you DO anyway?

> It was mainly an effort to fit in. I mean it was just what you did, the getting married. A friend of mine put it this way. She said she's in a group of people and everybody has a script except her. So getting back to me, everybody else kind of knew what to say and what to do and how to behave and what the next thing was, and what was coming up. I just sort of had no clue and I was just sort of improvising and trying to fit in and I never really did in any way, shape, or form.
>
> You know so many things didn't make sense to me, but everybody else just believed these things, and everybody else just lived their lives according to those beliefs, and so I felt I must be wrong. Everybody else had this knowledge and understanding of the world that I didn't have, and in my parents' generation, a female was about making everyone else happy, like you really just didn't have it all. So comments that people would make would get me thinking there must be something wrong with me.

By age 50, June had been married and divorced twice and had no children. At the time I met her, she had been divorced 15 years, lived alone, and was not in a relationship. June appeared to be quite serious about life and was very definite, confident, and self-assured about her views about marriage and motherhood. June was the youngest of three siblings, having one brother and one sister. Her sister had been married 25 years, and her brother was in a second marriage. She had four nieces and nephews whom she saw occasionally and did not feel especially close to. June was raised in the Midwest and lived there for 20 years of married life before moving to a major metropolitan city. Her first marriage lasted 10 years. She remarried 3 years after her divorce, and that marriage also lasted 10 years. She had remained single since her second divorce and had no plans to remarry. She had completed a master's degree in business and worked as an administrator for a financial institution. In her spare time, she dabbled in the arts, the career she had foregone for marriage.

Although June was married twice for 10 years each time, she felt the role of wife never really suited her very well. In both marriages she felt her emotional needs never counted. The result of two extremely unfulfilling marriages was depression and anxiety that all but paralyzed her as time progressed. At midlife June had come to the conclusion that marriage was not right for her. However, the prevailing social script to marry and mother was so strongly embedded in the culture that her natural response was to question herself and her desires to be different, rather than question the prevailing societal norms. In considering her feelings about marriage in the post-divorce phase, June recalled regret that she had married and had lost her original dreams for her life:

> I had no use for marriage as an institution or a contract, a legal instrument. I didn't have much use for it. But he [ex-husband] pushed very hard for it, and I felt like I got sold a bill of goods. I was very clear

> what I wanted to do. I wanted to travel, wasn't interested in material stuff, wasn't interested in getting married, and was quite happy living together. In fact, I didn't want to get married. So here I was with all this material stuff and married, and it had nothing to do with what I wanted for my life.
>
> I never, never would have gotten married at all. I would have had a career. But then again certain things had to happen to me before I was willing to take some risks. I mean, if you could erase all that, say well here you are you are a much more secure person at this point in life and you are much more capable of taking risks, well, yeah, everything would have been different. If you look at what was possible at that time and the choices that you made, then there are no regrets. I do look back and think, What if I had never gotten married in the first place. I wonder if I had gone into the fine arts to begin with. I think the possibility of doing that was zero, but I think if that had been possible, I would have had a much more interesting life in a much more interesting way. But I think there was zero chance of that happening, so what's the point of dwelling on it.

June's desire for children had always been extremely low since she could remember. She recalled having little to no interest in children throughout her adolescence and early adulthood. Also, she recalled babysitting as a teen and feeling little interest in the children she cared for. She had never particularly felt drawn to infants, and felt more of a sense of dislike about them. These experiences validated her belief that she did not want children. She also realized caring for a child would be her primary responsibility. She also had serious doubt that she could count on either of her husbands to partner with her around parenting a child.

June recalled her feelings about children in adolescence and early adulthood:

> I babysat as a teenager because it was what you did to make extra money, but I wasn't interested in those kids. I couldn't be bothered. I mean I just watched television the whole time. It's a wonder they didn't all die, but I just had no interest in those kids, never have been interested. Never have I been interested like "Let me take that baby from you." At one point early in the marriage we got a dog. It became very clear to me that I was the one who would be getting up and walking him and feeding him, and that was okay for six months, but ain't NO WAY I was doing that for no 18 years! NO WAY! So that got me over it.
>
> I can't stand newborns, they creep me out. They are all squirmy and I don't know what to do with them. And the smell, I can't stand the smell. Even when the puppy was really little, I couldn't stand it. I'm just not at all interested. Once they get to the cute stage and

> are kind of going around by themselves and are fun for 15 minutes, that's okay, but other than that, NO!

At midlife, June realized her lack of desire for children had been extremely strong throughout young adulthood. She recalled feelings of mild ambivalence, questioning, and review that quickly dissipated. June reported she had no feelings of disappointment, regret, or sadness about not having children, because she was sure she never wanted them. She did not recall any one decision point where she experienced the loss, or any periods of intense grief over time. She also recognized she had no interest in parenting by alternate means. She related:

> You realize that you are just flat out not interested in kids. I'm just not interested. My niece says to me when she is here, "You always notice the adults, but you never notice the kids." I'm just not interested, I really am not. I came to this realization probably about 10 or better years ago, which it took me a long time. And it really came because someone noticed that I am never interested in kids. Really, like, who I am right now and my life right now. If I had done anything differently, I mean a lot of shit happened to me, but none of it had an entirely shitty outcome. If none of that would have happened, or if one thing would not have happened, I'd be stuck for God's sake! Miserable with two kids and grandkids now—ugh! That would have been horrible.

Two years into her first marriage, June began to realize her emotional needs were not being met in her relationship. In retrospect, she believed she became involved in her second relationship and subsequent marriage as a way to exit the first. The thought of standing on her own outside of marriage was not a consideration for June. Thus, she quickly entered into a second marriage. June and her second husband separated after six years of marriage due to deterioration of the relationship and job opportunities in separate cities. After living apart as a trial for several years, the couple mutually decided to divorce.

June initially felt she had fallen into a black hole emotionally after both divorces. Indeed, marriage never seemed to fit her as a lifestyle. She recognized tremendous improvement in her emotional functioning after her second divorce and came to the realization she had been depressed and anxious most of her adult life. She connected that to her unfulfilling marital relationships. She recalled a sense of "losing herself" in relationships and increased feelings of depression and anxiety. Relationships with men had drained her of too much of herself emotionally and had contributed to chronic depression throughout most of her adulthood. She also expressed concern and awareness that her choices in men had not been good.

After June began to reorganize her life, she felt her depression lifting. She expressed contentment with her life, which she described as filled with job satisfaction, a variety of friends, cultural activities, and occasional visits with her nieces and nephews. June developed an extensive network of friends in her post-divorce life. She pursued interests she had lost track of in her married years and finally returned to her dream of studying painting. Achievement and positive feelings gained from work improved her sense of self. She was also proud of her ability to manage her own finances and prepare financially for her retirement years.

In terms of overall long-term adjustment, June was sure that she preferred single life and had always enjoyed and preferred being alone, even as a child. Looking back on her decisions to marry, she felt she had married due to social pressure, expectations of her family and the entire community, and lack of choice. June had no regrets about either of her divorces or not having children. She also had no interest in remarriage or even living with anyone. Since living alone, June felt her emotional functioning had improved greatly, and periods of depression and anxiety she experienced while married had ceased. She felt she was better at meeting her own emotional needs by herself rather than in marriage. She experienced a greater sense of well-being living on her own and felt that the experience had strengthened her survival skills. June related her feelings about the process of divorce and recovery:

> My husbands were a hard drag on me. They were both abusive in a subtle kind of way. What I wanted just didn't figure in, and it was like your turn will come someday, but that day was never coming, so what did I need it for? They were both very self-centered, very controlling. Everything else mattered and I really didn't, and everything revolved around them, and their friends, and what they wanted to do. My choices in men have not been good. I don't have a good history there.
>
> When I first got divorced, I was just so numb to everything. Everything! No emotions, no sadness, no anger, no happiness, nothing. It was just like completely null. I was really just mentally numb. I'd go to work and instead of getting seven things done, I'd get one thing done. Kind of like being at the bottom of a black hole and hoping to get out of it. It was just one miserable day after another. I knew something was wrong. I had no feelings, I was emotionally void.
>
> Once I started to recover, the horrible depressions that I had for decades seemed to be lifting. Since I've been on my own, I haven't had any of that. I think since the time I was 12, men in general make me feel unworthy. I am much better on my own than when I am with somebody. They end up taking too much of my life and I just think I've gotten to where I want too much. I've gotten selfish. I want to take control over my environment and you can't do that in a relationship. It's that kind of thing. I don't want to consider somebody else. Even if I did want a relationship, I would never want

to live with somebody. A commuter relationship would be perfect! Weekends and a week or two here or there but you lived your own life would be perfect.

I never want to live with anyone again. I don't have the energy for a relationship or to live with somebody. My physical resources are really limited, so between working and doing a few social things, I don't have the energy to deal with another person on a consistent basis. I'm very suspicious of my attractions because I have not done well two times. So I really don't trust that I would be attracted to somebody who would be appropriate, so why do that?

You have to make your own life. If you don't make your own life you are not interesting. No one is going to make it for you. You are the only person that can make your own happiness. Nobody else is in charge of making you happy. Only you make you happy. Especially when you are as depressed as I was. I think it's just managing yourself. Managing your stress and anxiety. Knowing what works for you. And being around people that have a positive impact on your life. I go shopping. I go to museums or hiking, or I'll take a walk into town and take a newspaper into the coffee shop. I've gone on vacation by myself. I did a tour last year of Alaska. It was awesome. There were a lot of people my age. I've also gone away with a single girlfriend. I keep myself busy. I also volunteer for Make a Wish Foundation. We just got to meet one of the children. It made me feel so great. The fact is, it ain't been easy, but I am as strong as I am and the person that I am because I haven't had the luxury of someone doing it for me. The fact of the matter is if I had someone doing it for me, I don't know where I would be. I don't know if it would have necessarily been a good thing. I think it has made me stronger and more capable and certainly more secure in myself.

Although June was very comfortable with single life without marriage and children, one of the most difficult parts of the experience was dealing with the biased reactions and assumptions of others. She believed even in the current day and age, others still perceived a sense of abnormality about her because she did not desire marriage or children. She recognized that aging is also perceived as an undesirable state for women more so than men. June expressed feelings of anger regarding others' assumptions that she was less valuable both as a woman and as a human being because she was not a wife or a mother. She felt she probably experienced less stigma than other women due to living in a large metropolitan city where it was easy to blend in, and her lifestyle was, for the most part, inconsequential to others. June described her experience:

Right from the start it kind of bothered me that it wasn't okay not to have kids. I mean, I thought it was a perfectly acceptable choice. I can remember someone commenting, "Well, what's wrong with her? She is selfish." And I remember thinking, Well that doesn't make any sense to me. Like if you don't have kids what does selfish have to do with anything? The only thing that bothered me was "Poor June, she couldn't have kids, she is putting all her maternal stuff into her dog." And that just made me kind of angry because it diminished me as a person and I wasn't interested in having kids. I didn't want that kind of life. And the thing about do I feel barren? It just made no sense to me. There's no logic to that. I don't get it, I don't buy into that.

I don't get reactions from other people so much anymore. I guess because it is commonplace. Most people know I am divorced and there is not a lot of reaction. I think people are surprised about my not having children, but people don't really ask anything about it. A lot of people don't even know I was ever married because I just really enjoy my life now. I don't dwell on it, I don't bring it up. If I do, it's in a joking fashion that it is so far behind me. No, everyone is happy that I am enjoying my life now.

One thing about the big city is it's a city full of misfits, so one more doesn't make any difference! Because it doesn't matter if you fit in here because everybody is so different. There is not the same kind of social pressure. One of the reasons I have felt more comfortable because there is diversity of human beings and it is like irrelevant what your neighbor is. Who cares? I think also, as you get older, you are less concerned about what other people think of you. It's not important anymore.

June related her thoughts about her future as a midlife woman without a spouse or children:

There was a period of time where I did do the aging thing, and I guess this is especially true for women. We are so inducted into what people think about us physically and how you can get around that, and you realize that the best that is ever going to be said about you by the casual passerby is "Oh, she looks very good for her age," and that was a hard one. Our model for aging as an institution is not valid, that most people stay healthy and active until their last six months of life. So that got me over a lot of worries. So as soon as you make that mental shift …

Work saves me every day. From day one I got so involved and had so much opportunity. It has become my out. It saves me because I have a purpose in life. It is my outlet, and that's where I get to succeed, my job. I never set out to have a career in business. I started out as a secretary. Just by a series of events I wound up in marketing. It just kind of was a path for me that I never foresaw. I think what surprised me the most was I took a really horrible time in my life and had this outlet which was my job. Everything just kind of fit.

Now I love my life! (*Laughs*) Some of it is environmental. Part of it is that I just really now found my place. I actually am very sensitive to my environment. I think a lot of people could live here or there on a farm, or in Iowa. I couldn't do that. I'm strongly responsive to my surroundings. Everything I could possibly want to do is right here. It's the kind of life I want to live. I have a small group of friends that I feel close to and can depend on if I need something. I am very independent and introverted at the same time.

NEEDING AND NOT WANTING MARRIAGE: THE STORY OF JUDY

Judy considered herself a feminist and was somewhat baffled as to why she pressured her ex-husband into marriage after 10 years of a live-in relationship. Her perspective could best be described as lifelong ambivalence about marriage and children. She regretted the decision to marry and was uncertain why she was driven to make such a mistake. Inexplicably, she began to feel internalized pressure to marry in her early 30s. Judy, who considered herself nontraditional, found herself not wanting to marry at all, and yet proceeding anyway. She regretted making this decision and felt she and her husband never recovered from making the mistake of getting married. She recalled the plan she assumed her life should take, and her view these roles were not choices, but rather prescriptions for how her life as a woman should progress. Judy was somewhat surprised by her behavior of pressuring her ex-husband to marry after a 10-year live-in relationship.

She discussed her perception about socialization that impacted her thoughts and behavior:

> I think I did it because I thought I was supposed to. It was the next thing you were supposed to do on the path. I think that there are stereotypical roles and you get programmed, and especially for a female, the expectation is that you'll get married. I don't think there was any other need I had to get married, because I didn't want children.

At 49, Judy was divorced eight years and had no children. She lived alone in a townhouse apartment in a large metropolitan city. Judy had a great sense of humor and expressed contentment with her lifestyle as a woman divorced at midlife without children. Judy was the oldest of two siblings, having a brother that she felt extremely close to. Judy held a doctorate degree in biology and worked as a researcher at a major medical institution. She earned a six-figure salary that she acknowledged enabled her to afford a comfortable lifestyle as a single woman, and also afforded her the ability to pay for many social and cultural activities after her divorce. Judy experienced significant losses in her early adulthood, having lost both her parents in her mid to late 20s. These losses seemed to have had a significant impact on her decisions in early adulthood, and contributed to increasing the bond to her brother.

Judy described her ambivalence about marriage:

> We lived together for 10 years and I felt like something was missing, like I needed to be married, so I was the one that pushed the issue. Even though we didn't want children, I felt like I should be married once. I don't really know why I did it. I think it was about a deeper commitment. It was a logical next step. And even though I knew things could work out even though you are married or not, it seemed like more of a commitment. I think it was a matter of trying it, that next step. And he said, "You know, if you really need this, then we'll do it," but it wasn't something he really wanted. It wasn't his thought that it was the best thing to do. He didn't see the need. I just felt like the need was the commitment. I really thought it was the right thing at the time. I really regretted that I did that because it was absolutely the wrong thing. But I didn't know it at the time. It's only in looking back.

Judy and her husband believed they did not want children while they were married, and the subject had been openly discussed between them. She also believed she never wanted children prior to marriage, nor had she ever been interested in exploring other means of becoming a parent. Although she was happy she did not have children, she described brief periods of ambivalence and regret in her late 30s. Judy did connect at least some of her lack of desire for children to her young adult experiences of loss of her parents, as well as her ex-husband's lack of desire for children.

Although never wanting the responsibility of raising children, Judy recalled a time in her mid-30s when she temporarily thought her feelings were changing. She also felt that despite several brief periods of re-evaluation, at midlife she still felt that having no children was the right decision for her as the caretaking responsibilities seemed unappealing. Judy described the conflict between her feelings of lack of desire for children and societal expectations:

> This thing about internalized feelings about getting married, it was the same thing with children. I think there was a period when I felt differently, like I might want children, was more, well, you had the marriage, and now we have the house, and now you are supposed to have a child, and now you have done this, and it's time for this, and that's where you go next.
>
> Mostly we thought we didn't want children, we had talked about it. We never acted on even trying. I couldn't say I really wanted to make a permanent decision, but we never tried either. When I hit a certain age, 35, 38, all of a sudden I started thinking maybe I really do want a child. But he really didn't, and then I just backed off. I

> never actually tried to get pregnant. It's funny because in my 20s and 30s I always thought that if I got pregnant I would have an abortion, and I never had a second thought about it. Then later when I was about 37, I thought, Gee, I don't know if I could have an abortion. Nothing against abortion, but there were these two little periods where I thought, Oh my god, I think I need a child, then I realized it was just a passing feeling and it wasn't a lifetime commitment.
>
> In my late 30s I went through feelings where I had some regret and grieving about not having a child and maybe it lasted two years, but it was never enough that I wanted to do anything about it, never. I never considered doing it by myself. Also, I had worked with abused children and single parents and I think that had an effect on me. But I don't think that was the only reason.

Judy continued to explain her feelings about lack of desire for children at midlife:

> I'm feeling no different at this stage. I'm really happy I never had children. I think I would be a good parent, but I was thinking the other day when my dog dropped to the ground and laid down and didn't want to move and she is 85 pounds, and I was thinking, What if that was a kid? I'm very happy with having to worry about me and nobody else. I think I have a very low patience tolerance. I think there was a little regret in my 30s, but no, I can parent through my nieces and nephews.
>
> And I've never thought about other ways to have a child because I really didn't want a child. I think those two periods in my late 30s were hormonal and needed to pass. I don't think it had anything to do with menopause. I think it had to do with a last chance kind of thing. That you either have one now or you never have one. I know there are other choices. I think I was just really ambivalent, and again maybe it was 40 to 50% for a little while, but it never went over 50%.

After ten years of living together and a pressured decision for marriage, Judy recalled increasing differences and decreasing compatibility in her marriage. Differences ranged from career goals to finances and spending to general life values. These differences between the couple seemed to intensify after the marriage. She also felt pushing her husband into marriage might have been a source of anger between them that they were unable to resolve. Judy identified the first two years after her divorce as very difficult emotionally, marked by depression and anxiety. She recalled her realizations about her divorce process:

> Basically I think the reason for the divorce was values. I think they became more diverse as time went on. It's just that he became so

> much more socially radical than I was. He didn't want to spend any money and that is just so different than me. I think that it changed. Even when I was working and he wasn't, he would be upset about me spending money, and I thought, Screw that. I'm working and bringing in all the money and that is not okay. School was another thing too. I think me going on for more schooling and him going to graduate school put a lot of strain on the relationship. I thought we were very competitive and that got to be very draining and not nurturing of each other. I kind of had my own life, went out with my friends. I traveled with other people. He didn't want to travel. He seemed depressed and became more of an isolate and never had many friends, and I thought, You know, that is not me either. It kind of happened over time. It seemed like we became more and more different and less and less compatible. Then I think he might have been angry about me pushing to get married, like I almost gave him an ultimatum about our relationship, and I don't think he recovered from that.
>
> Afterwards, I think I kind of had a delayed reaction, I think like six to nine months later, maybe even longer, even a year. I got on antidepressants. I was still functioning, but I just couldn't concentrate. I couldn't see that I just wasn't functioning as well as I had been, and I was having trouble concentrating at work. I just was in a mood. I'm a very hard worker, always had three jobs, and during that time I stayed home more than I ever had.

After the initial adjustment to divorce, Judy's emotional functioning improved greatly. She did not experience any significant difficulties with depression, anxiety, or physical symptoms. She maintained a great deal of satisfaction from her role as a researcher, and had not experienced any financial stress due to her lucrative salary. She identified the support of her brother, friends, and psychotherapy as important factors in her adjustment to the divorce. In regard to her future, she stated she has no regrets that she did not have children, and did not plan on being a parent by alternate means. She looked forward to continuing her dating, spending time with family and friends, and traveling.

Judy's narrative story regarding her life experiences included beliefs about herself as a strong, independent survivor who would always be able to care for herself, come what may. She also related her enjoyment of her perceived freedom and lack of missing the control issues prevalent in her marriage. Judy described her narrative of herself as a survivor:

> I think I have a sense of independence that helped me cope with the divorce. I think it's probably a survival thing, like whatever happens I am going to survive this. So survival skills really help with a divorce, that feeling that I can take care of myself. That no matter

> what happens I have to take care of myself and that makes it easier. I think I got through it because I had to, which is very interesting, the survival piece. It kind of follows me through life. That's when I do stuff in life, when I have to. When I don't have to, I don't do it. I think I'm really doing well because I have to.
>
> Since therapy and medication, I have really excelled. I continued in therapy. And I went back on medication about a year and a half ago because I realized my depression was more intractable than episodic. I went to a psychiatrist who said, "You know you can't do anything about what your brain is doing with this. You really need the support."

Judy also described difficulty and frustration in being unable to meet available, appropriate men. She felt adjustment to the role of dating at midlife had been more difficult than imagined:

> I think I was fantasizing a little bit about what it would be like, and actually that it would be a lot better than it actually was. I think in your 20s and 30s there are a lot more people around to date. As you get older there are not as many people around. People are married or whatever, and it is harder to meet someone. I didn't realize how hard it was going to be to meet someone, and that makes it hard.

Judy described the support that she perceived made it possible for her to recover from her divorce:

> My brother was very supportive and nurturing and he lived close. If I felt sick, he'd come over. If I felt bad, he'd take me out. He was always there. It didn't matter what the issue was, he would always be there. It wasn't financial. It was emotional and tangible. You know, if I needed a ride somewhere to take my car, he was there. He would help me when I was working on my schoolwork. He would do something kind of tangible.
>
> I had my friends around, so there were a lot of people who wanted to do things. I had a lot of friends that were mine and that made it easier. Also, I had a friend for a long time and she would always push me to do something. She would say, "Let's go do this," like parachuting. She didn't really have a lot of friends, but she did have a lot of things going on in her life. She was always like ready to go, to a bar, away for the weekend. She was great! Also, I think once I was able to function a little bit at work I became less depressed and started to go out a little bit more. I really like work. I really love what I do and I really like people. And I nurture a lot at work, and that is really where the relationships develop, at work, developing the friendships. I've always had three jobs and been a very hard worker.

Looking back, Judy realized the progress she had made:

> Now I'm really great with living alone and taking care of myself. I really like it! I don't have to negotiate to buy furniture, about what I buy, about what we are eating tonight. I'm very independent and I really like that. It's not that I don't like to take other people's feelings into account; it's just that it was such a struggle with us because we were so different. I do occasionally miss coming home to a partner and sharing aspects of my day. I think there is something else about being able to go home and share your day, and so that is the disadvantage. And they tell you what happened. And so now nobody responds right away. (*Laughs*) That's the irrational stuff. You know, nobody cares if you are working till eight. You know, those kinds of things are disadvantages, but I think the advantages outweigh it. I like living alone.

COMMITMENT TO A DREAM: THE STORY OF ALISSA

Alissa's beliefs about marriage were a contradiction in terms. Even though she received positive messages from her parents about not marrying, she still had internalized strong beliefs that marriage was the key to a woman's happiness. Growing up in a "happily married family," Alissa witnessed the experience of a good marriage firsthand. In some ways her high desire for marriage was not surprising, given her family experience. On the other hand, her high desire was in conflict with the messages she received from her parents that marriage was not the only choice for a woman, and that they supported whatever she chose for her life.

Alissa had always wanted to be married as long as she could remember. She recalled viewing marriage as a source of support to deal with the difficulties of life. She believed that meeting the right person would "just happen automatically." Her high desire for marriage was viewed by her as a gut feeling that it was the thing to do, rather than a conscious decision-making process. However, she recognized that much of her energy in young adulthood went into trying to meet a man to marry. She described her romantic, somewhat dreamy notion of her sense of knowing:

> I never got it drilled into me that I should get married and go out and have a family. I thought it was a wonderful thing that my parents saw me as a smart person who could do something with her life. They didn't say, "Honey, it's okay because you are going to get married and have children." So I was encouraged to grow and make a life for myself, and if that's what I wanted, great. So I was never given the message that marrying and having children was bad, but I was never given the message that it was the only choice by any means.

Even though her parents gave her positive messages about role choices, internally she still experienced a great deal of pressure to marry:

> I always wanted to be married from a young age. I had always wanted a partner in crime, and I always thought that would be a great thing. I always had a vision of what it would feel like to meet the person I was going to marry. The first time I went out with my ex-husband, it hit me like a bolt of lightning. I just kind of had this jolt. I think life is tough and I always wanted to share it with somebody, have a real rock, somebody that could support me. My parents had a really nice marriage. You know, I lived in a really happy family. Their marriage was happy and I saw what it was like. That model of their marriage probably propelled me into having a stronger longing for a male figure in my life, so that totally pushed me.

At 47, Alissa was divorced six years and had no children. She lived alone in a rented, one-bedroom apartment. After her divorce, Alissa began dating a man casually who lived several hundred miles away. The couple saw each other about once per month, and Alissa felt happy with this relationship as it was. She did not consider this a relationship to which she would desire to make a long-term commitment. Alissa was a well-spoken, intelligent, professional woman. She also impressed me as a woman content with her current lifestyle, having successfully recovered from a divorce she did not want. She firmly believed that a focus on spirituality had helped her recover from her divorce.

Alissa's family of origin was "an intact family," with her parents having been married 21 years. She perceived of her parents' marriage as a happy one. She had a graduate degree and worked as an administrator in the headquarters of an international corporation. Her six-figure salary per year afforded her a comfortable lifestyle and diminished financial distress after the divorce.

At the age of 35, Alissa married a man that she had known through her job and had developed a friendship with for two years prior to dating. The couple dated long distance for about two years before they married and moved together to a new state.

When it came to childbearing, Alissa was a classic "postponer" and eventually came to believe she had always had low desire and never wanted children. She remembered feeling relief when her fiancé revealed that he did not want children. She recalled different reasons for not wanting children throughout the various stages of her life, feeling it was never the right choice for her. She also described an ongoing process, never a firm, one-time decision. Rather, feelings evolved over time and periodically included ambivalence. Never feeling that having children was right for her, she continually reviewed her thoughts about the issue at various points in her young adulthood. Although she was ambivalent at times, her lack of desire remained consistent.

At times, women who feel they strongly do not desire children describe periods when they felt ambivalent and reconsider. However, many describe consistently arriving at the conclusion that they did not want children. Further confirmation of the lack of desire is evident in a woman's lack of active pursuit of pregnancy or becoming a parent by any other means.

Alissa described the process of delay and postponement of childbearing that eventually resulted in her realization that she did not want children:

> I never wanted children. It was for many reasons at different points in my life, but it was never a real drive for me to have a child. I love children, and I have a wonderful niece and nephew, but for me I just had different interests. I actually thought it would be fun to be pregnant and give birth, the actual physical aspects of it interested me as a woman, to understand what your body would go through. I thought, Gee, maybe this would be a good experience, but it was fleeting, it didn't last, it never lasted.
>
> As a teen I never wanted kids. I think at various times in my life there were different reasons for not wanting children. If you asked me at different points, there were probably different reasons and different answers. I can remember in my 20s it really wasn't of much interest to me. Part of it was the 60s mentality, like this world is awful, why bring a child into it? There's war, there's famine, the population is out of control, and everything. It was more like a political stance at that time, so it was more like a radical stance that having children wasn't a good idea for the environment, so that was my thinking in my 20s. I think I started to evolve. I started to think it's okay for people to have children, but then I started to think maybe I wouldn't be a good mother, that I wasn't stable enough, that I wasn't far enough in my career, that I really hadn't had a relationship, or I hadn't met somebody that I wanted to have a child with. That it wasn't right for me and I wasn't right for it, that kind of feeling.
>
> A few years ago I had a very large cyst. My ovary ended up needing to be removed, and my doctor at the time wanted me to have the other ovary removed, but I didn't want him to. It was probably the first time I said, "Gee, I better think about this." And it was mostly because I'm not quite done yet. What if I really did meet a man who really wanted it? So I did leave the door open, but it was pretty much leaving the door open rather than desiring it. It was pretty much you never know what is going to happen. I'm a person who says never say never.
>
> Then at another point I had an interesting experience with a newborn of a friend of mine. I spent a good length of time with them and I thought, Gee, maybe this would have been a good experience, but it was fleeting, it didn't last. Then a good friend of mine lost a four-year-old child who was killed in an accident right before I got married. I remember saying I could never live with that, I could not

> do that. I am not built, I don't have the courage to be a mother. You have to be willing to take the risk, and I realized at that point that the risk of that commitment and what it meant to have that commitment to see it through the good times and the bad. It was just a very tough experience. That was a painful loss, and I think it changed me. I was feeling like I didn't want to bring a child into a world that had so much pain. I think that was an underlying aspect to it, that boy life is painful.
>
> I considered other options at one point. I had a friend who adopted a baby from Korea and he was adorable. I fell in love with him. Again, the adoption piece for me was always attractive because of the gift of that. I remember talking to my therapist about that and we explored it for a little while. Like what would it be like to be a single parent? What would it take to do it on your own? And it didn't take me long to figure out that it would be too difficult, and that I didn't have that drive. If you did it by yourself, you had to have a dedication about it, even more so than doing it with somebody else, and I just didn't have that.

After a year of marriage, Alissa's relationship began to deteriorate, characterized by an increasing breakdown in communication and lack of responsiveness by her husband. It seemed her husband's career difficulties resulted in his distancing and withdrawing from her emotionally. The relationship continued to deteriorate for two years and worsened into emotional abuse. Alissa had a strong sense of commitment to her marriage and did not entertain the thought of initiating separation or divorce, even in light of the emotional abuse she experienced. This idea seemed unacceptable to her. She also felt a great deal of responsibility for making the marriage work.

The stalemate in communication persisted until her husband finally acknowledged wanting a divorce without any prior discussion or attempt at counseling. Even though her relationship had deteriorated into emotional abuse, she could not perceive of divorce as a choice. She recognized a destructive marriage was wrong for her, but she could not act upon breaking the commitment. This became an emotional barrier to her ability to initiate divorce. In her eyes, divorce was not a desirable option or solution. She recalled waiting two years in hopes of a reconciliation. After realizing there was no hope of saving the marriage, she reluctantly initiated divorce in order to move on with her life. She did not wish to divorce, and viewed her husband as the initiator of their divorce, even though she felt pushed to file the legal papers. Alissa described the breakdown of her marriage and divorce process:

> Three years and about six months into the relationship, and I can tell you exactly the day it happened, my ex-husband stopped talking to me. He was quite distressed over his job not working out. So the first three to four months of our marriage seemed fine to me, but

somewhere along the line he started to see me as part of the problem, rather than part of the solution, and there are a lot of nuances in that. And he stopped communicating with me and that was a big problem. The more supportive I got, the nastier he got, emotionally abusive, verbally, putting me down constantly.

He wasn't willing to try, not willing to work through problems, and that went on for about two years, until he finally woke up and said, "You're right, I want a divorce. I don't think I love you anymore. That's been the problem since the day this started happening and I couldn't tell you." He wouldn't go to counseling. He wouldn't do anything about it. I begged him to go to counseling to figure out how to end it. I said, "Okay, at least go to counseling to help me figure out how to get out of this," and he wouldn't do it.

I thought that once we got over the hump and realized we were on each other's side, we would be able to weather any storm. But I found out he wasn't willing to try, not willing to work through problems. That went on for about two years, and he finally, after all this time of me bugging him and saying what's wrong, he finally woke up and said, "You are right, I want a divorce. I don't think I love you anymore. That's been the problem since the day you started asking me about this and I couldn't tell you." He wouldn't go to counseling, I begged him and he wouldn't do anything about it.

The interesting thing was there were very few times where I felt like I should be apart from him. At that time my self-esteem probably wasn't the best, clearly wasn't the best, and he wasn't making it any better by this verbal abuse. I wish he had hit me, at certain times, I wish he had hauled off and hit me, because I would have walked out. It was all so kind of psychological that I don't think I even realized what was even going on at the time. And I look back and I think, Why didn't I get myself out of that? I don't know how much more I could have taken, but it was never in my mind that I would have done that, divorced. I don't know what would have happened to me had he not said it. I probably would have just lost my mind at some point.

I never considered saying I wanted a divorce.

The commitment I thought I had made to that marriage made it impossible for me to face getting out of it. We had talked about eloping and not having a wedding, but I realized the value of that wedding. It was not only about having a family and friends there ritual. It grounded me so deeply in that commitment, much more than I had ever imagined. Having my family and friends and everyone else witness it, and writing our own vows. I mean, my roots in that marriage went way deep. And it really took a lot to pull me out of it. I was committed, I would have done anything.

> I was so angry and I said, "I don't want to do this." I'm sure I was thinking that there has got to be a way to make this thing work, at the same time it was so devastating. But the other thing was he wasn't quite ready to let me go either. One time I said, "You've got to let me out of this and we've got to start divorce proceedings." But he didn't want to be pushed on it either. He knew he wanted the divorce, but when push came to shove … So finally I told him to get the divorce and to do all the work because I didn't want to do it because it was his choice. I didn't want to file; I said, "I'll go along with what we need to do," but I didn't want to file. I ended up doing it, and I finally ended up coming to the realization that it was time. I guess there was always the hope that it might work out.

Alissa experienced significant depression in initial reaction to separation and divorce. After the initial crisis passed, she began to mobilize herself and recover. She described work, psychotherapy, and antidepressant medication to be extremely important to her adjustment at that time.

> I would cry on the way home from work, go home, watch *Seinfeld*, take a bath and go to sleep. I probably did that for about six months. I did a lot of crying. I definitely was depressed. I did go to therapy at that time. I got on medication probably at the six-month point because I was really having a hard time. I remember trying to focus: Okay, what do I need to do to take care of myself? If I needed to sob into a pillow for six hours, that's what I did. If I needed to lay in a bathtub with hot water and take the phone off the hook, that's what I did. If I needed to watch six hours of rotten TV, that's what I did. So it was real important for me to get in touch with what I needed and giving myself permission to do exactly what it was that I needed to do, which was unusual for me. I was always a people pleaser and always did everything for everyone else. So if I needed to tell someone I can't support you right now because I am in too much pain myself, if I needed to call a friend, that's what I did. So I was very much in touch with my own needs, more than at any other time in my life.
>
> I had a very tough job, and actually my job probably saved me. I really compartmentalized it. I told no one at work because it was a fairly new job and I had a lot of responsibilities and I didn't want them to think I couldn't carry them out, so I literally worked 14-hour days.
>
> My divorce was final a month after I started my new job here, and it was a really good choice for me. Job satisfaction was always really important to me, and I am a career person. And I thought, Okay, what can I do with my career, where can I go? That was what I concentrated on. I think that was really survival instinct. I think it was survival mode, like I have to survive here. I've always been very

independent. I had income from the time I started to work. After I got my master's, I was financially independent. That was never an issue for me, never, no.

My mother was so sad for me. I remember because she knew how important it was for me to have a partner. She struggled, she was so supportive. Just knowing that I could call my mother at any time, that she was with me, that she was on my side unequivocally. That I could cry on her shoulder, that she would agree with me that he was a total louse. And that's always helpful! (*Laughs*) And she was always encouraging me that I had a life ahead of me, and that marriage and children weren't the end all. She never ever turned into the mother who said, "When are you going to have a child?" She was always the person who wanted me to be happy, whatever form that took for me, ALWAYS. And I am so blessed to have had that.

My therapist really helped me to understand my own feelings about it, my own anger, my own betrayal, and that it wasn't really my fault. I mean I went over and over it in my mind and thought about what I could have done differently, how I could have been a better wife, how I could have done this. And it truly was not me. It truly was him. I was thinking how I could be a better person in this, and truly there was no way, definitely no way. But she really helped me to understand that.

After the trauma and crisis of initial separation from her marriage, Alissa's functioning improved dramatically and she began to excel in various areas of her life. One year after her divorce, she obtained a prestigious job with a lucrative salary. The ability to focus on her competence at work saved her emotionally. A sense of competence and self-value also originated from her ability to care for herself financially. She continued in a casual, long-distance dating relationship that she felt met her needs and was satisfactory to her. She had become involved in various volunteer work with children. She also enjoyed cultural activities, which she often enjoyed alone or with friends. Alissa's recovery process was facilitated by supportive therapy that challenged her self-blaming narrative regarding her perceived failure as a wife.

Although almost all of the women in the study felt that loneliness was not a significant issue for them, several described occasional, brief periods of loneliness. However, these women also related confidence in their ability to manage feelings of loneliness. Alissa described her feelings of comfort in knowing how to respond to feelings of loneliness and shared her ability to pursue numerous, enjoyable activities on her own. Loneliness was not a major concern for her, and when she did feel lonely, she managed it well by making plans for herself.

She also appeared comfortable with her decision not to have children, even though she stated there was always some lingering ambivalence. She did not feel it was a completely final decision that she would never be a parent in the future in some way. Alissa had not ruled out adopting a child in the future, but did not foresee doing this without a spouse.

Looking back over her experience, as well as forward to the future, Alissa regretted the energy she had spent in her 20s and 30s in search of a man. She poignantly discussed her wonder at what else she might have achieved in her life had she placed her focus on her own development instead. She stated:

> Would I do anything differently? Yes, because I think that I spent a lot of time in my life worrying about men and male relationships, and when it will be permanent, and when I will find that one true love, and when I was going to get married before I got married. A lot of my energy in my 20s and 30s went toward finding that mate. And so I look back and I think, Gee, what could I have been doing? What could I have accomplished if I just sort of had not had that on my mind?
>
> I love my life now! It is so full and I feel so blessed and so lucky! I love being in my own space. I have my own little apartment, and having it fixed the way I want it and coming home and not having to deal with somebody else's problems, or even joys. Being able to function on my own, like if I want to do something, I don't have to see if anyone else wants to do it or not, or whether or not there's a conflicting problem.
>
> I think part of it is there is freedom to it. When I had someone living with me for a few months, I felt like I was taking care of him, cleaning up after him. Once he moved in, I was the one who was doing the cooking and cleaning. He didn't care. I was the one who wanted the house a certain way. We were very different. I liked planning ahead, he didn't. I felt all consumed with it. I felt getting time alone with my friends was difficult. I felt that managing the house was, although we got along great, we didn't fight, that I was the responsible one.
>
> I actually told someone the other day that I actually like my own company better than anyone else's right now! (*Laughs*) I think that getting an animal is as far as I want to go! I have so many activities! I do volunteer work. I do some work with hospice. I've been overseas. I've traveled to underdeveloped countries, and I've met wonderful people doing this work. I am active in my church. It's very stimulating! So I have a lot of things that are meaningful that fill my time. I have old friends, new friends. I have never lacked for friends.
>
> You know, I won't say I am never lonely, but I am really not. I have really been blessed with a lot of friends. So I always have enough people to do things with if I want to. I love living on my own! I love

the independence. If I want company, I have it. I'm very social. I have people over for dinner all the time. I just came back from wine country. I was there with four friends. So we are really lucky. There is really a large group, and these days there are so many single women out there you always have a buddy.

I'd really have to stretch to say that I feel lonely. I mean, when I was talking before about my marriage I felt like I could cry. But when I talk about this it feels okay. I'd very much like to be in a relationship, but I'm okay and I'm shocked about it! I know I've said that three times now! I was anxiety filled and now I'm not. I just don't get periods of loneliness. There's always something to do. No, I don't. All of a sudden here you are on your own again and all these things that you thought were going to happen were less definite. I think, I really don't have any kids, I really don't have to stay here. I could do anything.

Yes, there is some loneliness, but at this point in my life it seems very natural. It used to not be. I used to get very anxious about it. At this point in my life if I am lonely I am rarely bored. I can find something to do. It seems to me at this point in my life to be very manageable. I have no problem taking myself to the movies, museums, opera, doing anything by myself or calling a friend, or just staying home and watching TV or reading a book. I mean I don't need, I am able to figure out if I am lonely what to do about it.

Just sharing things with someone. I got this job and I'd love to have someone to share it with. Sharing the good things and the bad things. I think that's what makes it lonely, not having anyone to share the good things with. That gets lonely, not having anyone to talk to about what is going on in your life. And you don't realize it until you think about it. I try to connect with girlfriends, but some of them are too high maintenance, and I can't deal with wishy-washy. It's hard not having anyone to come home to, that's one of the hardest things.

I've thought about my old age and who's going to be around. I've thought of it more like I need to get my ducks in order. I need to make sure I have long-term disability insurance and that I have my funeral planned, and maybe I should get long-term care insurance. So I've sort of thought of it more practically, like what will happen if I get incapacitated and there isn't someone to take care of me. I really haven't thought about it in terms of WOW, what am I going to do? I've thought I need to plan for that, I need to plan that I'm gonna be alone.

I think that there have been times in my life where I have looked at my friends and have said, "Wow, they really have a lovely, warm family." I am sorry sometimes that it might have been nice to do, but it is not prolonged. At times I have felt a devastated feeling, but it has

> been very fleeting. You know, isolated moments for the most part when I am in a situation and I see a family and how they are interacting. I think, Oh boy, this is lovely. It does tug at my heart a little bit. I think, Oh boy, where did I go wrong, or why didn't I do this? But it doesn't last. It doesn't last.

She summarized the reaction of others:

> Mostly what I get is "I can't believe you didn't want to be a mother because you would have been such a wonderful mother." And I find when I am with my friends from long ago who are all married with children, that my activities feel less valuable in that context. They ask me what I've been doing and when I say I've been to Africa, working with hospices, raising money, and working with kids, they say that's really interesting and then they turn and say, "The other day my five-year-old ..." I don't think they understand. I think it is foreign to them and they don't know how to respond, like how different is my life. I don't think that it is at all a devaluing of it, but it feels less important because everyone is focused on their husband and their children and their house.

COMING OUT OF THE DARK: THE STORY OF PEGGY

Peggy is an example of a woman caught between traditional beliefs about the importance of being a wife and mother, and her role as a divorced woman at midlife without children. When Peggy first came to me, she was experiencing a high level of distress about her second divorce and the absence of children in her life. Although making attempts to recover, Peggy experienced a four-year period of depression and anxiety post-divorce. Despite many efforts, nothing seemed to decrease the distress she felt. The only solution to her distress, in her view, was to get remarried and have children. She could not imagine a future life without a husband and children. Her experience seemed bound to beliefs that the only valuable roles were those of wife and mother.

Peggy had wanted to be married and have children since the age of 12. Despite consistent high desire, Peggy also had a sense of knowing that she was "going along with the program" of what was expected of her. She recalled increasing pressure to marry in her early 20s as she observed many of her friends doing so. She addressed her belief that she *should* be married within a certain time frame as a precipitating factor in her marrying with doubts. She related her sense of "going along with it," rather than making a conscious choice:

> We dated for four months and knew each other casually for about a year before that. The conversation came up one day. He asked if I thought he was marriage material, and I said yes. I think at that point in my life I was just used to going along with things. I think

> the word *no* wasn't really a big part of my life at that point. When I think back at that point in my life, I always went along with things. I was going along with it. It seemed like the logical next step to get married at that age. I guess we thought we were at the right age to go ahead and get married, and we got married the following September. Looking back, I think there were signs it was the wrong thing.

At the time that Peggy came to therapy, she was 38 years old, had been divorced the second time for four years, and did not have children. She was not in a relationship when we began therapy and lived alone in a small house that she had purchased by herself after her divorce. Upon meeting for the first time, Peggy seemed moderately depressed and guarded. Her voice tone reflected a sense of frustration and hopelessness when she discussed her circumstances of being divorced at midlife without children.

Peggy was the oldest of four children, having two brothers and one sister. Her mother had also been divorced when Peggy was 12. She related having had a distant relationship with her father and having no contact with him in her adulthood. Peggy had a high school diploma and worked as an executive assistant for a large corporation, a job that she enjoyed and found satisfactory. Her job was also a source of support as she had made friends with her co-workers and spent time socializing with them outside of work. Peggy had been married twice, with her first marriage occurring at age 24 and lasting one year. She recalled marrying the first time because "it was time to do it," and she viewed that relationship as a mistake. She married for the second time after a one-year courtship.

Peggy always had a strong desire to have children since early adolescence. She was the quintessential little girl who loved only playing with baby dolls and always imagined herself as a mother. Peggy verbalized a strong desire for children before, during, and after her marriage and retained a high desire in the post-divorce period. However, despite her verbalized high desire for children, she also expressed some ambivalent feelings, manifested as a fear of pregnancy and "not being a baby person." She and her ex-husband began trying to become pregnant as soon as they were married. To her disappointment, she did not become pregnant. As therapy progressed, she expressed a realization of a possible connection between the conflict in her marriage and the stress of not becoming pregnant. She still retained high desire after her divorce; however, she felt that the divorce process had made her more cautious and realistic. She had become more aware of looking for traits in a man that would make him a good candidate for fatherhood. She still felt extremely hopeful she still had time to bear children into her 40s, and hoped to do so.

The couple divorced after a four-year marriage and a three-month separation. Peggy viewed herself as the initiator of both her divorces. She entered therapy shortly after her second divorce, feeling distressed and having difficulty functioning in her daily routine. Peggy stated the reasons for her second divorce were possible infertility, conflict, incompatibility, concern about her husband's immaturity and drinking, and her continued interest in a previous boyfriend.

Similar to Alissa, Peggy believed that marriage was for life and had not wanted to divorce. She also felt indirectly forced into initiating divorce by her ex-husband due to his lack of commitment to working things out. She further believed reasons for her divorce were her ex-husband's inability to meet her emotional needs, lack of trust, narcissism, and lack of his separation from his family of origin. She expressed a great deal of regret about her divorce and even after four years post-divorce still had fantasies of pursuing reunification.

Adjustment to life without a spouse and children over four years had been difficult for Peggy and had been exacerbated by lack of socialization and inability to find a suitable boyfriend or remarry. She also expressed dissatisfaction with a part-time relationship she had become involved in with a friend who was not interested in committing to a full-time relationship. Peggy had gotten involved in this relationship with a friend and acknowledged it was probably due to her extreme discomfort of being alone and feeling disconnected.

Peggy experienced a period of distress after her second divorce that lasted four years. Her distress seemed to revolve around incongruous feelings about wanting to be a wife and mother, and yet beginning to feel the need to adapt to single life. She described significant depression and anxiety that included general malaise and long amounts of time in bed sleeping. She utilized psychotherapy and anti-anxiety medication, which she found somewhat helpful. She related her feelings about her divorce process:

> I think I got remarried too quickly, just to do it and to not be alone. I think we didn't have things in common. Little things, like music. I know that is little, but mainly he wasn't home, and he was more of a drinker than me. Like we would go to a party and he would drink a lot with his friends, and I'm not into that. I'm more of a homebody. I'm not a partier, so I think we didn't have some important things in common as time went by.
>
> I was starting to feel it was all one-sided. When we would make plans with my friends or family, he didn't like that much and we wouldn't go out with them. So I was basically accommodating to HIM. I didn't feel like he was participating in MY life. I guess we were fighting a lot of the time, and part of it was about the issue of children. It was very stressful, very frustrating. I think that put a strain on the marriage as well. It was putting stress on him and me. We were fighting over it.

Although Peggy was clear about the reasons for her divorce, after four years of being single she had begun to have regrets about her divorce. She related:

> He was a good person; he would have done anything for me to make me happy. He knew a lot about me. He was very smart. He was a little immature, but basically he was a good person. I would do it different. I would have worked on it. And I would see the person I had. He respected me and he would have never cheated on me. The only thing I would say for people in a marriage, the grass is not greener, work it out. I would just give that advice to someone who is having problems, because a lot of people think the grass is greener and it is not.

Peggy related acting out during the time period shortly after her divorce for several months with a man whom she felt was dangerous and inappropriate for her. She had not repeated that behavior since that time, although experiencing anxiety and depression as a result of the downward spiral of her marriage and the first year after divorce. Peggy also expressed frustration and dislike for dating at midlife, and stated that she did not have much hope of meeting a suitable partner. Although she enjoyed the advantages of living alone and being independent, she also discussed the ongoing desire for a relationship and children.

> I don't think I have really coped. I slept a lot. I still sleep a lot. I am doing a little better. I feel like I want to be living my life and out doing things. I started going to therapy because I thought I was depressed because of the divorce. Towards the end I started to realize how much like his family he was, very cold and selfish, and I just couldn't stand that. I went to the doctor and actually it was more anxiety, and I got medication. I took it on and off when I would feel bad, like maybe once every couple of months when I couldn't get my head together.
>
> It has taken me four years to adjust! Maybe I'm not normal because I had this other thing going on with a friend who didn't want a relationship, that was a huge part of it. That was keeping me upset, and I didn't care about anybody else, anything else, my apartment could have fallen apart. Well, I did care about my cats and my mother. But I didn't care about anything else. I think it would have been different if I didn't have someone else in the picture. It might have only taken me two years to adjust to the divorce. I just didn't see how I could have been totally alone during those first few years. I think I didn't care about anything, even myself.

Although Peggy felt the first four years after her divorce were extremely difficult emotionally, she felt she finally had begun to "turn the corner." With the addition of a new female friend, her social life and dating life improved, and she became more optimistic about opportunities to remarry and have children in the future. Although experiencing occasional loneliness, she enjoyed living alone for the most part and was quite adventurous, doing many things she enjoyed by herself. She began to develop a large social network and many friends that "fixed her up" for dates.

Her family was also experienced as supportive, and she described feeling closer to them and more open since her divorce. Peggy also described utilizing older female family members and friends as mentors and role models for her single life. She had received several promotions and large salary increases at work, and found her career a source of satisfaction and fulfillment. She did not feel any financial strain due to the divorce.

Overall, Peggy appeared to be very optimistic about her life. She expressed a strong desire to remarry and have children. However, she also expressed a strong desire to be cautious about her choice of a partner and not make a third mistake. She expressed a desire to make her life interesting and diverse, and not have her happiness dependent upon the presence of a man. She had plans for herself and was reorganizing her life with definite ideas about interests she would pursue in her future, should she not remarry or have children. These included going back to school for artistic pursuits, traveling, and living in other locations. Although the idea of this lifestyle was still somewhat distressing to her internally, she had started to embrace the idea to make the most of her life without marriage and children. She stated:

> I think this new friend has helped me a lot. She knows a lot of people and she goes out a lot, and we go out a lot. We go out to dinner. We talk about guys. We have a lot in common being divorced and single. It's made a huge difference. I feel like I am starting to live again, like I am coming out of the dark. I was truly in a black hole and couldn't see my way out. It's the worst thing I have ever been through. But I'm better now, and I'm really starting to like my life. This is the first time I have ever been me on my own. I'm starting to see the light. You have to have your own life! If you don't make your own life you are not interesting! No one is going to make it for you. You are the only person that can make your own happiness. Nobody else is in charge of making you happy. You have to make you happy, especially when you are as depressed as I was.

PART III

A Relational Constructionist Approach

A clinical approach to women divorced at midlife without children, first and foremost, requires a nonblaming, nonvictimizing stance that considers them, at best, within an unresponsive social environment and, at worst, within a stigmatizing, devaluing environment that seeks to divide and oppress women. The goal is not to fit the client into rigid theory and assumptions. Rather, it is to meet each woman where she is, as a valued human being developing in a complex web of relationships with individuals, families, communities, institutions, and the larger society.

Developing an approach to clinical work with women divorced at midlife without children also requires meeting the challenge of working from an approach that redefines, supports, respects, and honors their experience. This means changing the "viewing and doing" of therapy in a way that disconnects from limiting, traditionally masculine-oriented theoretical models of development and adaptation. In effect, a clinical paradigm shift is needed, rather than repeating the destructiveness of biased social constructions that devalue and limit women. Rigid theories and thinking that utilize diagnosis to pathologize and stigmatize women who are not in relationship with either a spouse or children disrupt the therapist's capacity to join with the client at the deep, core level of her experience.

In Part I, several overarching theories were suggested as useful premises for clinical work with this group of women. These theoretical underpinnings will provide the framework for the clinical approach that follows here.

CHAPTER 11

Sponsoring, Re-storying, and Fostering Connection

For years psychiatrists have tried to "cure" their patients' conflicts by fitting them to the culture. But adjustment to a culture which does not permit the realization of one's entire being is not a cure at all, according to the new psychological thinkers.

—Betty Friedan, *The Feminine Mystique* (1997, p. 311)

If we were to gaze ever so closely through the kaleidoscope of clinical theories most of us have been trained to look through, we would still see evidence of the many colors of patriarchy, judgment, and exclusion of women who are "different" in some way. In thinking about presenting a clinical approach for work with women divorced at midlife without children, my hope is that the approach will provide you with an invitation to examining and shifting your own unique set of paradigms, to becoming aware of the underlying principles and beliefs that determine what you think about, what you bring to the therapy relationship and process, and how you can be most responsive to this group of women.

Over the last several decades of practice, training, research, and personal experience, I have arrived at a core set of beliefs about the purposes and benefits of therapy in general. This way of thinking undoubtedly reflects the sum total of my clinical training and experiences. These have resulted in firm convictions about the capacity of individuals to author their own solutions, the importance of storied beliefs on people's lives, and the importance of connection and belonging for human development. I have also arrived at beliefs about what is necessary and most useful in therapeutic response to the unique challenges for women and girls of all ages and circumstances, as well as women divorced at midlife without children. My work with this group, as well as my own experience, has provided me with the challenge of examining the beliefs at the core of my ideas and responses to others. I do not present these ideas as a clinical model from the position of self-proclaimed expert. Rather, my goal is to put forward to you, the reader, a way of thinking, an approach composed of many possible ideas and solutions from which you can choose. While this approach will be specifically focused on women divorced at midlife without children, I also hope you will possibly find many ideas that will be useful in your work with all women and girls.

GUIDING PREMISES FOR AN APPROACH TO THERAPY: CHANGING THE VIEWING AND DOING

Whatever one's clinical orientation and training, most would agree therapy is about the business of change. In the medical sense, therapy is defined as serving to cure or heal, concerned with discovering and applying remedies and treatments for diseases. From an Ericksonian view, therapy is about sponsoring the change, growth, and opening of another through the relational system of client and therapist (Gilligan, 2001). Based on respect and honor for the client, her capabilities, strengths, and potential for internal healing and growth, change occurs through a mutual process of conversation and relationship that results in the creation of new meanings and behaviors (deShazer, 1994).

Berg and DeJong (1996) described therapy as a process, consistent with a social constructionist view, that attempts to foster change by opening up new views of reality that relieve distress and result in a more satisfactory and productive life for the client. deShazer (1994) also called attention to therapy as a conversational process between client and therapist, rather than a didactic, authoritarian approach in which the therapist delivers strategized interventions from an omniscient stance. Rosen (1982) offered an interpretational definition of therapy from the Ericksonian view as focused on changing meaning through changing unconscious patterns via a relational experience with another (the therapist). Change is viewed as a self-reinforcing process that can lead to the ongoing development of the individual.

Although Erickson's thinking and actual technique were often elusive and confusing to his students and observers, his unrelenting belief in the uniqueness of the individual and in the capacity of human beings to heal and grow from within was remarkably clear. Viewing clients from this perspective results in a stance of hopefulness and encouragement that does, indeed, allow the therapist to sponsor clients in the service of "self-authorship" of their own growth, recovery, and self-discovery. Viewing clients as "one of a kind" requires fluid use of theory to best advance the growth process of the client.

I am reminded of the experience of observing my mother as a seamstress when I was a little girl. My mother was quite adept at sewing fanciful party dresses for my sister and me. She would begin with an idea we each had, a general pattern, and some fabric and accessories we each chose. As the dress took shape, my mother would create the vision I had for my unique dress, fitting exactly to my size, shaping, pinning, and adjusting until it was just perfect for me. My sister and I often had very different ideas for the visions of our party dresses. I was more red velvet and lace, my sister more neon, psychedelic, and "mod." The beauty of this process was that my mother was totally open to helping us create the vision we wanted for ourselves. She was the guide that brought the vision to life, making special, customized dresses that reflected our own special uniqueness. In the same way, in therapy it is important to follow the client's design and vision for her life. In order to do this, we need to start with a theoretical pattern, a creative idea allowing the client to choose the fabric of therapy and shape the final creation for her life.

In effect, although theories do provide guidance across cases, no case is exactly like any other case. Therapy needs to be responsive to the uniqueness of the individual and her life dilemmas. If we view clients from this position of uniqueness and capability, then attempts to fit them into rigidified theories are no longer useful to the therapeutic process. A flexible approach of "being with" the client that adapts to the uniqueness of the individual also renders the concept of resistance no longer useful.

Defining therapy from this perspective is especially relevant for work with women who are divorced without children since they are, by definition, in a role that is attached to negative meanings, vulnerability, isolation, and degradation. The ability to positively sponsor the client toward more functional, celebratory, and affirming meanings of her experience becomes a critical starting point for therapy.

REVISITING THE DEATH OF RESISTANCE

The risk of proposing a clinical model, complete with techniques, tools, and interventions, is that it will be viewed as a rigid prescription to be applied and used to "pigeonhole" clients into inflexible standards and expectations of mental health. Should the client "color outside the lines," so to speak, being unresponsive to the therapist's view and interventions, the traditional stance is to view the client as resistant. Such a process limits creative thinking about the uniqueness of each individual client, and the infinite ways she can author her own growth and development. My intent here is not to provide a recipe for change from which to "cook up" interventions. As both deShazer (1994) and Gilligan (2001) stated, there are many versions of therapy that have come in and out of favor in different eras. Rather than becoming entrenched in theory as scientifically proven "prescription" for the disease of the client, we can view theory as a guide for discovering the unique capabilities of the client for growth. As Gilligan (2001) so aptly stated:

> Every human being is like no other, and will respond to treatment as a unique individual, in a sense each requires a unique therapeutic "theory" made for him or her alone. To get to that distinct self, it is

the therapist's calling to engage in a kind of open-ended "not knowing"—to refrain from rushing to judgment or diagnosis or theoretical categorization or problem solving.

The concept of resistance implies a separation between client and therapist that is caused by the client's resisting, unwillingness, or inability to comply with the therapist's way of thinking. Resistance is defined in *Webster's Dictionary* as "opposition, the ability of an organism to resist harmful influences." In physics the concept of resistance defines the response of an object that is being pushed against. The more force applied to it, the more it will resist. Pushing against the client from an inflexible theoretical position prevents the client from feeling sponsored on a deep level. Rather, balancing support and empathy with challenge and demand for work is the stance that is most productive for the client.

deShazer's (1984) article on the death of resistance exposed the concept as a reified construct in need of revision. The idea that the therapeutic relationship and the client's progress should be judged by the client's willingness to comply with the suggestions, expert knowledge, and advice of the therapist was challenged. From this position, therapy can become an adversarial competition between therapist and client that is unproductive, and can often leave the client feeling misunderstood and judged.

The concept of clients as resistant or manipulative has not been useful to me for quite some time. If my goal is to "be with" the client at her deepest level of hurt, despair, or dysfunction, and to view her symptoms/problems as attempted solutions in the service of growth, then the concept of resistance no longer comes into play. I view myself as responsible for joining the client where she is, guiding her to discover her own capabilities for healing, and adjusting my approach according to the outcomes she desires.

The Ericksonian perspective positions the therapist in cooperation with the client, rather than as authority or expert. If we view therapy as a relational system in which both client and therapist bring themselves to the relationship, with both holding responsibility for the outcome of therapy, then the goal of the therapist becomes to "join with" and sponsor the client, not serve as an opponent. In such a position, the therapist then takes responsibility for failed interventions and lack of progress. If we use the concept of resistance, the question becomes why the client is resistant, and lack of progress is explained as a product of the client's own dysfunction. In my view, a more useful stance is to ask different questions that enable the therapist to recapitulate his or her initial hypothesis and continue to search to join with the client on a deeper level. Ask such questions as: What do I not understand about why the client is stuck? How can I change what I am doing to help her get unstuck? What are her capabilities and strengths I can draw upon? Through this perspective, therapy then becomes a fluid process of mutual work, rather than one that is limited by the therapist's "stuckness" in a theoretical stance that creates opposition. Gilligan (2001) further suggests the therapist's stance should be

> a receptive state wherein you allow yourself to be touched and awakened by the client's often hidden inner presence, which in turn allows you to awaken your client to his or her own inner core.

SHIFTING THE KALEIDOSCOPE OF PATRIARCHY

In her classic and timeless writings on self-esteem, Steinem (1992) identified three destructive components of patriarchal paradigms that need revision:

- Either-or thinking that divides everything into opposing parts
- Linear thinking that rates and grades others and places the roots of value and accomplishment in defeating and devaluing others
- The notion of hierarchy maintenances in which all authority flows from the top

She further suggests deconstruction of limiting paradigms:

> As a universal pattern with almost no alternatives, this paradigm limits us at best and destroys us at worst. It turns most human interactions into a contest that only one or a few at the top can win, and it teaches us that there is a limited amount of self esteem to go around, that some of us can only have if others do not. Fortunately this is just a cognitive construct. There is nothing biological or immutable about it, and therefore it can be changed. (Steinem, 1992, p. 187)

Despite the tremendous social progress that has been made since the first wave of feminism, the overwhelmingly powerful legacy of paradigms about women's worth, value, and identity as closely bound to their capacity to serve through marriage and childbearing still weighs heavily on the individual and collective unconscious of women. Surely it is not lost on us that these are the exact overarching paradigms that have been applied to women who are not wives or mothers. The "universal pattern" that Steinem speaks of here is that "all women must be wives and mothers." Only those who fit into these "gold standards" win the contest, so to speak. We assume that women who are not wives and mothers must not have the "prize" of self-esteem and must develop in an inferior way. Although progress has been made in shifting this paradigm, I concur with Steinem's idea that this construct needs to continue to be challenged in deeper ways, as it is often now underground.

The Stone Center authors (Jordan et al., 1991) also suggest separation from therapy models and paradigms that are based on distance rather than connection, and remind us that the use of diagnosis often creates a barrier that reflects the rigid standards of psychology models that are themselves larger reflections of institutionalized patriarchy in action. The Stone Center authors also call into question traditional models that uphold the value of impersonal, objective distance between client and therapist, rather than validating close connection in relationship.

AN EXPANDED LIFE CYCLE PERSPECTIVE

Based on the dramatic changes in relational arrangements, adult roles, and lifestyles in the last half of the 20th century, adults at any stage of the life cycle may find themselves without a spouse or children. With the increases in postponement of marriage and childbearing, and divorce, many adults may find themselves single at some point in their adulthood. Due to the many variations in family forms and relational experiences, this concept is also useful to describe other single adults, such as single, never married women without children, as well as adult males. Given recent cultural shifts, mature single adulthood without children should be viewed as a normative life cycle stage that may be arrived at through a variety of routes (Dafoe & Popenoe, 2006). These routes include remaining single and not mothering throughout young adulthood, divorcing, or becoming widowed.

Both individual and family life cycle theory need to be revisited and expanded to include a normative phase of mature single adulthood. This model would allow for the inclusion of both temporary and permanent states of mature single adulthood, rather than "pathologizing" this phase. Such theory expansion can facilitate a decrease in a "blaming the victim" ideology that often impacts women outside the norm.

Beginning from this perspective then, I am also suggesting that the phase of mature single adulthood can be facilitated by the development of *autonomous competence*. I have identified several coping skills that I consider key components of this concept. These are the capacities for increased self-nurturing, expanded intimacy and attachments, and multidimensional industriousness. While this term can be utilized in a general sense for adult development, for my purposes here, I am suggesting the utilization of the term *autonomous competence* to describe a developmental process for the increasing phenomenon of women who are divorced at midlife without children. I provide the following definition: those who have created and embraced new roles, and who function well outside the traditional roles of wife and mother.

The term *autonomous competence* is being suggested due to the absence of positive terms in the literature to describe women without a spouse and children. Previously, terms such as *ex-wife*, *divorced*, *voluntarily* or *involuntarily childless*, *childfree*, and *non-mother* have been pejoratively used. A previous shift in terms in the literature from *childless* to *childfree* was an attempt to provide a more positive connotation. This term still describes women only in relation to the absence of children (Casey, 2007; Letherby, 2002; Park, 2002). Women have been defined primarily in the *absence* of marriage and motherhood, rather than positively connoted as well functioning in their own right.

No term can be found in the literature that differs from this negative perspective. The absence of such terms is evidence of the pervasive, pro-natalist, pro-marriage social constructions that have been embedded in Western society and have limited women's roles and lifestyle choices.

Heatherington (2003) suggested the term *competent loner* to describe a general style of divorce adjustment for men and women. The word *loner* still retains a negative connotation. Literature regarding the family developmental life cycle has more recently included discussion of autonomous functioning and the mature interdependent self. However, theory development has stopped short of fully including mature single adulthood as a normative stage in either individual or family life cycle models (Carter & McGoldrick, 1999).

BEYOND STIGMA MANAGEMENT: IN SUPPORT OF ROLE INNOVATION

Adaptation to the role of divorced woman at midlife without children is facilitated by a woman's ability to challenge and overcome societal stigma and devaluation, and forge her way into new and fulfilling roles that foster well-being and growth. Approaching therapy from the position of supporting the process of role innovation is an important premise for clinical work with these women. Role innovation can be defined as the following:

> The process of challenging patriarchal cultural assumptions to construct multi-dimensional roles apart from the preferred roles of wife and mother, and thrive and function well within those roles.

A goal of this approach is to facilitate women's capacity for self-determination and increase their ability to neutralize the effects of a stigmatized role and "deviant" identity. A variety of defensive techniques are useful for women to manage and challenge pro-natalist biases and pejorative descriptions of childless women. Women's ability to surpass defensive techniques and utilize proactive techniques of role innovation to diminish internalized pressure and increase self-esteem regarding new roles and lifestyles is a critical coping skill. A therapist's ability to actively support proactive and creative efforts of the client for role innovation are a core part of treatment.

In a narrow sense, women are often defined in terms of their relation to others. Although one can categorize women according to role labels such as daughter, sister, or career woman, viewing role innovation as a broader process that consists of several critical coping skills can be more useful. This facilitates our thinking beyond relationship with others and focuses on beneficial coping skills. These include self-care and nurturing, expanded intimacy and attachments, and multidimensional industriousness.

Since divorce represents a major life crisis and significant loss, skills of self-care and nurturing are important to a woman's recovery. In therapy, exploration should include development of good capacity to be alone, ability to manage loneliness, positive financial adjustment, and other forms of self-care, self-nurturing, and self-preservation. Expanding intimacy and attachments includes increasing capacity to develop nurturing and supportive social networks, enhanced relationships with family members, parents, siblings, nieces and nephews, and other extended family members, and friendships. Multidimensional industriousness may include career directedness, pursuit of education, altruistic interests, cultural interests, and hobbies.

Initially, exit from the role of wife is an emotionally difficult process that results in a significant downward shift in functioning for almost all women. Role exit from preferred roles represents loss of status and perceived value. For most women, the end of marriage first represents an unwanted end to a significant, primary attachment. Initial grief reactions include significant depression, anxiety, numbness, psychosomatic symptoms, and general difficulty functioning in daily life. This validates the profound significance of connection, attachment, and relationships for women (Chodorow, 1978; Gilligan, 1982). Miller (1976) addresses the meaning of loss of relationship for women as loss of core sense of self.

However, after initial role exit, most women do actually adjust well to the role of divorced woman without children, and role innovation becomes a critical aspect of building feelings of competence and self-efficacy. Although divorce is initially traumatic and highly stressful, long-term adjustment has been found to be characterized by resilience, higher self-esteem, and enhanced ego functioning. Role innovation goes hand in hand with changing the meaning of exiting preferred roles into stigmatized roles. Shifting the narratives attached to these roles is also a critical goal of treatment. In effect, women who are able to develop narratives about the advantages of being single as a divorced woman at midlife far outweighing the disadvantages tend to fare better in the long term. This shift in meaning may include retrospective stories about the role of wife as somewhat emotionally oppressive and associated with lack of freedom, dependence, and inability to control one's life. Women also fare better who can relate beliefs regarding marriage as associated with negative experiences of primary responsibility for the relationship, home management, and many aspects of their spouse's daily life. Beliefs regarding a perceived sense of increased freedom in the absence of the caretaking aspect of the role of wife are also useful in adaptation to single life.

Another important aspect to explore in therapy is the emotional stress and disconnect that can occur after marriage, as women transition to the role of dating woman at midlife. This can undoubtedly be a difficult adaptation, and this process requires attention in therapy. In some cases, this transition takes place after 10 or more years of married life, thus representing a major shift in role and lifestyle. Some women relate tremendous frustration and disappointment regarding inability to meet appropriate potential partners at midlife. Activities for "singles" can be experienced as humiliating and devaluing.

In support of role innovation, it is important to be aware of embedded assumptions regarding bereft feelings about childlessness. Many women describe making a good emotional adjustment to exiting the role of potential mother, and it is important to support the positive narratives of their experience. In practice, the absence of descriptions of significant psychological symptoms such as depression, anxiety, psychosomatic illnesses, or suicidal ideation is significant. Some women also do not report a period of intense mourning or ongoing significant grief feelings. More recent research findings validate the lack of bereft feelings among voluntarily childless women who are comfortable in their role (Casey, 2007; Letherby, 2002).

FRAMING GOALS FOR THERAPY

The premises discussed above provide a guide that allows clinicians to support women in their search for fulfillment and a valued identity within their role as divorced women at midlife without children. Betty Freidan (1963/1997) suggested the need for detachment from theories that victimize women, are based in biological determinism, and define women only in relation to traditional and sexual roles. Such theories do not support the validation of women's basic need to grow and fulfill their potential as complete human beings. Furthermore, these premises provide a perspective that enables the therapist to approach treatment from a position that:

- Considers the person in relational and systemic context
- Defines therapy as a process of sponsorship and mutuality
- Focuses on cooperation and collaboration
- Attempts to detach from patriarchal paradigms
- Normalizes a life cycle stage of mature single adulthood
- Facilitates the development of autonomous competence
- Supports role innovation

As we begin to consider the clinical issues, clinical approach, and treatment case material, it is important to work from a knowledge base that grounds clinical thinking and the development of interventions. I view these theories as critical to thinking about my work with women in general, as well as the specific group examined here. Below, then, is a very brief review of the theories already outlined in Part I.

Social constructionist theory provides a critical backdrop for understanding women's experience in a patriarchal context in which rigid messages, beliefs, and prescriptions have long determined women's decision making, choices, and life experiences. The complex web of social constructions that impact women so pervasively needs to be a core consideration in this work, not an afterthought. Understanding the importance of connection and belonging for women from the feminist developmental perspective provides an important relational base from which to frame midlife women divorced without children. Normalizing women's need and their perceived responsibility for relationship prevents us from pathologizing their distress as well as their efforts to stay connected in the face of divorce and childlessness. Their status also requires adaptation to a major role loss, role exit, and transition to new roles. From this perspective, it is important to understand role theory in terms of the linking of preferred roles to socially valued status. Understanding the meaning of loss of value facilitates our ability to understand women's struggles to innovate new roles as they move forward. The family developmental life cycle also provides a guiding premise from which to view a woman as developing in connection rather than isolation. As one moves through the life cycle, considering the relational connection to immediate and extended family, friends, peers, community, and the larger society provides a critical context for viewing a woman's development. Ego psychology also provides a way for us to consider a woman's individual psychological development in relation to her adaptation to the social environment, in effect, her "fit" into the environment, or lack thereof. It is important to incorporate coping capacities, ego strengths, and functional defense mechanisms into our assessment of women's adjustment.

These theories then guide us toward an approach that enables women to recover, forge ahead, and create fulfilling lives for themselves as divorced women at midlife, apart from the roles of wife and mother. As a result of clinical experience, my research study, and my own experience with midlife divorce, I have identified several key coping skills and processes that have, for me, become the major overarching goals for therapy with this group of women. The primary goal for treatment is to facilitate the development of autonomous competence. Within this goal are the subgoals of meaning modification, expansion of intimacy and attachments, and role innovation.

Meaning Modification

The ability to find positive meaning and reconstruct life narratives in the face of loss and trauma has recently become a focus of theoretical attention (Neimeyer, 2000). The search for meaning in the divorce experience has also been identified as a valuable coping skill (Bevvino & Sharkin, 2003). In Parts I and II, considerable consideration has been given to the impact of negative reactions, perceptions, and beliefs about women who are outside the norm. The importance of viewing these women's experience from a social constructionist perspective also has been recommended. In light of these overarching contextual issues, the ability of women to externalize negative perceptions and meaning, and reconstruct positive meanings for the roles of unmarried and childless seems to be a critical coping skill for women divorced at midlife without children.

In therapy, women have described conflicting feelings of contentment about their lifestyles that are somehow diminished by underlying feelings of distress, discomfort, and sadness. It has become apparent to me that this distress often stems from a cognitive dissonance that reverberates from social constructions of shame and guilt about being unmarried and childless. These internalized messages can result in unexplainable anxiety and depression.

The process of loosening the internalized connection to these pejorative beliefs, in effect, deconstructing and reconstructing them more positively, is key in therapy. Externalizing and radically changing life stories, in my opinion, is a key to facilitating the emotional growth and well-being of these women. Exposing rigid prescriptions can free a woman to create new beliefs that support her value as a human being, and disconnect her from the constructions of shame, guilt, and failure regarding her status as ex-wife and non-mother.

Expanded Intimacy and Attachment

The loss of connection that results from midlife divorce, as well as the loss of future connection through relationship with children, places a woman in the vulnerable position of lacking the primary relational belonging that is gained from marriage and mothering. Given what is known about the importance of relationship to women's well-being and mental health in general, the ability to develop connection and belonging through expanded intimacy and attachments is another critical coping skill and a goal in therapy for these women. Positive divorce adjustment is related to a woman's capacity to expand close, supportive family relationships, friendship networks and socialization, and reference group support. Extended family support is an important factor in women's recovery process and adjustment to post-divorce life. Women usually relate that support and companionship of friends is critical, throughout both the divorce process and the post-divorce adjustment phase. Friends' ability to listen, provide unconditional support, and be available for companionship and social activities is important to adjustment. Reference group support, the development of friendships with other peers in like circumstances, divorced and single adults without children, is also an important factor in adjustment. Attention to the issue of expanding connections is another key goal for therapy. The ability of the therapist to be a consistent sponsor also represents another significant expansion of attachment that can be critical to a woman's adjustment to this role.

Role Innovation

The experience of exiting a role that is closely linked with preferential status and value and entering a role that is marginalized and stigmatized can be viewed as a developmental task that can be challenging for women. It requires a woman to develop value and meaning through the creation of new, fulfilling roles. Many women who are career focused feel that competence at work is a critical factor in their recovery and adjustment. The ability to focus and achieve at work during stressful periods facilitates feelings of mastery that are psychologically grounding for women experiencing midlife divorce. A sense of survival skill and resourcefulness in managing finances also contributes to feelings of competence and "survivorship."

Some women describe enhanced functioning as a result of divorce that has catapulted them toward impressive and significant professional and financial gains and advancements. When considering role innovation, one always needs to consider financial independence and a woman's ability to care for herself financially as a major source of perceived competence and self-efficacy. Positive socioeconomic status has long been correlated with positive identity change, improvements in competence, and higher self-esteem after divorce (Rahav, 2002).

Role innovation also needs to be broad enough to incorporate more than career and financial development. In therapy, it is important to consider and facilitate a variety of roles that can provide meaning and connection for women. From the relational perspective, a broad view that considers expansion of as many family roles as possible is useful. These include the roles of daughter, granddaughter, sister, aunt, and cousin. Broad exploration and support for expanded intergenerational connections through family roles can facilitate the recovery process. Some women have expanded their roles with relationships with extended family members such as aunts and uncles, nieces and nephews, and cousins. Expanded friendships are also critical to a positive adjustment. Some women have also branched out into other roles that have provided fulfillment for them. These have included volunteers and mentors to children, as well as other altruistic, spiritual, and religious pursuits.

Women who are divorced at midlife without children still face increased vulnerability and stress due to their status. In a patriarchal society, women have continually been expected to fit into rigidified roles that encourage division and competition among women. As therapists, we also are not immune to our own "societal training" to view wives and mothers as always altruistic, and non-wives and non-mothers as always substandard and narcissistic. This polarizing discourse continues to entrench women in positions of "other" and "stranger," rather than embracing all roles as valuable.

The surprising findings of the research study were the ability of women to develop extensive coping and mastery, and the lack of residual symptoms in the post-divorce state. The absence of ongoing depression, anxiety, loneliness, anger, bitterness, suicidal ideation, substance abuse, and eating disorders in the group I studied was significant. Most of the women I have worked with describe a sense of having gained their "voice" and a stronger sense of self, accompanied by freedom, independence, survivorship, and control over their lives.

While keeping these three overarching goals in view, it is important to work from a position of understanding the complexity of marriage, childbearing, and divorce decision-making processes for women. It is also important to consider the interplay between internal self-labeling and external stigma that continues to be promoted in a pro-natalist, pro-marriage society. Gutman (1995) suggests that clinicians consider a holistic view that normalizes the process of multiple decision points over the course of a woman's marital and childbearing career. The idea of a holistic view helps to identify, organize, and establish the interrelationship of the trends of marriage, divorce, postponement, and childlessness. By viewing women as gravitating ***toward*** and choosing roles they are attracted to, rather than as rejecting rigid roles and standards, the destructive impact of stigmatization on women can begin to be loosened.

A progressive way to view women's decision making about life choices is to normalize the conscious process of weighing costs and benefits of marriage and childbearing. This process has undoubtedly become more complex as women now have the opportunity to consider multiple choices for education, careers, and other forms of self-fulfillment. It is also productive to detach these decisions from socially constructed limiting narratives. A more productive view is to frame women's decisions from the position of traditional or untraditional beliefs regarding role expectations. Bias can be diminished if we view women as more traditional who are more focused on marriage and childbearing, and less traditional for those who choose other lifestyle paths. This in effect normalizes both experiences and diminishes value-laden biases about either choice.

An important component of therapeutic work is facilitating women's ability to construct narrative descriptions regarding their circumstances and choices that enhance and validate their view of self and fracture the meanings attached to the "woman must equal wife and mother" equation. It is equally as important to facilitate the development of coping strategies that foster positive adaptation to the social environment.

For me, the overall goal of this clinical work is my ability to sponsor the client in a way that respects and honors the pace of her own growth process and promotes her search for strengths and internal ability to solve her own dilemmas. The important role that psychotherapy can play for these women is to facilitate the sorting out of confused and doubtful feelings about life choices and desires, and the exploring of perceptions of self, reactions to perceived stigmatization, reactions of others, and the meaning attached to these experiences. Many women have described support in therapy as the most critical factor in enabling them to forge forward through the most difficult periods of grief, confusion, and distress. For the therapist, the process of self-examination of beliefs and biases can increase the ability to approach this group with a progressive view that breaks through long-standing beliefs that devalue women who are not wives and mothers.

THE CLINICAL APPROACH: A THREE-PART GUIDE

In considering these goals as the overarching objectives of treatment, I have arrived at a relational constructionist approach that incorporates three clinical perspectives: solution focused/Ericksonian, narrative/meaning modification, and relational/intergenerational. Although I am separating these perspectives out for the purposes of clarity and learning for the reader, in actuality, many aspects of these concepts/models are intertwined and draw from each other. I caution the reader not to apply these as prescriptions. Rather, I suggest that these perspectives be used fluidly and simultaneously to weave a tapestry of treatment that supports and responds to the uniqueness of each individual client, while at the same time being coherent and guided by theory. Maintaining openness and flexibility enables one to detach from rigid theoretical positions of black or white, that is, pathology or health. I prefer to use these perspectives as a base from which to increase my ability to see the rich kaleidoscope of colors of each client's unique life experience, and the unique meaning it holds for her. From this starting point, then, client and therapist work synergistically to compose solutions, growth, and healing that "fit" the unique goals and desires of that client.

SPONSORING, SOLUTIONS, AND STRENGTHS

> If one advances confidently in the direction of one's own dreams, endeavoring to live the life one has imagined, one will meet with success unexpected in common hour.
>
> **—Henry David Thoreau**

In his quote from more than a century ago, Henry David Thoreau captured what, for me, is the essence of therapy from a solution-focused/Ericksonian perspective: sponsoring the client's dreams for her life and facilitating her ability to live the life she has imagined. This approach is first and foremost one that respects and honors the client's desires, wishes, dreams, and goals for her own life. The therapist's role is to act as sponsor, guide, and coach to facilitate the client's ability to move forward on a self-defined journey of growth and development. As defined by Berg and Dolan (2001), this approach is one of hope, respect, and honor for the client, with the therapist coming from a position of "gentle thoughtfulness, reverence for the client's wishes, and respectful desire to restore the client's dignity in the least intrusive and most empowering manner possible" (p. 175). The approach was further defined by Berg and DeJong (1996) as a mutual problem-solving process of client and therapist with the goal of co-constructing competence. The therapist's role is to facilitate the client's ability to define what she wants to improve in her life, and identify the internal resources and strengths the client can utilize to bring about change and growth. From this perspective, a critical starting point for treatment is a firm belief in the internal healing capacity of the client and her internal ability to find unique solutions to her own life dilemmas. Also, imparting a firm belief to the client that change and growth are not only likely, but inevitable, provides the lending of hope and a vision of a positive future.

Such a hopeful approach is synergistic with the needs of women divorced at midlife without children. As they experience the crisis of divorce and the subsequent challenges of reorganizing their lives without a spouse or children, an approach that lends hope, vision, and a belief in the client's ability to succeed seems more than apropos to this work. The role of divorced woman without children is isolative by definition, so a therapist's ability to provide positive sponsorship can be very affirming. The focus on creative solution development is especially useful in supporting the goals of role innovation and positive adaptation to a stigmatized status.

I will be referring to the model of solution-focused brief therapy that is the body of work of its originators, Steve deShazer, Insoo Berg, and their many colleagues at the Brief Family Therapy Center in Milwaukee. I will refer to ***solution focused*** and ***Ericksonian*** interchangeably, as the solution-focused model has its theoretical roots firmly in Ericksonian premises. For the most part, I consider them one in the same. For the purposes of this book, my intent is to present a brief synopsis of my understanding and application of the basics of the approach, and more specifically how it can be useful in clinical work with women divorced at midlife without children. I would not presume to attempt to rewrite the classic body of literature that has evolved over the last several decades on this model. I highly encourage the reader to pursue the study of deShazer and Berg's complete works as well as the Ericksonian literature.

Originally defined as a "systems theory" therapy that utilizes client strengths and capacities to promote change and problem resolution quickly, the model initially received attention for deShazer's groundbreaking redefinition of the focus of therapy, interpretation of Ericksonian premises, as well as his use of systems principles and generic solution-focused techniques. The Milwaukee team and their many associates have advanced the model over the years through literature that furthered the model's application to many specific client populations and social issues, including parenting, child welfare, substance abuse, work with children in the school setting, and trauma. Originally, the model was recognized for solution-focused techniques and questions such as the miracle question, the scaling technique, the first session formula task, and other generic techniques. As I have followed the development of the model through the writings of deShazer, Berg, and others over the last several decades, my understanding of deShazer's emphasis has evolved from a more technique-oriented model of practices and "solution mapping" to an approach that focuses on the relational/conversational aspects of therapy in which change in meaning and behavior is a result of a mutual process between client and therapist. Berg and Dolan (2001) refer to therapy as a linguistic process of "spinning straw into gold," with the client providing the raw materials for the storytelling process.

In the mid-1980s, I had the good fortune to train with deShazer and Berg in New York City at the Center for Adoptive Families. Having professionally grown up in social work education, the eco-systems approach, and cognitive behavior therapy, I found this approach appealing for several reasons. I was initially attracted to it due to its hopefulness, respect, and focus on strengths and solutions. This approach lends itself well to the social work values of starting where the client is, honoring the unique value of each individual, and supporting the client's right to self-determination. This fit my style much more than theories that focused on pathology, rigid classifications, and approaches that, in my view, attempted to judgmentally fit clients into reified theory. Considering a client "resistant" if they did not fit into the therapist's theory and technique also never sat well with me. I was attracted to the pragmatics and "doability" of the model, and the applicability to short-term work and crisis intervention. In my years of working in a child welfare/family service agency, I also came to find the approach very appealing to children and parents who enjoyed actively and creatively participating in the process of solution development. The child welfare system has not been known for its sensitivity to clients, often victimizing them and treating them as second rate from a position of authority and power. I found that utilizing this approach with such a vulnerable population increased strengths, helped families and children to focus on what they were good at and what they did well, and provided hope in the often hopeless child welfare system.

When I began my work with divorced women, it was a natural transition to utilize this approach with this vulnerable population. The results of lending hope to clients, the power of compliments and constructive language, inexplicable "miracles" that stick, and the impact of sponsoring clients toward their own growth have proven remarkable at best, and extremely valuable at worst.

As the model was developing in the earlier years, professional conversations often focused on the concreteness of the model, whether the techniques were generic enough to be used as a computerized program, and whether they required a therapist at all. Although deShazer consistently spoke his belief in the purity and concepts of the model, it was not intended to be a "computerized recipe" for therapy. deShazer was always clear that working in this model was by no means simplistic, nor was it a process of looking for positives that required little skill on the part of the therapist. He was also clear that relational skill and empathy were not "the babies to throw out with the bathwater" with the inception of the solution-focused model. In fact, the relational and joining skills of the therapist are core components of successful treatment and the use of the solution-focused model.

IN ANOTHER'S SHOES

The ability and willingness of the therapist to "be with" the client at a deep level of her emotional experience is the basis for establishing a therapeutic connection that is a catalyst for change in the solution-focused approach (deShazer, 1994). Therapeutic sponsoring requires the opening of oneself in order to be at the core of another's experience of pain, disturbance, and despair. As challenging as this may be, it is this deep connection that provides the impetus for growth and re-storying, and prevents therapy from becoming routine and unresponsive to the client. As deShazer (1994) noted, it is the establishment of relational connection that keeps therapy from deteriorating into rote technique, unproductive interventions, and eventually a process of uncreative, boring psychobabble. While solution-focused interviewing techniques and interventions have been the hallmarks of the solution-focused approach, the importance of the role of the therapist in building a deep connection with the client is an equally important cornerstone of the approach.

Berg and Dolan's (2001) concept of the therapeutic relationship suggests the therapist needs to begin from a position of "curious not knowing." Their concept of "leading the client from behind" evokes images of gentle support and safety, rather than pushing or pulling the resistant client where the therapist thinks she should go. From Berg and Dolan's view, building the therapeutic connection from a posture of sponsorship involves acceptance of the client's stories, beliefs, values, and symptoms at face value, the ability to deeply listen, and respect for the client's wishes for change. Approaching from this posture facilitates a collaborative approach in which the therapist holds responsibility for cooperating with the client's goals, rather than becoming stuck in rigid expectations that the client fit into the therapist's chosen theoretical model. I would not presume to know in advance where a client should go. In effect, I truly cannot walk completely in her shoes, nor do I know the depth of her dilemmas or the consequences of change for each individual.

Sponsorship in the Ericksonian sense refers to the process of establishing a deep connection with the client's inner experience that goes beyond support and empathy. Gilligan (2001) defines the therapeutic sponsor as one who seeks to awaken, nurture, and inspire the deepest aspects of the client, in the service of facilitating the client's ability to author her own growth and solutions. Gilligan further described the therapeutic relationship as a sanctuary in which the therapist allows himself or herself to "be with" the client at the deepest level of her emotional experience, and supports the client in facing her deepest fears, thoughts, and destructive impulses within the safety of an unconditionally caring relationship of acceptance. Erikson was known for his uncanny ability to join with his clients on deep levels, often understanding the client's physiological functioning in great detail. His capacity to join in such a deep way, to positively sponsor, allowed him to discover the client's deepest fears and disturbances, accept her unconditionally, and in turn use her to facilitate change and growth (Gilligan, 2001). His belief in the capacity of others to change on a deep unconscious level through experiences with others validated the importance of sponsorship in the therapeutic relationship (Rosen, 1982).

Sponsoring the client through deep connection requires the willingness of the therapist to leave the position of directing the client from a posture of superiority and authority. It also requires disconnection from rigid adherence to models and theories, standard questions, interview outlines, classifications and diagnoses, and strategized interventions that are prescribed and delivered to the client. This shift in focus allows a deeper understanding of the client's "stuckness," the dilemmas of change, and her capabilities for fostering her own growth. Gilligan (2001) cautions that in order to sponsor this deep connection, the therapist must be willing to know what might be exposed from his or her own deep core of being, dilemmas, pain, and despair. In effect, being with the client in her experience will undoubtedly awaken in the therapist his or her own biases, dilemmas, and fears. In the work at hand, it is important for therapists to search for their own core beliefs about divorced women, single life, childlessness, and women who do not desire either marriage or children. Also, early adulthood decisions, marriage, childbearing, midlife crisis, life review, aging, and family relationships are just a few of the issues that will undoubtedly be awakened in this work. Deeper fears regarding loss and abandonment, life regrets, and lost dreams can also be anticipated to be awakened if the therapist allows a deep connection with the experiences of these women.

Clients most often appear for therapy at the worst moments of life, when they are vulnerable, feeling panic, despair, and unable to cope. From the Ericksonian perspective, these states of disturbed functioning and increased symptoms are viewed as attempts at growth by the client, albeit clients' attempted solutions are sometimes ineffective, dysfunctional, and even dangerous to their well-being. These symptoms are viewed as attempted solutions, and periods of disturbance or crisis can be viewed as opportunities for growth, in effect an unconscious, internal "waking up" in the service of growth and development (Gilligan, 2001). Crisis theory has long validated the concept of crisis as opportunity for growth and improved ego functioning. Sponsoring, then, involves accepting the client in her deepest level of disturbance and working toward transformation of symptoms into resilience and improved functioning.

Women divorced at midlife without children undoubtedly experience a vulnerable state of disorganization and disequilibrium as their world as they know it, and the original dreams for their lives, are often shaken to the core. Reorganizing life without a spouse or children can raise deep fears, panic, anxiety, and disturbance. The legacy of shame, guilt, and deviance that is attached to this role often exacerbates women's emotional experience and ability to recover.

The approach taken by the therapist can play a critical role in a woman's capacity for recovery and can result in either positive or negative sponsorship. The relational experience between client and therapist can have a critical impact on the client's ability to feel safe, supported, and understood. Negative sponsorship of women in therapy often stems from adherence to theory entrenched in patriarchy. For women, a negative experience in therapy can repeat the devaluing experience that results from the socially constructed denigrating beliefs of the larger society. Utilizing a deviance model that pathlogizes women through pejorative assumptions about problems with intimacy, narcissism, dysfunctional family relationships, and inadequate mothering can create separation and competition between client and therapist. Such an approach further institutionalizes denigrating beliefs from earlier eras, in which divorced women without children were viewed as inferior, worthless, dangerous, sick, and immoral (Popenoe, 1936). Positive sponsorship is a critical posture for counteracting the negative impact of patriarchy through a relational experience that supports the woman being "in the lead," authoring her own recovery, and designing her own future experience.

A relationship with a therapist in which a woman is expected to be obedient by fitting into the therapist's expectations of a good patient (hence a good woman), or risk being viewed as resistant, manipulative, or sick, not only repeats devaluing experiences, but also replicates relationships characterized by power, domination, and submission. As Belenky et al. (1986) state:

> Women see blind obedience to authorities as being of utmost importance for keeping out of trouble and insuring their own survival, because trying to know why is not thought to be particularly possible or important. (Belenky et al., 1986, p. 28)

Women are socialized throughout their lives to see others in positions of authority as all powerful and all knowing. In order to remain connected to this paradigm, the silencing of women's own sense of voice, self, and knowing through submissiveness and powerlessness is a prerequisite (Belenky et al., 1986). In their classic work, Belenky et al. defined the developmental goal of subjective knowing for women as a process of redefining authority and radically changing views of experts and those in power. In this way, a woman's sense of knowing and personal authority begins to shift from the external world to the internal sense of knowing of herself. The goal is a state of connected knowing in which knowledge originates from the personal experience of the woman herself, rather than the expertise of outside authorities.

The ability of the therapist to positively sponsor and detach from a position of authority and power has critical implications for women's growth and development. In work with women divorced at midlife without children, such an approach facilitates the fostering of a woman's own competence to shape and direct her own life, and to change her story from one of denigration to one of empowerment. Belenky et al. (1986) found that many women "hear their own voice" throughout young adulthood, but are unable to fully embrace their own sense of knowing until their 40s and 50s.

Working with women divorced at midlife presents an opportunity for the therapist to provide the opening for the client to begin to listen to and act in accordance with her inner voice—that voice that may have been a whisper, barely able to be heard for decades. Facilitating a woman's ability to hear her own voice in therapy through subjective and connected knowing can result in her ability to develop her own solutions, change the meaning of her life experience, and "self-define" innovative roles for her future. As sponsors, if we cooperate with the client and listen closely enough, we will hear the voices and inner knowing of women who are fulfilled without marriage and motherhood, who are not bereft or lonely, and who view their life as full of infinite possibilities. We may also begin to see the richness of the colors in a kaleidoscope of beliefs that embraces difference and promotes belonging and value, rather than division and competition among women.

FOLLOW THE YELLOW BRICK ROAD

The ability to sponsor and be with the client provides a necessary foundation for solution-oriented therapy with women divorced at midlife without children. Starting from this sponsoring relationship as the core catalyst for growth and improvement, I view the original solution-focused model, interviewing techniques, and interventions as complementary tools to promote change. A model that promotes competence and teaches clients the process of solution development is especially relevant for women in a vulnerable role. The solution-focused perspective enhances women's perception of their ability to care for themselves and solve problems independently, a skill they may have minimized in their married years.

As advanced by deShazer and Berg's work, several overarching Ericksonian premises are the cornerstone of solution-focused therapy. For my purposes here, I am presenting a brief overview of solution-focused/Ericksonian premises for the reader. I encourage readers to pursue the solution-focused and Ericksonian literature for further depth and learning (Berg & Dolan, 2001; deShazer, 1985, 1988, 1994; O'Hanlon, 1987).

Thinking Systemically

The solution-focused model utilizes systems principles in which the client is viewed as a part of a complex system of relationships. Systems thinking involves avoidance of looking for the root cause of a problem, instead focusing on the circularity and relational aspects of the interconnected system. Thinking circularly, then, there are infinite possibilities for change within the system. One of the hallmarks of deShazer's (1986) work was his clarification of the concept that change was not dependent upon interventions being connected to the presenting problem. In fact, he proposed that change could be facilitated with the therapist actually knowing very little about the details of the problem. deShazer also utilized an "if it ain't broke, don't fix it" minimalist approach in which the search for change and potential solutions was the goal. From this perspective, the therapist avoids gathering voluminous information that may be interesting, but may not make a difference to the client. Although parts of the system are interconnected, it is not necessary to change the entire system to bring about change. Change is also viewed as a given and can occur in any part of the system. Also, small changes can lead to bigger changes, in effect snowballing into other parts of the system. Systems thinking from this perspective also involves the assumption that every system holds within it the seeds of solutions. From this systems orientation, the therapist maintains the following.

Maintaining a Solution Focus

Therapy focuses on the search for solutions, with less attention paid to detailed descriptions of presenting problems, complaints, or the history of the problem. The assumption is made that for every problem there are always exceptions and the seeds of solutions somewhere in the client's experience. Problem-saturated conversations are avoided and "solution talk" is amplified. Once exceptions and potential solutions are identified, work can focus on improvement and guiding the client to increase the solution state. Presenting problems are constructed as workable complaints and transformed into manageable goals.

Forward Thinking: Present and Future Focus

In addition to searching for exceptions and potential solutions, focus is also maintained on what is currently going well for the client in the present, and hypothesizing about a future in which the problem is either solved or improved, even just a little (Berg & Dolan, 2001). This approach is forward thinking, and the past is utilized primarily to explore possible solutions or clues to hypothetical solutions. Little attention is paid to the history of the problem, how it got that way, or the length of time it occurred.

The Expectation of Change and Success

The therapist maintains the posture of expecting solutions and use of strengths by the client. Success is a presupposition that the therapist reflects in words, conversation, and storytelling. The details of success originate from the client, guided by the therapist as sponsor and coach. Assumptions that change is an inevitable constant, that every problem has a solution, and that every client has the capability of developing unique solutions are utilized.

A Theory of Cooperation

The therapist cooperates with the client by listening closely to her goals and where she feels she is stuck. The client is not viewed as resistant if she does not complete tasks or interventions. The therapist maintains responsibility for revising the treatment focus if progress is not made. By cooperating with the client in a flexible way, the door can be opened for an infinite number of possible solutions. In addition to avoiding rigid use of theory or model, cooperation also includes minimizing the need to prove cause and effect (O'Hanlon, 1987).

Utilization of the Client's Natural Strengths

Erikson's work was characterized by being responsive to the client's world-view and utilizing the unique capacities of the client as a catalyst for change (Crenshaw, 2004). Even when the client brings rigidified symptoms, patterns, or behaviors, she is embraced as the seeds of unique solutions. This requires a shift on the therapist's part to view symptoms as benevolent attempts of the unconscious to solve a client's unique life dilemma, rather than destructive impulses (O'Hanlon, 1987). Such a posture does not mean condoning destructive symptoms; rather, it is providing the client with an environment of openness and acceptance to share even the most shameful of feelings or symptoms, accepted at face value. The strengths the client brings are amplified and utilized in solution development. The therapist works from the belief that the client has the natural ability to overcome her own difficulties, and holds the answers within. Therapy is natural conversation that is used as the tool to promote change (O'Hanlon, 1987). Symptoms are accepted at face value as attempted solutions on the part of the client, no matter how dysfunctional. Symptom transformation to potential solutions is a core catalyst for change.

CHEERLEADING FOR CHANGE: CONSTRUCTIVE COACHING

Anyone who has ever been involved in a sport knows the purpose of a coach is to guide and motivate the athlete toward success and reaching his or her maximum potential. The concept of constructive coaching further describes the role of the therapist in solution-focused work. We have discussed the posture of the therapist as sponsor for the client, as well as premises utilized in solution development. The "nuts and bolts" of solution-focused therapy are the utilization of solution-focused conversation, interviewing techniques, and interventions all geared toward producing improvement and change for the client. The overarching goal of constructive coaching and solution-focused conversation is to push toward identification of strengths and solutions, and search for the capabilities of the client to solve her own dilemmas. There is minimal focus on detailed problem descriptions, unhelpful storylines, or what is not working in the client's life.

The process of constructive coaching involves facilitating the emergence of solutions through the process of conversation and the therapist's ability to ask questions that influence solution-focused thinking on the part of the client. Listening with an empathic ear is utilized as problems are identified; however, problem talk is kept to a minimum. Theory-based generic solutions are not presented by the therapist; rather, through inductive interviewing, the coach facilitates the development of solutions that the client owns.

Constructive coaching takes place through conversation, composed of words and language that are infused with meaning. Every word or phrase used has meaning for the listener and is a message to the unconscious that either validates or invalidates stories, perceptions, and feelings. I like to think that every question or statement posed by the therapist is itself an intervention. Relabeling and reframing conversations with positive connotations and direction is the heart of constructive, solution-focused coaching. Utilizing key words, phrases, and stories used by the client is helpful in building solutions in a cooperative way. The use of complimentary language creates a positive connection to the client that furthers the sponsoring/coaching relationship in the service of change. Once again, I encourage the reader to reference the body of work of deShazer, Berg, and others for more depth on these techniques.

Several guidelines are a useful starting point for constructive coaching/solution-focused interviewing:

- Maintain the solution focus through words and language.
- Speak from the position of expecting change.
- Use words such as *what*, *when*, and *how*, not *if*, to impart belief in the inevitability of change.
- Keep on track by actively searching for exceptions and possible solutions.
- Politely ignore problem-saturated details and descriptions.
- Use four to five direct and indirect compliments each session.

The following constructive questions are useful in solution-focused interviewing:

- What is going well now that you want to continue?
- What happens when the problem isn't happening?
- What is different at those times?
- Tell me about a time in the past when things were better.
- What will things look like when the problem is solved?
- How will you know when the problem is solved?
- How will others know when the problem is solved?
- What has improved since we last talked?
- What needs to happen in order to keep improvement going?
- On a scale of 1 to 10, where are things now?
- What would have to happen to raise the number higher?
- Make a list of all possible solutions. What is the easiest of these to do?

In addition to constructive/solution-focused questions, deShazer, Berg, and the Milwaukee team (deShazer, 1985, 1988, 1994) also developed several generic interventions that are intended to guide the client toward solution development through observation and shifting focus away from problem descriptions. These generic interventions are not meant to be prescriptions; rather, they are intended to orient the client toward concrete and specific solutions through vague, solution-focused suggestion. These interventions can evoke problem-solving capacities out of the unconscious and shift the client's thinking from problem focused to solution oriented. These interventions are not meant to be "fit" to problems; rather, they can be utilized as suggestions at any point in the course of treatment, for any problem description. It is important that the therapist be instructed to keep the delivery of the instructions vague and brief, and not be drawn into conversation that might undo the intervention before it is attempted. It is also important that the therapist follow up on the task during subsequent sessions. Clients often change these interventions to fit their needs better, and they are to be complimented for their initiative in this regard. Should a client not find the intervention useful or not complete it, the constructive coach/therapist takes responsibility for adjusting treatment and for the lack of fit with the client. Brief descriptions of several useful techniques follow:

First-session formula task: The client is instructed to observe what is going well that she wants to continue. This is especially useful when there is no clear complaint or it is difficult to obtain descriptions of exceptions or possible solutions.

Pay attention to task: The client is instructed to pay attention to what is happening when the problem is not happening, and what she and others are doing that is different at those times. This is useful in response to a client's complaints about her own behavior, and presupposes the behavior is within the client's control.

Do something different task: Instruct the client to do something different or do one thing different. This can serve as a pattern interruption and evoke many possibilities for change.

Prediction task: Instruct the client to predict or guess each morning what kind of day it will be: problem free or not, good day or bad. The client then keeps track of the predictions, logs them, and checks back on her predictions later in the day. Follow-up should include conversation focusing on the differences in good and bad days. This is especially useful when a client reports random exceptions or solutions.

Miracle question: Ask the client: If you woke up tomorrow and a miracle happened overnight, what would be different? This question helps the client define an improved future state and visualize the changes that would need to take place to arrive at a more hopeful future.

Scaling question: Ask the client to rate herself or her progress utilizing a scale of 1 to 10. Use of numbers can clarify for both client and therapist more concretely how they view progress, and can also clarify how much or little distress the client is experiencing. The use of numbers facilitates the client's ability to be self-observant and to assess herself very quickly separate from emotional states. Scales can also be constructed to be more specifically related to the client's focus, such as a confidence scale, a hopefulness scale, or an independence scale.

In summary, Betty Friedan (1977) proclaimed that it is in a woman's defining herself by her own actions, according to her own deepest sense of knowing, that she can break through to authenticity and liberation. A women's recovery from divorce at midlife without children can be greatly enhanced through a sponsoring relationship with a therapist who complements and utilizes her natural abilities and strengths from the solution-focused/Ericksonian perspective. It is in the empowerment of a woman through her own redefinition of self and development of unique solutions that she can become more authentically herself. Sponsoring and constructively coaching a woman toward the blending of her own unique attributes and capabilities can lead a woman into a new world, one she shapes and directs according to her own free will. It is in this process of solution and strength building that the meaning of her experience, and in fact her very self-concept, can begin to change (Belenky et al., 1986).

RE-STORYING A LIFE: MEANING MODIFICATION

> Only becoming conscious of old and unchosen patterns allows us to change them, and even so, change, no matter how much for the better, still feels cold and lonely at first—as if we were out there on the edge of the universe with the wind whistling past our ears—because it doesn't feel like home.
>
> **—G. Steinem, *Revolution From Within* (1992, p. 38)**

Being *unmarried* and *childless* in a society that has been traditionally marriage centered and pro-mothering represents a collision of meanings regarding a role and status that conflicts with dominant social discourse. Becoming stuck between traditional and untraditional beliefs can result in internal psychological conflict that can paralyze a woman and result in an inability to sort out life choices. As Steinem (1992) states, women can perceive themselves as "out there on the edge alone" in a role that is at once unfamiliar and often unplanned. A woman who is not a wife or mother, or who does not desire marriage, children, or remarriage, is in opposition with long-standing standards that women *should* marry and mother. The stigmatized meaning that is attached to these experiences often impacts a woman's internalized view of self. Despite significant social change that has resulted in more acceptance of choosing not to marry or mother, the legacy of underlying devaluing paradigms still remains.

Redefining a life story through the conversational process of therapy can provide a woman with the opportunity to begin to reshape her experiences through different lenses of meaning that minimize distress and foster the construction of competence. In addition to listening more closely to her own intuitive voice, a woman's ability to re-story her experiences of early marriage, midlife divorce, and absence of children by developing positive beliefs can greatly diminish distress and emotional discomfort with her life circumstance. The opportunity to deconstruct original expectations regarding roles and lifestyle choices, and reconstruct more meaningful experiences that are congruent with the inner voice, is an important process in divorce recovery. Women who can loosen the emotional bonds to culturally prescribed roles are able to reconstruct beliefs and internalized narratives to broaden the definition of femininity apart from marriage and motherhood.

A client who was a midlife divorced woman without children shared the following story in a therapy session:

> I was traveling through an airport recently over the holidays, and a security guard commented to me, "Oh, traveling alone over the holidays?" When I replied yes and said I was divorced and without children, he spontaneously stated, "Oh, incredibly lonely?" When I replied no, he quickly stated, "Oh, I get it then, free and adventurous!"

She continued:

> You know, I just don't get where other people are coming from. They assume things that are just based on what you are SUPPOSED to think and do. You know when I really think about it, mostly I am quite content and happy with my life. But sometimes there is this nagging sadness and panic that pops up from somewhere that I don't understand, and I just don't get where it is coming from. Then I think, Wait a minute, who says being married and having kids is better? Where did we get that from? And sometimes I just think it is these expectations about what everybody else thinks I SHOULD be doing that are making me feel bad. It's like these ideas got trapped in my head, and they are in there way down deep. Then I think, What if my life is totally great as it is and I am missing it?

This brief interchange captures the essence of meaning modification: revising a life experience through words and story, thereby changing its meaning in the service of growth and change. The purpose of changing narrative descriptions is to shift negative, harmful, or destructive meaning to more constructive, hopeful, and celebratory meaning to further the client's life and goals. Working in meaning modification is a primary goal of work with these women, and entails working in complex, overlapping levels of meaning around such issues as marriage, mothering, divorce, childlessness, single life, and more. It is through the intricate linguistic weaving of new descriptions, meanings, and labels in story that the therapist can have a major impact on diminishing the harmful impact of pejorative social constructions on women, and in turn decrease their distress. As Steinem (1992) suggested, shifting major paradigms and changing organizing principles that underlie what we think about and our concepts of self and the world are necessary for women's self-esteem and growth.

AN INTERCHANGE OF WORDS

Therapy is a relational/conversational process in which the telling and retelling of stories between client and therapist is a catalyst for meaning modification (deShazer, 1994). Gilligan (2001) describes the process of therapy as helping the client to author a life poem, bringing it to full expression. Berg and Dolan (2001) liken the process of meaning modification to linguistically "spinning straw into gold," with the client providing the raw materials for the story. Berg and Dolan further describe the therapy process as one in which the therapist gently directs the flow of conversation, uncovering hidden resources and strengths in the service of change.

It is this reshaping of stories that facilitates the client's ability to break free from limiting, devaluing meanings, construct more useful meanings, and grow in the direction of her inner voice. The process of externalizing problems and creating alternate narratives can diminish the impact of a life experience that conflicts with dominant cultural discourse. In turn, re-storying can promote a sense of coherence, continuity, and validation for an expanding identity (White & Epston, 1990). Neimeyer (2001) refers to this as "sense making" of an experience. He offers the following:

> From a relational constructivist view we are shaped and sustained by our shifting patterns of attachment to people, places and possessions that largely anchor the meanings of our lives. The loss of these attachments challenges who we are and prompts revisions in our life narratives that can sometimes be deep going. (Neimeyer, 2001, p. 289)

Neimeyer suggests that the stages of grieving are not a rote process to be completed. Rather, grief recovery is a unique process of meaning making for each individual, in which the narrative construction of self and changing meanings to more responsive connotations facilitate coping with loss as a lived experience.

The telling and retelling of life stories has long been suggested as a core process in psychotherapy. The concept of distress reduction through re-storying life experiences via alternate narratives also has theoretical roots in Freudian theory (deShazer, 1994). Shafer (1992) discussed modern psychoanalysis as a process of reauthoring lives through an array of narratives. It is also noted that versions of the self may be comprised of many inside storylines in which an individual tries to develop a consistent and coherent account of his or her life. Freudian theory delineated a fundamental change in the way a problem is defined as an important process in structural change (Shafer, 1992). deShazer's concept of a therapeutic process in which client and therapist alike are co-creators of storylines is not dissimilar from the concept implied in Freud's earlier work.

From the Ericksonian perspective, meaning is viewed as a co-constructed product of the client-therapist relationship. deShazer (1994) emphasized the mutuality of this process, describing meaning as a synergistic product of the relational interchange among client, therapist, and others. This mutual process involves the utilization of the worldviews and life experiences of both client and therapist. Utilizing the client's unique conceptualizations, meanings, stories, patterns of response, and language is the catalyst to moving forward. The therapist's part in the mutual process is to be responsive to the client's worldview, also using what he or she brings to the process from his or her own worldview and experience in service of the client's growth. In the Ericksonian tradition, this utilization of the therapist's self is often shared through embedded storytelling, rather than through direct self-disclosure (Crenshaw, 2004).

Such a mutual approach departs from an individual focus in which the client is seen as troubled, sick, or a product of dysfunctional family dynamics, and minimizes the viewing of problems as stemming from internal deficits of the client. A starting point for therapy, then, is exploring the client's life experiences through the meanings she attaches to them. Language and words are filled with meaning and implications, and are the primary tools through which client and therapist alike discover the storied life experience of the client. Change is facilitated through the deconstruction of meaning and the reconstruction of new meanings in the service of improved present and future functioning and minimizing distress.

Although meaning deconstruction and reconstruction have been written about extensively, little connection has been made to a process critical to women's development and role exit and transition. For the purposes of working with this group of women, I am defining meaning modification as a process by which socially constructed meanings regarding women's identity, roles, and status are deconstructed and reconstructed in order to adapt positively in a patriarchal culture to a stigmatized role outside the prescribed norm of marriage and motherhood.

RECONSTRUCTION OF THE MEANING OF LOSS

In the last decade, recent work on bereavement, mourning, and divorce adjustment has suggested that the search for meaning and meaning reconstruction are critical adaptive processes in recovery from loss and trauma (Bevvino & Sharkin, 2003; Neimeyer, 2001). The essential construct of this theory includes viewing the individual as searching for and developing positive meanings and narratives for traumatic losses to enhance growth and recovery. Revisions in self-narratives can transform identity, resulting in positive effects and greater adaptation after loss (Bevvino & Sharkin, 2003; Heatherington, 2003; Neimeyer, 2000).

Bevvino and Sharkin (2003) examined the relationship between searching for and finding meaning and divorce adjustment. It was concluded that the ability to search for and construct positive meaning from divorce experiences was positively related with psychological well-being. Women were generally found to view divorce as an opportunity. The ability to find new, positive meanings in their circumstances seems to be a critical factor in enhanced recovery and role adaptation.

The externalization of socially constructed narratives, the re-storying of lives with more positive connotations, and the internalization of reconstructed meaning are important therapeutic processes in loss recovery. Meaning modification is a critical factor in positive adjustment and a proposed explanation for the lack of poor adjustment and psychosocial symptoms. In effect, a process of meaning modification enables women to reauthor the events of their lives and perceptions about role changes in positive ways. Meaning modification facilitates healing and increased comfort level with a stigmatized identity.

The benefits of meaning modification can also be viewed in the context of cognitive dissonance theory. This theory of human motivation suggests that the holding of two contradictory cognitions, beliefs, or perceptions can result in psychological distress or cognitive dissonance (Festinger, 1957). Festinger noted that human motivation tends toward reduction of psychological tension caused by beliefs or behaviors inconsistent with underlying beliefs (Wicklund & Brehm, 1976). Festinger suggested three modes of reducing distress: changing beliefs, acquiring new beliefs, and reducing the importance of dissonant beliefs (Cooper & Fazio, 1984).

In summary, socially constructed meaning has a powerful impact on how women experience and interpret their world. A woman's reactions to divorce at midlife without children must be viewed within the patriarchal context of a complex web of meaning. Despite tremendous social change, the legacy of narratives that devalue unmarried, childless women is still embedded in Western culture. If negative meanings remain unchallenged, it is often difficult for a woman to make sense or find positive meaning in her experience of loss.

Meaning modification is a critical area of intervention in therapy. A primary function of the therapist is to bring internalized negative meanings into awareness, facilitate disengagement from them, and assist in composing new tales of the client's life story. deShazer (1985) states that from a polyocular view, an infinite number of meanings is always possible. The positive re-storying of a woman's life experience can facilitate healing and growth, minimize distress, and provide the fundamental basis for coping and recovery.

FOSTERING CONNECTION: WORKING IN THE RELATIONAL CONTEXT

> Feeling connected and in contact with another often allows us our most profound sense of personal meaning and reality; at its best, therapy works toward developing and honoring this relational presence.
>
> —**J. V. Jordan et al., *Women's Growth in Connection* (1991, p. 289)**

CONNECTION AND INTIMACY: THE TOUCHSTONE FOR WOMEN'S WELL-BEING

Connection, belonging, and relationship have long been at the core of women's definition of self, well-being, and value. As Benjamin (1988) states:

> Recognition is so central to human existence as to often escape notice, or, rather, it appears to us in so many guises that it is seldom grasped as one overarching concept. There are any number of near-synonyms for it; to recognize is to affirm, validate, acknowledge, know, accept, understand, empathize, take in, tolerate, appreciate, see, identify with, find familiar, ..., love." (Benjamin, 1988, p. 15)

A woman's capacity to recover from divorce at midlife needs to be understood in the context of her development of self in relationship and mutual connection to others. Miller (1976) conceptualized women's sense of self as closely bound to the capacity to develop and maintain relationships. Identity and connection are often fused together in women's perception of themselves. Women's growth at all life stages has been connected to mutual relationships in which they feel heard and validated. Since most women do not aspire to separation and isolation, the transition to single life can be distressing, and the striving for relationship and mutual recognition often continues throughout the separation, divorce, and post-divorce processes. Transitioning from married life to single life can trigger severe loneliness, meaninglessness, and a core sense of detachment from others.

The relational losses that occur through the experience of divorce at midlife without children can cause considerable distress and emotional discomfort for many women. Loss of the roles of wife and potential mother, and the perceived value of those roles, is also significant. The sense of well-being and attachment women often experience as wives and mothers is absent for these women. These losses can be far reaching and encompass not only the real loss of the primary relationship, but also multiple losses of relationships with in-law family, friends, and acquaintances connected to the marital relationship. The impact of loss can reverberate throughout every stage of the post-divorce life cycle.

These losses can be best understood in the context of the importance of attachment, connection, and responsibility for relationship as central to women's well-being. The meaning of loss of relationships to women has been described as not simply loss of the primary object, but also loss of identity and core sense of self. The end of relationship at midlife can threaten a woman's sense of well-being and lead to despair and depression (Gilligan, 1982).

Major losses and disruptions, if viewed as life cycle transitions with the potential for change and growth, can result in an increase in a woman's capacity to improve self-care and be responsible for her relational life in healthy connection and separation with others. Sponsoring a woman's unique solutions to her needs for connection fosters her competence and ability to be self-directing, and in turn her sense of knowing and self. In the post-divorce stage, supporting a woman's ability to broaden connections in positive ways through expanded intimacy and attachments is a necessary and important focus of work.

A LIFE COURSE DISRUPTED: THE RELATIONAL CONTEXT IN FLUX

In addition to significant loss of connection, divorce also represents a major disruption of a woman's individual and family life cycle, and often results in extensive ripple effects throughout the extended family system and other relational networks. These far-reaching implications can impact the flow of the family life cycle and the subsequent stages that follow post-divorce (Herz Brown, 1991). It is important to consider how these women continue on the life cycle course as a part of a complex family system moving through time, generation to generation. Given that they are "out of sync" with other family members' and peers' normative stages, the divorce crisis not only requires a transition out of familiar family roles, but is further complicated by the life cycle tasks of midlife and aging. It is especially important to consider the family context for women divorced without children, due to the isolative nature of the role itself. It is important to link women to their family of origin, rather than view them as moving forward in isolation (Kaslow & Linzer Schwartz, 1987).

The complex relational changes in the extended family that accompany divorce are an important focus for treatment and intervention. It is important that therapy focus on the restructuring of relationships not only within the extended family of origin, but also with other relationships as well. Distance and closeness to various family members may need to be renegotiated as the woman proceeds on her journey through the family life cycle. In effect, the family structure and hierarchy may be forever changed in ways that were not anticipated, and may ripple throughout the family system in all the life cycle stages to come (Carter & McGoldrich, 1999). Healthy disengagement that may have occurred upon marriage and leaving home may now need to be renegotiated. Enmeshment may also be exacerbated by the woman's change in status. Since these women are part of a family system developing and transitioning over time, it is important that treatment include discussion regarding the impact of their role status on changing family relationships and future family development. As women experience family rituals, transitions, and expectable life stages such as holidays, celebrations, illnesses, and loss of older generations, it is important to prepare them for the possibility of journeying through these experiences as single adults without the supports of spouses and children.

HONORING CONNECTION: FOSTERING DIVERSE ATTACHMENTS

In approaching treatment with women divorced at midlife without children, it is critical to honor a woman's need for connection and attachment, rather than pathologize it. The need for relationship should be framed as self-enhancing, not as weakness or incompetence. An approach that promotes separation and independence can invalidate a woman's need for connection throughout the process of divorce and recovery. For many women, independence is associated with isolation, intense loneliness, and meaninglessness. The approach should support a woman's development in both healthy connection and separation with others, and foster her ability to be responsible for the direction of her own life and expand her relational network in the way she so chooses (Herz Brown, 1991).

Working within the relational context, as sponsor and coach, it is most useful to follow the client's lead to support her desires in her quest for intimacy, attachment, separation, or independence. From a nonjudgmental stance, the therapist needs to accept all possible creative solutions the client brings that promote healthy attachment and separation. The client may arrive at a variety of creative solutions to obtain intimacy and connection that may include relationships with significant others, extended family members, friends, mentors, work colleagues, and acquaintances.

An individual woman's need for connection can vary greatly throughout the divorce process. Some women have extreme difficulty tolerating separation and being alone, others find it appealing, and still others grow to enjoy it in time. Some women spend incredible amounts of emotional and physical energy trying to "regroup" from the relational losses of divorce, and attempt to quickly retrieve "lost objects" in the form of new relationships. Other women commit themselves to building skills of independence and are not interested in remarriage. Normalizing these efforts is in keeping with the feminist view of women's development and the Ericksonian premises of sponsoring and accepting symptoms as attempted solutions. Framing efforts to remain in connection throughout divorce and post-divorce stages as attempts at stabilization and growth can further the therapy in positive ways. Sponsorship also needs to include acceptance and normalization of the experiences of women who may not experience such distress, who enjoy living alone, and who do not plan to enter into a full-time relationship with a spouse, or to mother children in any way. Viewing them as deviant or dysfunctional can detract from the sponsoring relationship with the therapist and decrease effectiveness of treatment.

Many women explore a variety of different types of relationships during the separation, divorce, and post-divorce process. They are often hesitant to enter full-time relationships after divorce due to fear of repeating past mistakes and poor relationship choices. However, there may still be a strong need for connection and intimacy with a significant other. Some women enjoy part-time relationships as a solution to this dilemma. However, these relationships can often be accompanied by shame and guilt. From a sponsoring position, it is often useful to explore how the relationship is helpful to her, and what she feels she *does* get from it. Then the choice becomes hers as to whether this is a relationship that suits her.

In treatment, some clients have shared various stories of feeling devalued and chastised in therapy, both for needing connection and for desiring separation and independence. One woman shared an experience in which she felt criticized by her previous therapist for entering a new relationship very quickly after her marital separation, stating this was a rebound, was "not healthy," and was proof of her difficulty with "real intimacy." The therapist also warned the client that her goal should be to increase her ability to be alone. While that may be a reasonable goal of treatment for some, to assume this perspective would be useful for a client who does not share this goal only creates a barrier to treatment. Another option is to accept this client's ability to find a relationship as a strength and a creative attempted solution to intolerable loneliness in the service of her own growth.

Another client shared her view that she had made extremely poor choices for relationships, and that she was committed to living alone and complimenting her life with part-time relationships and friendships. Her experience was that she drank less and felt much less depression, more competence, and more emotional stability on her own. She felt she "turned into a victim" when she was in relationship. Thus, single life was a better solution for her. Rather than viewing this as difficulty with intimacy or reaction formation, one could compliment the client for knowing her self well enough to devise a solution that increased her functionality, rather than diminished it. In this woman's case, it was less harmful for her to remain alone and fill up her life with a variety of connections and fulfilling activities.

As sponsor of the client, I view my purpose as facilitating a woman's ability to find solutions that fit her unique needs, not delivering preconceived prescriptions for connection or separation. This allows the therapist to join with the client and facilitate her progress at her own pace. The client is the captain of the ship, navigating toward her own unique desires to meet her relational needs.

A woman may or may not seek a relationship with a significant other, part-time, full-time, temporary, or permanent. It is important that whatever she seeks out to meet her relational needs be supported in therapy, as long as these relationships are helpful and not harmful. A wide range of potentially valuable connections and relationships also need to be encouraged and explored. Expansion of a woman's network needs to reach beyond immediate and extended family, and should include exploration of other family members as possible sources of closeness, support, and mentorship. This may include parents, grandparents, siblings, aunts, uncles, and cousins. In addition, expansion of relationships with long-term friends, new friends, colleagues, and acquaintances is also valuable. Fostering connection through the creative expansion of intimacy and attachments can increase a woman's sense of well-being and fulfillment, during and after midlife divorce.

As Jordan et al. (1991) state:

> It is not because of relationships per se that women are suppressed or oppressed. The issue is the ***nature*** of the relationships. In fact, without the recognition of the importance of relationships to women, we do not help women find a path that leads to growth and development. Some psychologists fall into a tendency to encourage "independence" and "separation," which is not what many women want. (Jordan et al., 1991, p. 22)

In summary, an effective clinical approach for work with women divorced at midlife without children requires a commitment to fracturing connections to entrenched paradigms about women's development that limit one's ability to sponsor their growth as complete human beings. A nonvictimizing stance respects and honors each woman's unique needs and desires to continue her journey through life in the most fulfilling way possible. It also requires a deep commitment to solution development, meaning modification, and fostering expansion of connection and intimacy. Focusing on these overarching goals can facilitate these women in their quest to build mastery and confidence in the face of a world that continues to judge, disapprove, and divide. Friedan (1997) reminded us that treatment must be detached from the idea of cure by fitting into the prevailing cultural norms.

CHAPTER 12

No Time Is a Good Time for Goodbye

The Case of Sara

> Many of the younger generation of wives who marry early have never suffered this lonely terror. They thought they did not have to choose, to look into the future, and plan what they want to do with their lives. They only had to wait to be chosen, marking time passively until the husband, the babies, the new house decided what the rest of their lives would be.
>
> **—Betty Friedan, *The Feminine Mystique* (1997, p. 77)**

One crisp October evening, an intriguing message was left on my office answering machine by a sweet, but somewhat frustrated sounding female voice:

> I don't know if you can help me. I've been to a few other therapists, and I can't seem to find anyone who can help me. I'm divorced, and I don't have children, and I heard you have done a lot of work with women. I'd like to see if I could make an appointment with you.

LOOKING IN ON THE PARTY: PRESENTING PROBLEMS/COMPLAINTS

I met Sara for her first session a few days after her phone call. After introductions, I invited Sara to tell me why she was there. She began with further frustration and skepticism:

Sara: I've been trying to find a therapist who can help me, and so far I'm not having any luck. I just can't seem to find one who understands what I'm going through. It feels like there is something wrong with me because my life is not like everyone else's. I've been divorced for six years, and I'm having some feelings I just can't shake, and I don't know what's wrong with me. I'm not sure I'm recovering okay. There are just these things that I can't solve, no matter how hard I try. And these other therapists I've been to, well, I think they made me feel worse, you know, more like there is something wrong with ME.

DC: Tell me what you think the problems have been with these other therapists?

S: Well, I feel like I am kind of stuck, and I can't help myself out of where I am no matter how hard I try. You see I got divorced six years ago, and I met someone, Jeff, a week after I separated, and we have been some sort of friends, kind of on and off part-time ever since. That was six years ago. I think I know that he's not right for me as a full-time relationship, and I met him so quickly. But I really want a full-time relationship. I've been looking since the day I got separated, but it just hasn't happened. Everybody is telling me it's because of my relationship with Jeff. And I can't get out of it, I tried, and I just can't. I know I should say goodbye, but it seems like no time is a good time for goodbye.

DC: You don't feel like you want to say goodbye?

S: I feel like I should, but I can't do it. That's what is upsetting me so much. I can't get myself out of it.

DC: And what did the other therapists you saw say about this?

S: Well, the first one kept telling me I had problems with real intimacy, and that things weren't going to get any better for me until I learned to be alone. She felt since I was divorced quite awhile and hadn't found anyone, I must be sending out the wrong vibes. She thought that I would have to be alone for a period of time before I would be ready for complete relationship. Another one told me I must be too picky, since I hadn't found a man yet, and I should put all my effort into finding one. Another one kept calling me by the wrong name. She couldn't even remember my name, so how could she understand me? With most of them I just came away feeling worse than before. I feel like they have tried to fit me into some mold or something, judging me, and they just don't get it, they just don't get ME! I felt like they are not seeing ME and what the struggles of my life are right now. I think its easy to say I should be alone, or I should be able to find a man. You know, living in this world as a single woman and with no children, sometimes it just feels like I am pressing my nose against a glass window, looking in on everyone else enjoying the party of life, and you're not in it. You just feel like an outcast or something. It just seems like everyone has someone—a partner or kids. You know for the most part I love my life, and I don't regret the divorce for one minute, but deep down I just have this nagging feeling like I don't belong anywhere.

DC: And so I take it Jeff helps you feel like you belong somewhere, even though its not 100% what you want?

S: (***In silence, starts to well up with tears and shakes her head affirmatively***)

DC: I can see why it would be hard to give that up. So this idea of separating from Jeff, how did you feel about that?

S: Well, it just made me feel like what's wrong with me that I can't be alone? Everybody's pressuring me to do it. I felt so incompetent and damaged. Plus I have tried to break off from Jeff a couple of times and I just can't do it. I can't do it for more than a few weeks now. It's getting harder and harder to do. The most I ever made it was a few months.

DC: What happens when you try?

S: I get so scared, I just get this panic, and I feel sick. I get pain in my stomach and dizzy. I feel like I am screaming inside when he's gone. I feel like I am all alone in the world. I feel like I'm not going to make it. A couple of times after a few months of being apart from him, I had a few drinking episodes and I started to feel really down.

DC: So it doesn't really seem to be good for you right now to separate from him?

S: No, it seems too hard.

DC: How much of the time are you feeling this kind of distress, let's say on a scale of 1 to 10? [Scaling question]

S: Well, when I am in contact with him, most of the time I'm really okay, it's just once in awhile I get feeling this way, like I have to stop being with him and it seems overwhelming. Probably 90% of the time I am okay, but when the panic comes, it's really bad.

Maintaining a solution focus, I chose to focus on the 90% of time that Sara was feeling okay, rather than search for further details of the presenting problem.

DC: So WOW—90% of the time you feel pretty good? That's a really high number. What do you think keeps you feeling so good so much of the time?

S: Gee, I never thought of it like that, that I was good most of the time. I just was thinking about how upset I am.

DC: There must be a lot of good in your relationship with Jeff that helps you to feel good most of the time. I want to hear a lot more about what's good about your relationship with Jeff, but before we do that, tell me more about the other therapists you went to see.

S: Well, another one, she was kind of the opposite of the first one. She felt I hadn't made enough effort to meet a man, and that was what she was pushing me to do. She said I'd have to get away from Jeff, and if I just went out there, there were a lot of men out there. She actually looked out the window when she said it, as if the men were lined up outside waiting. I had this sinking feeling that she didn't understand why I was upset either. I felt so frustrated I wanted to scream. She didn't bother to ask me what I had already done to try to meet somebody. If she only knew! I told her I had spent the first five years going to singles events, going out to activities, traveled, learned to play golf, joined the Internet dating service, and joined two "matchmaking" services. I can't bear to do any of it anymore—I'd rather stay home by myself. It's too painful.

DC: Wow! You did ALL of that? That is really impressive, and brave of you to try all that! That must have taken a lot of energy on your part. It must have taken a lot of strength to try all that.

It was important to begin to frame Sara as self-preserving, attempting solutions in the service of her own growth. Building competence rather than validating failure was a beginning step toward a sponsoring relationship in our first meetings.

S: (*She starts to cry again*) I have done SO MUCH and I can't do it anymore, and then there is this situation with Jeff that I feel I should be getting out of. I feel so trapped. You know, I really like living by myself, I can't say I feel lonely on a daily basis, but the thought of being totally alone without a main connection to someone, that scares the hell out of me. And the funny thing is, you know its weird because when I REALLY think about it I am really happy with my life—I just think I don't BELIEVE that I am, or that something is stopping me from believing that I am—like there is something not letting me be happy as I am and I can't figure out why. It's like, what's really hurting me? I can't get it, solve it by myself, and so far I haven't found a therapist that gets it either. They keep trying to tell me these suggestions that don't help.

Sara's first words in the first hour of therapy were very telling. Sara's story is unfortunately all too common. The pathologizing and stereotyping of women who are, for whatever reasons, divorced, not remarried, not living with anyone, not in a traditional full-time relationship, and *childless* limits the capacity of the therapist to begin from a position of sponsorship. It is also a reflection of continued attachments to patriarchal paradigms about expectations of women's roles and functioning. Sara had "tried out" several therapists, and each attempt solidified in her mind that her unique experience of divorce at midlife without children was not understood. She left with depleted feelings of self-worth, feeling she did not "measure up" in a number of ways. She *should* be able to be alone, *should* be able to attract a man. The fact that she was having difficulty with both these scenarios was proof that she was incompetent and "damaged goods" in her own eyes. The remainder of the first therapy hour primarily focused on going slowly with Sara at her own pace to hear about her presenting dilemma and her previous experiences in therapy.

In the solution-focused perspective, it is important to explore and understand what has been useful or not useful for the client in the past, in order to avoid repeating unhelpful solutions that do not resonate as useful for the client. It is often important to hear from the client what other therapists have done that has or has not been helpful. In Sara's case, her initial complaint was that she felt she had not found a therapist that fully understood her dilemma. It was also important for me to understand what she perceived the barriers were to the development of these previous therapeutic relationships. Rather than competing with past therapists, this exploration was in the service of building an effective sponsoring relationship with her. It was my sense that how we began together and how I accepted at face value and understood her previous experiences would have a great impact on the capacity for us to move forward together with her treatment.

The client's answers to this line of questioning can provide a guide in order to avoid repeating solutions that have not been useful or made a difference to the client. In the end, it is "the differences that make a difference" to the client that are the key to successful treatment. It is important to explore what the client wants to be different in therapy, and how she would know therapy was helpful.

I observed deShazer to sometimes use the following as an opening question of a first consultation: "How will you know when you can end therapy?" This question can help the therapist and client move quickly into understanding the client's goals for therapy. In effect, it also begins the conversation at solution development, rather than problem description. Sara's response to this question was the following:

S: Well, I think the only thing I want is to stop feeling bad and so stuck between two bad choices. I have been thinking that I have to get out of this situation with Jeff. I guess that's my goal. I feel like I have to, it is hurting me so much. And the other therapists all kept telling me that is what I thought I have to do.

DC: Do you think there are any other possibilities?

S: No, I can't think of any other way to help myself. That's the problem, that's where I'm stuck, and that's why I called you. I feel like I can't go on like this.

In this first session, I had several goals in mind. I began from a position of acceptance of Sara's symptoms at face value as attempted solutions. I also began to set the tone for a sponsoring relationship by listening deeply to her, and to begin to focus conversation on possible solutions and meaning modifications. In my mind, I also wanted to normalize her need for connection, respect her difficulty in breaking an important attachment, and began to think about what limiting social constructions of meaning may be at the core of her distress. I also began to challenge myself about how I could help Sara get unstuck and change the meaning of her experience, rather than viewing her from a deficit or dysfunction perspective. I surely did not want to repeat what did not work in her previous experiences of therapy.

An important tool for building the sponsoring relationship is the use of compliments throughout sessions. Sincere expression compliments that can focus on the client's strengths also builds a positive rapport. Complimenting Sara for her bravery, expressing understanding of the importance of her relationship with Jeff, and inviting her to tell me more about the positives of that relationship were opening attempts in sponsorship. In addition to listening deeply to the client's story and allowing her to describe the problems as she sees them, it is also important to "push for" beginning solutions in the very first session. Beginning and ending with conversation about the "good things" can lend hope and vision to the client. The session ended with the following:

DC: So, I am beginning to get a real understanding of why you're feeling stuck and how important a decision this is about the relationship with Jeff. I always like to hear about "good things," so tell me before we end today, what is going well for you now?

S: Gee, I haven't really thought about that too much, because I am so upset about my situation. I didn't really think anything was going good.

DC: Well, between now and the next time we meet, I'd like to ask you to think about two things, and keep track of them on paper if you can. First, what is going well for you that you want to continue. Because we will want to keep that and have more of that happen for you. [First session formula task] Secondly, what are you getting out of the relationship with Jeff? I really want to hear more about how that relationship is helpful to you right now.

S: You mean you are not going to tell me to get out of it? You think it's helping me? (*She looks stunned*)

DC: Yes, I think it might be actually helping you in a lot of ways, and no, I wouldn't pretend to know if it is the right thing for you to get out of it. That's a very personal decision. And yes, to your credit, I think you may have found in Jeff something that you need right now, just when you needed to. Let's talk about it more next time.

S: (*Looking surprised with a slight glimmer of a smile*) I haven't really been thinking about what's going good, just what I'm crummy at. And about Jeff, everybody has been telling me how bad it is for me, I just have mostly felt a lot of guilt and ashamed of it. I feel a little better already, and I do want to come back.

Sara seemed to lack hope that another therapy experience could be helpful. Sara's initial complaint was that she felt emotionally trapped and desired to get out of a part-time relationship that she felt she had been using as a crutch since shortly into her marital separation. Her desperation about wanting a full-time relationship was palatable, and much of Sara's distress seemed to center on not being remarried. She was distressed that she had not found a permanent relationship or remarried, despite heroic efforts venturing into the world of single life. Sara "bought into" the narratives of previous therapists, as well as many of her friends. She believed that she should succeed at being alone for awhile, and then she should put all her energy into finding a man and "real relationship." Sara had attempted to get out of her relationship with Jeff several times, and each time she experienced considerable symptoms of distress, anxiety, and mild panic, including dizziness, hyperventilation, stomach pain, and depression. Each time she became increasingly afraid to try again.

Although most of the time Sara felt she had recovered from her divorce and was generally happy with her life (her number of 90% on the scaling question), she described periods of distress, emotional upheaval, overwhelming loneliness, and sadness. She described this as "just not feeling right or at home with myself." She felt she could not put her finger on what was causing it. Sara felt she had tried a lot to cope with these periods of distress and could not heal herself.

Sara seemed emotionally trapped in a world in which independence felt comfortable to her, and yet she remained distressed about still being single. On some level, she felt she would never feel valuable as long as she had not remarried and did not have some kind of family. My beginning thoughts centered on how I might be able to help Sara modify the meanings of her experience to be more in alignment with her current life and her emotions. In effect, diminishing the cognitive dissonance between the two sets of beliefs and creating cognitive consonance. Sara was trapped between two sets of beliefs: traditional and untraditional. Her comfort with living alone and having diverse connections was transposed against a backdrop of damaging beliefs regarding her self-worth if she stayed in a part-time relationship and was unsuccessful at finding another marriage.

Sara was in a considerable amount of emotional distress when she arrived at her first appointment. She felt out of sync, describing herself as pressing her nose against a glass, looking in on a party that she could not be part of. From the Ericksonian perspective, Sara's distress can be viewed as an opportunity for growth on a deeper level. I interpreted her distress as her internal "waking up" and a push toward healing and improvement. Gilligan (2001) describes the client in distress and upheaval as exposing the "tender soft spot" that is in need of care and healing. Although a client may be functioning well in many areas, as turned out to be the case with Sara, the vulnerable soft spot is what they bring to us. We must accept it with open arms, sponsoring the growth they often desperately desire.

A LIFE IN TRANSITION

Sara was married at the age of 20 to her first boyfriend. They met at the age of 18, with Sara having done very little dating prior to this relationship. In retrospect, she felt that marriage at such an early age was a mistake. She was divorced at age 38 after an 18-year marriage. She entered therapy with me at the age of 44 after being divorced six years. Looking back, Sara felt the need to be married was "deeply buried inside" (unconscious) when she was younger. She described "not thinking" about her decision, but feeling that this was automatically what she should do. When her ex-husband "showed up" with an engagement ring when she was 19, she recalled feeling euphoric and putting all her other goals "on the back burner." Sara described her marriage as deteriorating throughout the years. The relationship was characterized by lack of intimacy and emotional disconnection that continued to increase over the years. Sara described distressed feelings and depression that increased over time. She was silent about her needs and unhappiness throughout her entire marriage. She stated:

> The thought of expressing my needs and unhappiness never occurred to me. That's the way it was, and my way was to be silent. That's what I learned in my growing up, to stay silent and not upset anyone, especially my father. That's what you did to be "good." The thought of talking to my husband about what was wrong never even came into my mind. I didn't tell anyone else either—not my closest friends, not my family. I just suffered for a lot of years by myself.

Sara's discomfort in her marriage increased in her mid-30s. She believed her thought process regarding leaving the marriage took place over a decade. Sara returned to college to complete a bachelor's degree in nursing while she was still married. Retrospectively, she felt this was her way of preparing to improve her financial situation and her ability to care for herself. In effect, preparing herself to improve her finances expanded her opportunities and choices to leave the marriage. Sara entered therapy when she felt her unhappiness in the marriage was intolerable. She also was experiencing an increase in anxiety and mild panic symptoms. Sara remained in therapy for three years during her separation and divorce process. She eventually filed for divorce after several attempts at therapy with her husband and a two-year separation period.

Regarding her childbearing decision-making process, Sara continually delayed having children over the 18 years of her marriage. Over the course of our therapy, Sara was able to discover an understanding of her delay of this decision. Sara described a weak desire for children throughout her adolescence and early adulthood. She did not recall a strong interest in having children. Sara also wondered if her lack of interest was exacerbated by her deteriorating marriage. She felt on some level she had a sense of knowing that she did not want to remain in the marriage. She recalled:

> I wonder if my not making any effort to have children was because I knew somewhere in my heart that I didn't want this marriage. The unhappiness was getting worse and worse. I didn't realize it at the time, but having children would have meant I would be stuck in that relationship, and the depression was increasing. I just never dealt with it. I just didn't do anything about it. I never really tried to get pregnant, and he never brought it up. We didn't talk about it at all, and it just kept getting dragged out.

LISTENING TO SILENT TEARS: THE ART OF SPONSORING

Sara experienced several therapists as judgmental and giving advice precipitously that did not fit her experience or capabilities. The experiences that Sara described included feeling incompetent and dysfunctional. Somehow she did not feel sponsored or "connected to" deeply at her immediate level of need and despair.

In Sara's view, several therapy experiences represented a dichotomy of blame. One disregarded Sara's need for connection by suggesting she needed to succeed at being alone. Another criticized her inability to find a relationship, implying her goal should be to find a man. The implication to Sara was that she was not succeeding at either one of these scenarios. These theoretical reflected beliefs either devalued her need for connection or connected her worth to her capacity to find a man.

Her experience replicated the classic "blaming the victim" stance for Sara. Messages seemed to stem from utilization of deviance/deficit models that increased Sara's feelings of incompetence and difference.

It should be recognized that these were Sara's perceptions of her experiences. Whether this was intended by the therapists was unknown to me. My concern was the meaning of these experiences to Sara, and how I could listen to her closely enough to hear how I might be successful in attempts to sponsor her.

Listening as deeply as possible to Sara's silent tears was the beginning of the sponsoring relationship. My initial goals were to "be with" her at a core level, to listen to her dilemma without rigid hypothesis, judgment, or preconceived strategies and interventions. I initially approached Sara from a position of "curious not knowing," beginning with no assumptions about her dilemma, behavior, choices, or what might be useful solutions to her problems.

The purpose of deep listening is to gain as deep an understanding as possible of the client's perception of her "stuckness." The therapist then begins to test out this understanding in conversation reflected back to the client for validation. Any attempt at advice or intervention without this deep understanding would possibly be viewed as more of the same of her other experiences. I checked myself not to view Sara as "resistant" to her other therapists' interventions and ideas. Rather, I wanted to make more effort to cooperate with her where she was, and discover what she wanted from therapy.

I viewed Sara's distressing symptoms as a struggle with herself for her own growth. Although her initial solution of her relationship with Jeff had worked for her on many levels, Sara was telling me through her distress and tears that she was striving for something more for her life. I accepted her symptoms as attempted solutions in an effort to sort out myriad issues of connection, intimacy, separation, independence, abandonment, and loss in her post-divorce years. Her need for connection with Jeff, and indeed her willingness to allow herself to attach to him in the process of growth, was indeed brave and courageous in the face of all her previous losses. It was important for me to normalize and applaud her desire for connection, not devalue her for it. Sara was waking up to her soft spot, a great opportunity for healing and growth (Gilligan, 2001).

As solution-focused sponsor and coach, it was my role to start from a position of honor and respect for Sara's despair and her stuckness in a life circumstance that was becoming increasingly intolerable to her. My stance of gentle guidance, rather than expert advice giving, provided the beginning foundation for the therapeutic relationship. From this stance, Sara could begin to focus on her capacity to solve this dilemma with her own strengths and capabilities. I trusted in her ability to know what would ultimately make a difference to her and enable her to advance in the direction of her dreams. As I left the first session, my thoughts turned to how I could support Sara, keeping her "in the lead," guiding "from behind," so she could find her way where she wanted to go. Looking for diagnosis and pathology could result in my being stuck in an ineffective experience with Sara. Rather, I focused on listening to the meaning of her silent tears, lending hope, pushing solution development, discovering storylines to change, and fostering connections in the service of her growth.

CALLING ALL POSSIBLE BOATS: THE SEARCH FOR SOLUTIONS

Sara's distress upon entering therapy resulted in a twofold solution-focused approach to her treatment. Sara was in immediate emotional and physical distress, with significant symptoms of panic and depression when she first came to see me. In keeping with a solution focus, a present and future focus, and searching for Sara's natural strengths, the following second session took place:

DC: Sara, the first time you were here, you described to me two things that were bothering you the most: your upset feelings right now and your feeling that you need to leave the relationship with Jeff. Which of those do you feel would be the best for you to work on first?

S: I think it seems too hard to think about leaving Jeff, so I need some help with my upset feelings right now, if you can help me with that.

DC: So tell me what is bothering you the most.

S: Well, I'm just having periods of time when I feel distressed, and I get dizzy, and I can't think straight. Sometimes I feel like I can't stay in my apartment. I just get such a panicked lonely feeling. I can't collect myself.

DC: So tell me what have you been able to do to help yourself at those times?

S: Sometimes I take a bubble bath and get under the covers and sleep it off. Other times I get myself dressed and go out to the mall, but sometimes I can't figure out what to do. That's all, just those two. I haven't been able to do anything else and I don't know what else would help.

DC: So it sounds like you have been really good at caring for yourself and found some ways to get yourself through it. That's very brave of you. So why don't we think of some other possibilities? So, Sara, when you could look in the future and see yourself feeling better, let's say next week or a few weeks from now, what would you see yourself doing?

S: The two things I know I can do now, stay in bed and sleep it off, or go out and try to change my mood. I guess if I called my friends more and asked them if I could spend time with them, that might help. Also, I think keeping busy helps, like going to lectures and the movies. Oh, also, if I go to the gym and exercise it really changes my mood a lot.

DC: Oh really, that sounds good. What else seems to change your mood a lot?

S: Probably now that I think about it, the exercise seems to be the thing that helps the most because it really helps to get out the bad energy.

DC: So of all these things, which do you think is the easiest for you to do more of?

S: Probably two, probably exercising more and calling friends. I haven't really done that. I think I can do that.

DC: And when you call friends and exercise, how will you be feeling different?

S: I think both things would help calm me down and stay peaceful and not so alone. I could see myself just enjoying being with my friends.

DC: And which friends do you think would be most willing to help you if you get lonely or anxious?

S: Probably a couple of friends—Kathy, Jane, and Tara—they are friends I can count on, any time of day or night.

DC: Great—they sound like awesome friends. I'm so impressed with how you are helping yourself through hard times. So it sounds like doing more of what you already know how to do will help you to feel better. Between now and the next time we meet, I'd like you to keep thinking about things you know how to do to help yourself to feel less scared or lonely.

In this second session with Sara, it was important to allow her to take the lead regarding what she was most able to work on first. Sara chose to work on her immediate symptoms of physical and psychological distress. Should I have pursued her ending the relationship with Jeff, I could have become "out of sync" with her capacity for growth and change at that point in treatment. Using constructive language such as "What was she already doing that she knew how to do?" and "When you are doing better, in a week or a couple of weeks, what will that be like?" accomplished several things. It implied the expectation of change and presupposed that she already had the capability to utilize her own strengths to solve her current symptoms. The use of compliments also served to reframe Sara's perception of herself and supported sponsoring her to see herself as competent and strong. Sara had become somewhat stuck in finding solutions to her periodic symptoms of panic. The technique of guiding Sara through devising a list of all possible solutions and her choice of the easiest one to do put her in charge of authoring her own plan for self-care and responding to these symptoms. Little attention was focused on the details of Sara's symptoms; rather, focusing on solutions set the process in motion to begin to teach Sara solution construction.

Over the course of therapy, Sara continued to develop concrete self-care solutions for her periods of anxiety and panic. She became increasingly more comfortable with periods of "alone time" and doing things on her own. She ventured out to dinners, movies, and cultural events, sometimes with friends, sometimes alone. She also returned to school to complete a master's degree in nursing. This was an educational, emotional, and financial achievement she was rightfully proud of. This enabled Sara to obtain a better-paying job that provided her with more income and a feeling of security. My hope was that this first phase of treatment would set the stage for further solution development regarding the more entrenched distress around her relationship with Jeff.

SAFE HARBOR: RELATIONSHIPS IN REVISION

In addition to working on solution development around self-care and coping skills, another important area of intervention with Sara was the work on re-storying the meaning of her experiences of divorce and post-divorce relationship. Sara seemed to be emotionally trapped in storylines that were resulting in emotional and physical distress. It seemed that the actual relationship with Jeff was not the source of her distress. Rather, the narratives she attached to this relationship were resulting in feelings of incompetence and lack of value. I had inklings in the first few sessions that helping Sara re-story her experience, as Berg and Dolan (2001) suggest, "spinning straw into gold," would enable Sara to move on in whatever way she chose—whether that be in connection with Jeff, searching for someone else, or contented on her own.

While Sara continued to make improvements in the practical areas of self-care in response to her immediate symptoms, her inability to leave her relationship with Jeff continued. Despite several attempts to break the attachment, Sara was be unable to maintain the separation for more than a few months. The usual pattern involved Jeff contacting her and both of them gravitating back to each other once again. I viewed Sara's desire to break the connection as an attempt at growth on her part, as her desire for a complete relationship increased.

Solution development continued around Sara's distress about her relationship with Jeff. Exploration of the meaning of this relationship to Sara was a major part of the work. Sara was in the lead determining that her goal was to separate from Jeff. The following is an interchange in which we explored all possible solutions to her dilemma with Jeff:

S: I really want to try to find a way out of this relationship with Jeff. I just feel too upset all the time that I can't move on.

DC: Tell me what has happened when you have tried to break off before.

S: Well, usually it has been these horrible "breakup" conversations, where I tell him I am not happy like this and he leaves, and then there is no more contact. Cold turkey. It's horrible, and I don't want to go through that anymore.

DC: You don't feel you can break it off directly like you did before?

S: No, the feelings just get worse and worse each time. I just feel this horrible emptiness and longing to get him back. It gets worse as time goes along, not better. Then I am afraid I might drink or go out and be with someone just to be with someone.

DC: We should talk about how being with Jeff seems to be helping you, but let's stick with right now, since you want to try to change something about your contact with him, some other ways you might do that.

I gave Sara the task of developing a list of all possible solutions to her dilemma with Jeff. Sara arrived the following week with the following list, which I present in her words:

1. Horrible breakup scene
2. Write a breakup letter
3. Break up over the phone
4. Just stop returning his phone calls cold turkey
5. Stop being available little by little
6. Make a lot of effort to meet someone else
7. Do nothing until forced into it
8. Stay with it and somehow be okay about it

DC: Sara, which of these do you feel would be easiest to do?

S: I don't know, they all seem hard to do, too hard. I've been through the horrible breakup scene too many times, four or five, I can't do it anymore. It is too hurtful. I feel so sick when I do that. I tried the not calling back once, and I actually made it a few months. But that was really hard too.

DC: So maybe we should just put most of these ideas off the table for now. Now what about this one at the end, about staying with it and being okay with it? What is your idea about that?

S: I'm not sure what I meant, but sometimes I think maybe there is some way to cope with it that I haven't thought of before.

DC: What's your idea about?

S: I can't seem to get out of this, so what if I kept it and felt different about it? Like if there was some way I could make it okay. See, I always feel like its not healthy for me. I know he's not a full-time relationship for me. He's 10 years younger than me. We have so many basic differences, and he tends to be a little depressed, which scares me. I also think he drinks once in awhile when he is feeling depressed. And I couldn't commit to something like that.

DC: It sounds like good judgment on your part to think about these risks, and good knowing of yourself to know what you don't want to be around permanently. That's not easy to do. So let's try to figure out what this means to you and why you are getting stuck. It is a possibility that we could help you see it differently. So tell me, what is it about Jeff that keeps you in the relationship?

S: We are okay companions, we do a few things together, movies, some concerts, but in many other ways we don't have much in common. He is 10 years younger than me, and I think our life experience is too different. So when I really think about it, I guess it's not so much the actual relationship, but the thing I like the most is that he calls me every day. I guess it is this sense of security that I am not alone. It just gives me that feeling of safety and being cared for somehow. And I still do everything I want to do in terms of going out and trying to meet people. He doesn't stop me.

DC: What do you think you have learned from these years of this relationship with Jeff?

S: I think I have tried to work on talking more, you know, speaking up for myself when something bothers me. I think that was my part of what ruined my marriage, the fact that I didn't speak up and I kept things in for so many years. Then when I spoke up, it was too late, I was so angry and it was too late.

DC: So you are learning to speak up with Jeff? How is that going?

S: It's getting a little better all the time. It's still hard to do, but I take a deep breath and do it.

DC: That seems like a really important thing that you are learning to do that! WOW! That is really impressive. That should help you a lot in your next relationship. Sounds like your relationship with Jeff is good practice, and it keeps you feeling safe.

S: (*Smiles a little*) I never thought of it at all as good practice before. I also think the companionship that I do have with him, and the closeness is much better than my marriage was. So that has been a nice thing.

DC: That's very big!!! So why think about getting out of it?

S: Everybody has been telling me I have to or I won't find a real permanent relationship. And I still do think that is what I want.

DC: You know, I was thinking about how you go out exploring to meet new people, and then you kind of have the safety of coming back to Jeff to touch base and provide you with that secure feeling. It reminds me of how the sailors go out and explore the seas and have many adventures, and yet they always know where the safe harbor is when they need it. That's kind of how I see your relationship with Jeff. It's like he is your safe harbor. I think its very smart of you to keep that safe harbor.

S: I hadn't thought of it that way. I never thought if I could change how I feel, or how I could make it work for me.

DC: So what would you need to think in order to change it and make it work for you?

S: I guess if I thought of him as a friend, a safe harbor like you said, a safety zone while I am trying to find what I really want, that makes it feel a lot different.

DC: So then, if you thought of it that way, would there be any need to get out of it?

S: Hmm, maybe not. I could see it as like a temporary solution while I am still trying to meet someone for a full-time relationship. I guess its just what other people think—that it is keeping me from something else. That doesn't have to be true.

DC: You're right, that doesn't have to be true at all. Could you see yourself as in control of this for yourself?

S: Yeah, if it is my plan, then it's up to me.

Conversations continued between us in therapy regarding the meaning of her relationship with Jeff. Sara's distress seemed to originate from the meaning she and others attached to it, rather than from the actual relationship itself. The view of it as a symbol of weakness, dysfunction, and a crutch was a core storyline underlying the pressure Sara felt to leave the relationship. However, just the thought of leaving was intolerable to Sara. This coupled with the distress she had experienced during previous breakup attempts resulted in her feeling paralyzed and trapped. The pattern of focusing on degrading beliefs, perceived incompetence, and inability to change things developed into a cycle of panic and depression.

As time progressed in therapy, the conversational focus about Sara's relationship with Jeff shifted to solution rather than symptom. Many discussions clarified the advantages and strengths of the relationship, and Sara's creativity and competence. Viewing this relationship as a friendship, wisely chosen by Sara to provide security and emotional safety throughout her post-divorce period, enabled Sara to view herself as competent rather than dysfunctional and destructive. I continued to support this positive view through compliments and stories that implied new meanings. It would have been easy to get myself stuck in the same unsuccessful patterns as Sara's previous therapist, attempting to convince Sara to leave Jeff and be alone. It was important to respect Sara's need for this connection and to follow her lead about the pace for her growth. Interestingly, as we continued to work on solidifying meaning modification, Sara's panic symptoms gradually decreased without ever being the primary focus of this stage of the therapy.

Another critical storyline that required meaning modification was the narrative of Sara's divorce experience. Sara's marriage was characterized by lack of intimacy and connection, which she internalized over the years as reflection of her undesirability and inability to be "good enough" and make the relationship work. The divorce process further validated Sara's initial story in that her husband refused to commit to therapy to save the marriage. She internalized this as further proof of his devaluation and lack of desire for her, and had intense feelings of abandonment.

Reconstructing the meaning of the loss of Sara's marriage and her divorce was an important redefinition that increased her coping ability. Looking at her story through a different lens of meaning changed her internalized experience and perception of her divorce. Rather than holding on to stories of abandonment, victimization, and undesirability, we began to construct stories of bravery, survivorship, and self-advocacy. We conversed about the process of Sara's recognition that she was not fulfilled in her marriage, and that she desired more for her life. Complimenting Sara as bravely acting on meeting her own needs, taking charge of her own life, and wisely leaving an unhealthy relationship increased her pride and self-esteem. Reframing her initiation of separation and divorce to be seen as a healthy reflection of her need for closeness and intimacy decreased her emotional distress. The story "spun from straw to gold" was one of a woman courageously finally listening to her own voice, a voice that had been speaking to her for almost two decades as an internal whisper of panic and depression. Sara's description of her "wake-up call" was the following:

> I realize now I was having panic attacks for like 10 years. Then I started to realize it might have been because the marriage was bad. I thought there had to be more out there for me and that I deserved it. I had to take a chance that I could find it. I couldn't live with myself if I didn't try to find a better relationship. Living with that emotional neglect was killing me, little by little every day. I was scared as anything, and didn't even know how I could do it. I had never lived on my own or taken care of myself, but I knew there had to be a way. It became so painful that I couldn't live that way any more. I finally said I want and deserve more than this.

ENDURING ENDEARMENTS: EXPANDING ATTACHMENTS

In addition to re-storying her experiences of relationship and divorce, it was also important for Sara to expand her connections in as many ways as possible. Eventually, as Sara expanded her relationship network and found closeness and security from multiple sources, her intense need for the security of Jeff lessened. In working within the context of Sara's relational sphere, we explored who else might be able to provide her with close connection and emotional security.

Beginning with her family of origin, Sara made efforts to improve her relationship with her brother, sister, and nephews. These relationships were sometimes helpful, sometimes disappointing and unreliable. Since Sara did not always feel fully connected with her siblings and nephews, we also explored the extended family as a source of other possible lost connections that Sara could reconnect with. She discovered an aunt and uncle who were more than willing to reconnect with her. Even though living at a distance in Arizona, Sara was able to bridge this connection. She especially found her aunt a source of support, and they were able to connect frequently by phone and occasional visits to Arizona. Reconnecting with her aunt and uncle also resulted in renewed connections to several cousins she had spent quite a bit of time with as a child. Although initially the relationships with her cousins required reacquaintance, eventually they did become a source of reference group support. Several cousins in her age group were also divorced, one without children. These expanded connections gave her a sense of family she felt she had lost with the death of her parents in her late adolescence.

Exploring Sara's friendship network also provided her with expanded connection and emotional security. Sara's increased ability to "use her voice" to ask friends for more closeness and connection had positive impact. As Sara shared more of her feelings of distress and loneliness, her best friend of 20 years, Sue, became another safe harbor. Sue had not been fully aware of Sara's struggles, and so she began to "watch over" Sara in a more connected, sisterly way. She increased her calls to Sara to several times weekly, and she provided Sara with an open invitation to visit or spend holidays. As Sara continued to ask for support, other friends followed with similar open invitations. Another single girlfriend made an agreement with Sara that they could call each other day or night for emergencies and the other would come. As Sara ventured out, sometimes traveling alone, attending lectures and seminars, she also made several new female friends that she met by chance.

Sara's return to graduate school and her move into a professional nursing career also expanded her network, providing her with a variety of additional friendships: single, never married; divorced; and married. At work Sara also developed some relationships with older women who became mentors to her, both professionally and personally. We also discussed other areas of need for Sara, such as who she might live close to later in life, who might help her financially, and whom she could depend upon should health problems arise.

LEARNING TO BE NEW: ROLE INNOVATION

Sara's expansion of her life in many areas provided her with new roles and experiences that helped to diminish her distress about her life circumstance. Therapy focused on role innovation in a broad sense, rather than just in terms of relationships with others. Role innovation was intertwined with the therapeutic goals of solution building, meaning modification, and fostering connections. In Sara's case, role innovation was characterized by an evolving sense of herself as an autonomously competent woman, who was expanding her self-care and nurturing, intimacy and attachments, and diverse industriousness.

Sara's initial exit from the role of wife was extremely distressing, resulting in an escalation of grief, panic, and depression. In my view, Sara's relationship with Jeff provided her with the stability and connection she needed during her initial period of role exit and grief. She experienced this period in her life as highly traumatic. Over time, Sara made a good adaptation to her exit from married life and potential motherhood. Returning to school and completing a master's degree in nursing was an accomplishment that she was extremely proud of. This also provided her with networking, professional, and friendship opportunities that expanded her life and decreased her loneliness. As she expanded her professional, friendship, and family roles, her capacity to withstand being alone also increased. Sara's ability to reach out to others and use her voice to express her needs resulted in re-establishing lost connections with extended family, with friends becoming more "family-like" and girlfriends becoming more "sisterly."

Regarding the exit from the role of potential mother, Sara recalled very brief periods of curiosity and mild sadness about not having children; however, she never experienced any intense or extended grief regarding the absence of children. She did not recall a strong desire for children, and described inactivity in the pursuit of pregnancy throughout her marriage. She described interests in many other pursuits in early adulthood, including pursuing a career in nursing. This goal was delayed when Sara married early. Sara's case was a classic case of postponed childbearing that eventually drifted into permanent childlessness. Sara connected this to an awareness on some level that her marriage was not fulfilling, and that eventually she would move out of it. In effect, pursuing childbearing would have trapped her in that relationship.

It is important not to assume that the lack of bereft feelings or lack of desire for children is dysfunctional. We developed a narrative story in which Sara was able to recognize she had a weak desire for children since adolescence. We also worked to detach her story from paradigms of shame and guilt, and validated her feelings of comfort regarding having no children. Sara did not have a particularly strong focus on beliefs about childlessness as a deviant identity. Nor did stigmatizing reactions of others cause her distress. Since this was not a particularly distressing area of meaning for Sara, it was not a primary focus of treatment.

It was important to follow Sara's lead, guiding her on the path she wanted to travel. There were no prescribed solutions. Rather, I attempted to stay true to my roles of solution-focused guide, constructive coach, and mutual storyteller. Meeting Sara at her "soft spot," collaborating and cooperating with her in a "one-of-a-kind" framework for therapy, enabled Sara to define her own goals and solutions.

Sara came and went from therapy as needed over the course of six years. Her comings and goings were normalized as "tune-ups," rather than viewed as resistance. Over time, I saw Sara grow in her own comfort in being alone. She stopped feeling the desperate need to meet someone and remarry. Her goal became having as happy a life as possible. She never did become comfortable leaving Jeff. A critical shift in story enabled Sara to see her relationship with Jeff as a great long-term friendship. She also viewed it as a testament to her ability to provide herself with a relationship that met her basic emotional needs. When we ended therapy the last time, Sara was still in the relationship with Jeff; however, the meaning of it had changed for her. She viewed it as a friendship that provided her with important support and stability. She and Jeff had decided they would be friends, whatever else happened or did not happen in their lives. This worked for Sara. In addition, the meaning of her marriage, divorce, and childlessness was forever changed in ways that enabled her to move on with a different sense of self as an autonomously competent woman. In our last session, Sara recalled:

> I remember how panicked I felt when I first separated. I think I was numb for a long time. I don't even know how I made it to work. In the first weeks I used to lay on the floor of my living room and just cry until I couldn't cry anymore. It has been a long, hard road, but I'm here. I feel like I have gained a lot of peacefulness through the divorce. I take good care of myself, and the relationships that I do have are really happy ones. My long-time friends I consider family in every way. Other new friends I think I will know for a long time. Some of us talk about how we can help each other when we get older. I have one single girlfriend, she has been through a lot of dating and broken relationships, and we share a bond about helping each other when we are starting a relationship and going through breakups. We are just there for each other 24/7, no judgments. The relationships with my family that have improved have been great too. I have started to draw on them when I do feel in an emotional slump. My work has been great, I love what I do, and I have a lot of friends at work. Now that I'm settled, I've been enjoying a lot of things, with other people, and with myself. I consider those times my times of relationship with me.
>
> As far as Jeff goes, he's still there, but I just feel different about it now. I consider him a friend who we help each other and give stability to each other. I'm not really "looking" for anybody anymore, but if someone comes along that would add to my life, that's what I would want. But now I'm okay to say I'm living my life just as it is, and I want to make it as happy as it can be, with or without a marriage. It's like I've had to learn to be new.

She smiled in contentment. Thinking back to her silent tears in that first session, now replaced by a contented smile, I could only respond with a contented smile of my own. There I sat, watching her advance in the direction of her own dreams, proud coach, cheering for her all the way!

In the solution-focused approach, the client takes the lead in identifying the issues and goals for therapy. deShazer and Berg's solution-focused principle—"if it ain't broke, don't fix it"—suggests that therapy should focus on issues that the client wants to attend to, rather than attempting to fix what isn't "broken." It is important for the therapist to use restraint from focusing on areas that may be of interest for him or her, but may not be especially useful for the client. In the cases of both Sara and Susan (discussed in Part I), it was important not to apply a "cookie cutter" theoretical approach to either of these clients. Rather, treatment was individualized based on each unique experience of divorce at midlife without children. In neither case did I assume that I knew what was best for the client.

In summary, the overall thrust of the therapeutic process for the cases of both Susan and Sara focused on guiding them toward solution building and conversations regarding new storylines that changed the meaning of their experiences to healthier constructions. This eventually resulted in the decrease in initial presenting symptoms for both. In the end, it was a combination of sponsorship, solution construction, meaning modification, and working in the relational sphere that made the difference in both clients' ability to cope effectively. Throughout treatment with both, it was important to continually check my beliefs and the underlying premises guiding my thinking. Looking back on my experience of therapy with Sara and Susan, the "differences that made a difference" for me as the therapist were:

- Sponsoring through a mutually defined process of collaboration
- Staying consistently committed to the solution focus
- Utilizing conversation as the primary tool for meaning modification
- Reconstructing the meaning of loss in the process of divorce
- Normalizing mature single adulthood and autonomous competence
- Validating the need for connection and attachment as strength
- Exploring expanded connections in the relational context
- Solidifying positive feelings about new roles
- Individualizing the unique needs of the client within a flexible theoretical and clinical framework

CHAPTER 13

Epilogue

Looking to the Future

Who knows what women can become when they are finally free to become themselves?

—Betty Friedan, *The Feminine Mystique* (1997, p. 378)

Women, finally free to be themselves. It is official: Women's very identity is under revision! Embracing and advancing the concept of complete freedom of choice for women requires redefinitions of theory, culture, and institutions that detach from limiting patriarchal social constructions that have long been barriers to such freedom. The ongoing process of social redefinition now needs to be expanded and detached from value judgments regarding women who are not wives or mothers, by either circumstance or design.

The social trends and changes of the last several decades have undoubtedly resulted in an expanded array of choices for women. As the social change of this era becomes institutionalized in coming decades, it is anticipated that an increasing number of women will be divorced at midlife without children. Although the advantages of such changes are apparent, the downside is that women are now faced with complex decision-making processes that were not even considerations for previous generations. These include decisions regarding whether to remain single, marry, bear children, or divorce.

In a society in which preference for the roles of wife and mother is still pervasively embedded in the culture, these experiences are still intensified by devaluing narrative meanings attached to this role. The legacy of patriarchy and rigid standards for women's roles still lingers in both overt and covert ways. It is important to disconnect from beliefs regarding these roles as alternate and substandard in order to consider them as valuable in their own right. By no means have the external or internal barriers to complete freedom of choice for women been eradicated.

THEORETICAL IMPLICATIONS

Although considerable theoretical expansion has occurred over the last few decades, theories of women's individual development and psychology, as well as family life cycle developmental theory, need to be further broadened in scope. This is necessary in order to incorporate more recent social change and the experience of this group of women. I suggest we begin with inclusion of a normative life cycle stage of mature single adulthood. In this way we can normalize the development of autonomous competence for women, as well as all adults. A focus on autonomous competence provides for inclusion of such skills as increased self-nurturing and self-care, expanded connections and attachments, and creative innovation of diverse roles. This proposed stage not only is applicable for midlife women who are divorced without children, but also can be a useful concept in consideration of other adults who find themselves single in adulthood.

CLINICAL IMPLICATIONS

In thinking retrospectively about my work with women divorced at midlife without children, it seems to me that several perspectives stand out with important implications for clinical work. Given that this role places women at risk for vulnerability, isolation, and disenfranchisement, it is first and foremost important to begin with a sponsoring stance from a solution and strength-oriented perspective. It is also critical to work from a broad developmental perspective that fractures the "woman must equal wife and mother" equation.

The ability to work from a supportive, multipositional approach also requires professionals' awareness not only of their clients' internalized narratives, but also of their own beliefs. Rather than working from a pathologizing theoretical framework, professionals need to normalize their view of women who are not wives or mothers and view alternate choices as equally valid, fulfilling, and healthy roles. This awareness is critical in order to be able to effectively facilitate exploration of meaning and meaning modification with the client. It is important to deconstruct one's own pro-marriage, pro-natalist biases.

The internalization of social constructions has a pervasive impact on women's behavior and decisions and often drives women's behavior in destructive ways. Internalized beliefs regarding the universal "requirements" that all women should desire marriage and childbearing make it extremely difficult for women to voice ambivalent or "prohibited" feelings. Expressing lack of desire for either has been so taboo that most women are never able to do so. Internalized narratives regarding lifelong commitment to marriage and responsibility for success of relationships often act as prohibitions to divorce. These beliefs often contribute to many women's inability to initiate divorce, even in the presence of emotional abuse and neglect.

It is important to help women challenge constructs regarding marriage, childbearing, and divorce. Professionals need to assist women at all developmental stages in identifying these prescriptions and consciously exploring all possible role options and choices. This includes working through the process of integrating traditional and untraditional beliefs that may come into conflict by midlife. In this way we can play an important role in helping women explore their true sense of knowing and the desires and role choices for their lives. Encouraging women to remain open to all possibilities and explore the dilemmas of choices outside the norm can facilitate a sense of "voice," independence, and control, regardless of whether those choices include marriage and motherhood.

My clinical work as well as the research study has provided important information about the clinical areas that need attention in assisting women who either are considering midlife divorce or are already divorced. A comprehensive approach needs to include four critical areas: development of autonomous competence, meaning reconstruction, fostering expanded connections, and role innovation. It is also important to explore such issues as the client's capacity to be alone, techniques for managing loneliness, changes in family relationships, building and maintaining supportive social networks and friendships, dating at midlife, financial adjustment, career planning, and midlife and aging. Family support is an especially critical factor in adjustment, and expanding relationships is an important area of resource for recovery.

Knowledge gained from working with women divorced at midlife without children also provides valuable information that is useful in work with women in young adulthood, as well as couples considering marriage and childbearing. Individuals and couples alike should be encouraged to explore beliefs and expectations about marriage and childbearing. Couples experiencing possible infertility should also be assisted in openly communicating these concerns and feelings to each other, rather than acting out painful feelings that can sometimes lead to midlife divorce. Most of the women I have interviewed note that they have not been asked questions regarding the issue of childbearing decision making in therapy. Many have related stories of lack of preparation for all the aspects of midlife divorce.

POLICY RECOMMENDATIONS

Recent social change has brought about examination of social constructions and norms that have traditionally dominated cultural discourses regarding women's roles. However, societal supports have not kept pace with these changes and have not been sufficiently institutionalized. Many advancements in recent social policy have been family focused, to the exclusion of women who are not married and not mothers. Recent policies such as the Family Leave Act and child care tax credits do not address the needs of those women who do not have children (Park, 2002). Other corporate benefits such as on-site day care and flex time for parents are also exclusive of women without children.

While these family-focused policies are needed improvements, social policy and programs should also consider that not all women are in traditional family roles. I would recommend creative policy that would support women who are not married and do not have children. This may include local mental health services such as support groups and appropriate socialization activities, tuition credits to assist in obtaining education and career advancement, and tax credits to assist in financial adjustment. Another suggestion is cafeteria-style benefits in which benefits are equal for all workers, with the individual choosing how his or her benefit money will be spent. This may allow single women without children to spend their allotment on benefits that would be more useful to them (Park, 2002). Examples may include tuition for educational pursuits, additional retirement contributions, and "corporate sabbaticals" for those who do not anticipate utilizing family leave.

In my research, I was surprised by the women's unanimous views regarding the unacceptability and difficulty of mothering alone and perceived barriers to doing so. It is possible that some women who *do* desire to parent children would be more open to considering alternative methods such as foster parenting and adoption if enough supports were in place. Supports might include increased subsidized adoption benefits, available and affordable day care, guaranteed health care, more extensive family leave provisions, better college tuition benefits for single mothers, and better workplace support for single mothers.

FUTURE RESEARCH RECOMMENDATIONS

As clinical experience with this group of women develops in the coming years, more research will be needed to ground practice and advance clinical knowledge. As a result of my practice and research, the following issues have come to light that could be useful foci for further study:

1. The impact of social constructions on young women's desire to marry and mother, and on actual behavior and decisions, and exploration of shifting social scripts and narratives on young women's role choices
2. The study of women's narratives and beliefs about divorce and adjustment
3. Current factors involved in women's lack of desire for marriage and children, and ability to act upon alternative role choices
4. The relationship of role conflict to women's decisions regarding marriage and motherhood
5. Exploration of the differences between women who pursue single motherhood and those who do not

6. Further study of women divorced at midlife without children with inclusion of samples that are more culturally, educationally, geographically, and economically diverse

PARTING THOUGHTS

As I was finishing the final touches to this book, I participated in a clinical case conference with several highly respected colleagues of mine. One began presenting the case of a woman who had been divorced at midlife without children. She had been single for 13 years and was still experiencing distress over the fact that she had not remarried. To my dismay, the opening words of my colleague's presentation reflected a "blaming the victim" hypothesis. She stated:

> Of course since she is still single we know that she must have problems with intimacy and must be pushing people away. We all know that a woman who is alone must be doing something wrong. And then there is the issue of her not wanting or even liking children. There is some deficit there that needs to be explored.

After pondering whether I felt more anger or sadness, I thought to myself, "Well, the entrenched legacy of patriarchy is still very much alive and well."

I return now to William Ryan's (1972) challenge of almost 40 years ago. Ryan's work championed the idea of ending victimization of others by ceasing to place blame on individuals. He suggested that we focus on equality rather than inequality, and look to address the deficits of a dehumanizing society. Rather than devaluing others who are outside a prescribed norm, we need to institutionalize beliefs of inclusion and flexibility. Without a blaming the victim ideology then, women who are not wives and mothers can be viewed as complete human beings developing in a society that is supportive and responsive to their unique needs.

As a society we are coming out of the dark, so to speak. There is no turning back from the "quantum leaps" of recent social change. But there is still a long way to go. We must continue on with the struggle to bring in the next wave of feminism—a wave that pushes us all further forward in fracturing faulty beliefs on a much deeper level; a wave that institutionalizes new beliefs that champion equality; a wave that invalidates beliefs that continue to diminish the experiences of women who are "different." In fact, it is this very core social construction of stigmatization of difference that needs to be de-institutionalized.

Although professionally we have come a long way in revising and expanding theory, we still need to continue to push the envelope further. We must continue to detach from theories of exclusion, deviance, and deficit. The first step in this process is our awareness of assumptions about women who are not wives or mothers as dysfunctional, bereft, and limited in their capacity for individual development. My research validated that women can successfully adapt to this experience and create meaningful identities and fulfilling lives apart from the roles of wife and mother. In so doing, they gain their "voice," independence, and control of self.

We must also ask ourselves important questions that challenge us to rethink reified theories that developed in earlier eras. Such questions as:

- What is our need to diagnose, categorize, and judge?
- Can we simply "be with" the client in the struggle of their human condition?
- Can we leave behind theories that blame the victim through ideological discrimination and devaluation of women?
- Can we detach from judgments that limit our ability to sponsor each woman's unique plan for her life?
- Can we truly support *all* choices for women?

My hope in embarking upon this book was to give voice to the story of women who are divorced at midlife without children. I hope that I have provided you with thought-provoking information. As you move forward, I hope it will help you to shape your work with women and girls, as well as your personal beliefs. I ask you to be aware of women who are out there struggling to forge new paths for themselves. Sponsor them in any way you can. Be a friend, be a "sister," be there for them at the deepest level you can.

On a personal note, I have been a "no marriage, no kid" woman for the past 14 years, since my midlife divorce. I would like to be able to tell you that my journey is totally smooth going at this point, but I cannot. On the positive side, my journey has been remarkably full of wonderful new life experiences. Many long-term connections have grown much deeper through these years. They have sustained me in the best and worst of times. There have been many new connections that have met my needs for attachment and closeness. As I age, I look forward to these younger friendships growing through the coming years. There have been awesome professional experiences. There have been wonderful adventures of travel. I have been fortunate enough to see many of my dreams come true. I appreciate that I lead a mostly happy, contented life. I would describe it as peaceful, fulfilled, adventuresome, independent, and sometimes envied by others. In many ways I have succeeded at finding my strengths, re-storying the meaning of my life, fostering connections, and innovating a new identity for myself. My story has surely been revised: from victim to survivor, from stigmatized to privileged.

Have I fractured the fairy tale of long ago? In many ways yes, and in some deep ways no. The fairy tale still whispers to me from somewhere deep inside. The out of sync feeling lingers on, still entrenched somewhere within the deepest part of my psyche. It is that small feeling of discomfort that the shape my life has taken does not match up with what was supposed to be. At times it surfaces as sadness, other times as feelings of inadequacy, difference, shame, and guilt.

As for me, I will continue on my journey in a continuous process of redefining my own life, helping others to redefine theirs, and hopefully arriving at a place of comfort and fulfillment with who they are. I wish for you the same, a continuous process of growth and redefinition professionally and personally, however you so choose. I hope you will "surf the next wave," the one that champions the cause of redefining society in a way that truly supports complete freedom of choice for women. If we can successfully navigate the wave to a different shore, we can support the potential in all women as human beings first of all, of value in their own right, regardless of whether they are wives or mothers.

Appendix: Interview Guide

DEMOGRAPHICS

Name
Current age
Age at divorce
Race/ethnicity
Income
Education
Profession
Family of origin composition
Subject's place in birth order in family of origin

MARRIAGE

Describe when and how couple met
Length of relationship
Date of marriage
Age at marriage
Number of marriages
How would you describe your marital relationship?
What were the strengths and weaknesses of the marriage?
Were there any other significant losses for the couple during the marriage?
Any pregnancies? Outcomes?

CHILDBEARING DECISION-MAKING PROCESS

What were your feelings about having children before your marriage?
What were your feelings about having children while you were married?
How was the decision made about childbearing during the marriage?

What do you perceive were the factors involved in your not having children?
How do you feel now about not having children?
How have your feelings about having children changed or stayed the same over the course of being single, married, divorced, and now single again?
How do you feel about possibly approaching the end of the childbearing years?
How do you feel about the possibility of not having any children in the future?
How do you feel about not having a spouse at this time in regard to not having children?
How would you go about having children if you decided you wanted them now?
Have you considered adoption as an option?

PROCESS OF DIVORCE

Length of time since divorce
Length of time it took to divorce
Age at divorce
What do you perceive are the reasons for your divorce?
What do you think were the precipitating events of the divorce?
Who initiated it?
Who physically left?
Were there any third-party affairs?

ADJUSTMENT ISSUES

Describe the experience of being divorced at midlife without children.
What impact has this had on you?
What impact has this had on you financially?
What meaning do you attach to your circumstances?
What feelings do you have about it?
What meanings do you think others place on your circumstances?
What are your thoughts about the roles available to you and your identity as a woman without a spouse and children?
What have been the difficulties, challenges?
What has your grief process and recovery been like?
Have you noticed any change in behaviors or physical symptoms that concern you?
Did you have any of these symptoms before the divorce?
How do you feel you are functioning now?

How are you adjusting to single life?
How is your life organized and structured now?
How is your social life going now (quality and quantity)?
Are you dating now?
What has the dating experience been like for you?
What qualities are you looking for now?
How do you feel about being without a spouse or children (loneliness/isolation vs. freedom/independence)?
How do you feel when you are around people who are married and/or have children?
How do you feel about aging at this time?

REACTIONS AND SUPPORT FROM OTHERS

What reactions have you gotten from others?
What reactions have you gotten from your family members?
What type of support is most helpful to you?
From whom do you have support?
How are your friendships and social network since your divorce?

POSITIVE ASPECTS

What are the positive aspects of your life at this time?
What positive aspects are there to your divorce?
What are the opportunities of this phase for you?
What do you think your strengths are in dealing with this?
What coping skills do you think have helped you?
What achievements have you had?
What are you looking forward to in the future?

FAMILY OF ORIGIN

Age and circumstances of separation from family of origin
How would you describe your childhood?
How would you describe your relationships with family members, mother and father?
Describe your parents' marital relationship.
What do you think you learned from your parents about marriage and children?
Were there any significant losses throughout childhood?
Have your relationships with your family of origin changed since your divorce? If so, how?

References

Abrams, L. S. (2000). Guardians of virtue: The social reformers and the "girl problem," 1890–1920. *Social Service Review, 74*, 436–451.

Ahrons, C. (1994). *The good divorce: Keeping your family together when your marriage comes apart*. New York: Harper Collins Publishers.

Anderson, C. M., & Stewart, S. (1994). *Flying solo: Single women at midlife*. New York: W.W. Norton & Company.

Arnold, K. D., & McKenry, P. C. (1986). Divorce and the midlife transition: Some preliminary findings. *Journal of Divorce, 9*, 55–63.

Ban Breathnach, S. (1998). *Something more: Excavating your authentic self*. New York: Warner Books.

Basch, N. (1999). *Framing American divorce: From the revolutionary generation to the Victorians*. Berkeley: University of California Press.

Belenky, M. F., McVicker Clinchy, B., Rule Goldberger, N., & Mattuck Tarule, J. (1986). *Women's ways of knowing*. New York: Basic Books.

Benjamin, J. (1988). *The bonds of love: Psychoanalysis, feminism, and the problem of domination*. New York: Pantheon Books.

Berg, I. K., & DeJong, P. (1996). Solution-building conversations: Co-constructing a sense of compentence with clients. *Families in Society: The Journal of Contemporary Human Services, 77*, 376–391.

Berg, I. K., & Dolan, Y. (2001). *Tales of solutions: A collection of hope inspiring stories*. New York: W.W. Norton and Company.

Bevvino, D. L., & Sharkin, B. S. (2003). Divorce adjustment as a function of finding meaning and gender differences. *Journal of Divorce and Remarriage, 39*, 81–97.

Bisagni, G. M., & Eckenrode, J. (1995). The role of work identity in women's adjustment to divorce. *American Journal of Orthopsychiatry, 63*, 574–583.

Bursik, K. (1991). Adaptation to divorce and ego development in adult women. *Journal of Personality and Social Psychology, 60*, 300–306.

Callan, V. (1983). Factors affecting early and late deciders of voluntary childlessness. *Journal of Social Psychology, 119*, 261–268.

Carter, B., & McGoldrick, M. (1988). *The changing family life cycle: A framework for family therapy*. New York: Gardner Press.

Carter, B., & McGoldrick, M. (1999). *The expanded family lifecycle: Individual, family, and social perspectives*. Boston: Allyn and Bacon.

Casey, T. (2007). *Pride and joy: The lives and passions of women without children*. Hillsboro: Beyond Words Publishing.

Chapman, S. F., Price, S. J., & Serovich, J. (1995). The effects of guilt on divorce adjustment. *Journal of Divorce and Remarriage, 22*, 163–177.

Cherlin, A. J. (1992). *Marriage, divorce, and remarriage*. Cambridge, MA: Harvard University Press.

Chodorow, N. (1978). *The reproduction of mothering: Psychoanalysis and the sociology of gender*. Berkeley: University of California Press.

Cleveland, M. (1979). Divorce in the middle years: The sexual dimension. *Journal of Divorce, 2*, 255–262.

Cooper, J., & Fazio, R. H. (1984). A new look at dissonance theory. In L. Berkowitz, *Advances in social experimental social psychology* (Vol. 17, pp. 229–264). Orlando, FL: Academic Press.

Crenshaw, W. (2004). *Treating families and children in the child protective system*. New York: Bruner Routledge.

Dafoe Whitehead, B., & Popenoe, D. (2006). *The state of our unions: The National Marriage Project*. Piscataway, NJ.

Daniluk, J. C., & Herman, A. (1984). Parenthood decision-making. *Family Relations, 33*, 607–612.

Davis, N. (1982). Childless and single-childed women in early twentieth-century America. *Journal of Family Issues, 3*, 431–458.

deShazer, S. (1985). *Keys to solutions in brief therapy*. New York: W.W. Norton and Company.

deShazer, S. (1988). *Clues: Investigating solutions in brief therapy*. New York: W.W. Norton.

deShazer, S. (1994). *Words were originally magic*. New York: W.W. Norton and Company.

Dever, M., & Saugeres, L. (2004). I forgot to have children: Untangling links between feminism, careers, and voluntary childlessness. *Journal of the Association for Research on Mothering, 6*, 116–126.

Dion, K. K. (1995). Delayed parenthood and women's expectations about the transition to parenthood. *International Journal of Behavioral Development, 18*, 315–333.

Duran-Aydintug, C. (1995). Former spouses exiting role identities. *Journal of Divorce and Remarriage, 24*, 23–40.

Erikson, E. (1950). *Childhood and society*. New York: W.W. Norton and Company.

Erikson, E. (1968). *Identity: Youth and crisis*. New York: W.W. Norton and Company.

Erikson, E. (1975). *Life history and the historical moment*. New York: W.W. Norton and Company.

Erikson, E. (1982). *The life cycle completed: A review*. New York: W.W. Norton and Company.

Enright, E. (2004, July/August). A house divided. *AARP, The Magazine*, 62–68.

Festinger, L. (1957). *A theory of cognitive dissonance*. Stanford, CA: Stanford University Press.

Fields, J., & Casper, L. M. (2001, March). *America's families and living arrangements* (Current Population Reports, P20-537). Washington, DC: U.S. Census Bureau.

Friedan, B. (1997). *The feminine mystique*. New York: Norton. (Original work published 1963)

Gander, A. M. (1991). After the divorce: Familial factors that predict well-being for older and younger persons. *Journal of Divorce and Remarriage, 1*, 175–192.

Gergen, K. (1985). The social constructionist movement in modern psychology. *American Psychologist, 40*, 266–275.

Gergen, K. (1991). *The saturated self: Dilemmas of identity in contemporary life*. New York: HarperCollins Publishers.

Gillespie, R. (2000). When no means no: Disbelief, disregard, and deviance as discourses of voluntary childlessness. *Women's Studies International Forum, 23*, 223–234.

Gilligan, C. (1982). *In a different voice*. Cambridge, MA: Harvard University Press.

Gilligan, S. (2001, January/February). Getting to the core: Mastering the art of therapeutic connection. *The Psychotherapy Networker*, 22–55.

Goldstein, E. G. (1984). *Ego psychology and social work practice*. New York: Free Press.

Goldstein, J. R. (1999, August). The leveling of divorce in the United States. *Demography, 36*, 409–414.

Goode, W. J. (1956). *After divorce*. Glencoe, IL: Free Press.

Gutman, M. A. (1995). Fertility management: Infertility, delayed childbearing, and voluntary childlessness. In D. C. Goldberg (Ed.), *Contemporary marriage: Special issues in couples' therapy* (120–159). Homewood, IL: The Dorsey Press.

Hansson, R. O., et al. (1984). Femininity, masculinity, and adjustment to divorce among women. *Psychology of Women Quarterly, 8*, 248–260.

Hartmann, H. (1939). *Ego psychology and the problem of adaptation*. New York: International Universities Press.

Hayes, M. P., Stinnet, N., & Defrain, J. (1980). Learning about marriage from the divorced. *Journal of Divorce, 4*, 23–29.

Heatherington, E. M. (2003). Intimate pathways: Changing patterns in close personal relationships across time. *Family Relations, 52*, 318–331.

Heaton, T. B., Jacobsen, C. K., & Holland, K. (1999). Persistence and change in decisions to remain childless. *Journal of Marriage and the Family, 61*, 531–539.

Heidemann, B., Suhomolinova, O., & O'Rand, A. (1998). Economic independence, economic status, and empty nest in midlife marital disruption. *Journal of Marriage and the Family, 60*, 219–231.

Herz Brown, F. (1991). *Reweaving the family tapestry*. New York: W.W. Norton and Company.

Hird, M. J., & Abshoff, K. (2000). Women without children: A contradiction in terms? *Journal of Comparative Family Studies, 31*, 347–366.

Hollingsworth, L. S. (1916). Social devices for impelling women to bear children. *American Journal of Psychology, 22*, 19–29.

Houseknecht, S. K. (1977). Reference group support for voluntary childlessness: Evidence of conformity. *Journal of Marriage and the Family, 39*, 285–292.

Houseknecht, S. K. (1987). Voluntary childlessness. In M. B. Sussman & S. K. Steinmetz (Ed.), *Handbook of marriage and the family* (317–353). New York: Plenum Press.

Jordan, J. V., Kaplan, A. G., Miller, J. B., Stiver, I. P., & Surrey, J. L. (1991). *Women's growth in connection*. New York: Guilford Press.

Kaslow, F., & Linzer Schwartz, L. (1987). *The dynamics of divorce: A life cycle perspective*. New York: Bruner/Mazel.

Kaufman, G. (2000). Do gender role attitudes matter? Family formation and dissolution among traditional and egalitarian men and women. *Journal of Family Issues*, *21*, 128–144.

Kelly Raley, R., & Bumpass, L. (2003). The topography of the divorce plateau: Levels and trends in union stability in the United States after 1980. *Demographic Research*, *8*, 245–259.

Kitson, G. C. (1988). *The impact of age on adjustment for women at thirteen months post death or divorce*. Paper presented at the 41st Annual Scientific Meeting of the Gerontological Society of America, San Francisco.

Kitson, G. C., & Morgan, L. A. (1990). The multiple consequences of divorce: A decade review. *Journal of Marriage and the Family*, *52*, 913–924.

Lampman, C., & Dowling-Guyer, S. (1995). Attitudes towards voluntary and involuntary childlessness. *Basic and Applied Social Psychology*, *17*, 213–222.

Landa, A. M. (2004). The lives and development of voluntarily childless men and women. *Dissertation Abstracts International A: The Humanities and Social Sciences*, 65(6), 2379. (University Microfilms International)

Langelier, R., & Deckert, P. (1978). The late-divorce phenomenon: The causes and impact of ending 20-year-old or longer marriages. *Journal of Divorce*, *1*, 381–390.

Lawler Dye, J. (2004, June). *Fertility of American women* (Current Population Reports, 20-555). Washington, DC: U.S. Census Bureau.

Letherby, G. (1999). Other than mother and mothers as others: The experience of motherhood and non-motherhood in relation to infertility and "involuntary childlessness." *Women's Studies International Forum*, 22, 359–372.

Letherby, G. (2002). Childless and bereft? Stereotypes and realities in relation to "voluntary" and "involuntary" childlessness and womanhood. *Sociological Inquiry*, *72*, 7–20.

Lloyd, S. A., & Zick, C. D. (1989). Divorce at mid and later life: Does the empirical evidence support the theory? *Journal of Divorce*, *9*, 89–102.

Longman, P. (2004). *The empty cradle: How falling birthrates threaten world prosperity and what to do about it*. New York: Basic Books.

Lund, K. L. (1990). A feminist perspective on divorce therapy for women. *Journal of Divorce*, *13*, 57–67.

Marks, N., & Lambert, J. D. (1998). Marital status, continuity, and change among young and midlife adults. *Journal of Family Issues*, *19*, 652–685.

McDaniel, A., Kusgen, C., & Coleman, M. (2003). Women's experiences of midlife divorce following long-term marriage. *Journal of Divorce and Remarriage*, *38*, 103–128.

McManus, M. J. (2006, July 23). Life without children. *Washington Times*, 22, 28, 39.

Mejumder, D. (2004). Choosing childlessness: Intentions of voluntary childlessness in the United States. *Michigan Sociological Review*, *18*, 108–135.

Miall, C. E. (1986). The stigma of involuntary childlessness. *Social Problems*, *33*, 268–282

Miller, J. B. (1976). *Toward a new psychology of women*. Boston: Beacon Press.

Miller, N. B., Smerglia, V. L., Gaudet, P. Scott, & Kitson, G. C. (1998). Stressful life events, social support, and the distress of widowed and divorced women. *Journal of Family Issues*, *19*, 181–203.

Moen, P. (1998, Spring). Recasting careers: Changing reference groups, risks and realities. *Generations*, 40–45.

Morell, C. M. (1993). Intentionally childless women: Another view of women's development. *Affilia*, *8*, 300–316.

Morgan, L. A. (1991). *After marriage ends: Economic consequences for midlife women*. Newbury Park, CA: Sage Publications.

Mosher, W. D., & Bachrach, C. A. (1982). Childlessness in the United States: Estimates from the National Survey of Family Growth. *Journal of Family Issues*, *3*, 517–543.

Mueller, K. A., & Yoder, J. D. (1999). Stigmatization of non-normative family size status. *Sex Roles*, *41*, 901–919.

Nathanson, I. G. (1995). Divorce and women's spirituality. *Journal of Divorce and Remarriage*, *22*, 179–189.

Nave-Herz, R. (1989). Childless marriages. *Marriage and Family Review*, *14*, 239–250.

Neimeyer, R. A. (2000). *Meaning reconstruction & the experience of loss*. Washington, DC: American Psychological Association.

Norlin, J. M., & Chess, W. A. (1988). *Human behavior and the social environment: Social systems theory*. Boston: Allyn and Bacon.

O'Hanlon, W. H. (1987). *Taproots: Underlying principles of Milton Erickson's therapy and hypnosis*. New York: W.W. Norton.

Park, K. (2002). Stigma management among the voluntarily childless. *Sociological Perspectives*, *45*, 21–45.

Poelker, D. A., & Baldwin, C. (1999). Postponed motherhood and the out-of-sync life cycle. *Journal of Mental Health Counseling*, *21*, 136–147.

Popenoe, P. (1936). Motivation of childless marriages. *Journal of Heredity*, *27*, 469–472.

Popenoe, P. (1943). Childlessness: Voluntary or involuntary? *Journal of Heredity*, *34*, 83–87.

Rahav, G. (2002). Divorced women: Factors contributing to self-identity change. *Journal of Divorce and Remarriage*, *37*, 41–59.

Reading, J., & Amatea, E. S. (1986). Role deviance or role diversification: Reassessing the psychosocial factors affecting the parenthood choice of career-oriented women. *Journal of Marriage and the Family*, *48*, 255–260.

Rosen, S. (1982). *My voice will go with you: The teaching tales of Milton H. Erickson*. New York: W.W. Norton.

Russo, N. F. (1979). Overview: Sex roles, fertility, and the motherhood mandate. *Psychology of Women Quarterly*, *4*, 7–15.

Ryan, W. (1972). *Blaming the victim*. New York: Vintage Books.

Schafer, R. (1992). *Retelling a life: Narration and dialogue in psychoanalysis*. New York, Basic Books.

Schoen, R., & Standish, N. (2001). The retrechment of marriage: Results from marital status life tables for the United States, 1995. *Population and Development Review*, *27*, 553–563.

Sclater, S. D. (1999). *Divorce: A psychosocial study*. Brookfield, VT: Ashgate Publishers.

Sheehy, G. (1995). *New passages*. New York: Random House.

Shields, S., & Cooper, P. (1983). Stereotypes of traditional and non-traditional childbearing roles. *Sex Roles*, *9*, 363–376.

Shober, M. M. (1994). Psychosocial development in women: Childfree vs. childbearing women. *Dissertation Abstracts International A: Humanities and Social Sciences*, 54(10-A), 3902. (University Microfilms International)

Slater, L., Banks, A., & Henderson, D. J. (2003). *The complete guide to mental health for women*. Boston: Beacon Press.

Steinem, G. (1992). *Revolution from within: A book of self esteem*. Boston: Little, Brown, and Company.

Thabes, V. (1997). A survey analysis of women's long-term post-divorce adjustment. *Journal of Divorce and Remarriage*, *27*, 163–175.

Thornton, A., & Young-Demarco, L. (2001). Four decades of trends and attitudes towards family issues in the United States: The 1960s through the 1990s. *Journal of Marriage and the Family*, *63*, 1009–1037.

Twenge, J. M., Campbell, K. W., & Foster, C. A. (2003). Parenthood and marital satisfaction: A meta-analytic review. *Journal of Marriage and the Family*, *65*, 574–583.

Veevers, J. (1980). *Childless by choice*. Toronto: Butterworths.

Veevers, J. (1973). Voluntarily childless wives: An exploratory study. *Sociology and Social Research*, *57*, 356–366.

Wallerstein, J. S. (1986). Women after divorce: Preliminary report after a ten-year follow-up. *American Journal of Orthopsychiatry*, *56*, 65–77.

Walter, J. L., & Peller, J. (2000). *Recreating brief therapy: Preferences and possibilities*. New York: W.W. Norton and Company.

Walters, M., Carter, B., Papp, P., & Silverstein, O. (1988). *The invisible web*. New York: Guilford Press.

Weedon, C. (1987). *Feminist practice and post-structural theory*. New York: Basil Blackwell.

Welles-Nystrom, B. (1997). The meaning of postponed motherhood for women in the United States and Sweden: Aspects of feminism and radical timing strategies. *Health Care for Women International*, *18*, 279–299.

White, M., & Epston, D. (1990). *Narrative means to therapeutic ends*. New York: W.W. Norton and Company.

Wickes, H. (1993, March). Childless women in midlife: A case study from a feminist and Jungian perspective. *Dissertation Abstracts International*, 53(9-B), 4935. (University Microfilms International)

Wicklund, R. A., & Brehm, J. W. (1976). *Perspectives on cognitive dissonance*. Hillsdale, NJ: Erlbaum.

Wijnberg, M. H., & Holmes, T. (1992). Adaptation to divorce: The impact of role orientation on family-life cycle perspectives. *Families in Society: The Journal of Contemporary Human Services*, *73*, 159–167.

Williams, J. H. (1987). *Psychology of women: Behavior in a biosocial context*. New York: W.W. Norton.

Woodward, J., Zabel, J., & DeCosta, C. (1980). Loneliness and divorce. *Journal of Divorce*, *4*, 73–81.

Wu, Z., & Penning, M. (1997). Marital instability after midlife. *Journal of Family Issues*, *18*, 459–478.

Yogev, B., & Vierra, A. (1983). The state of motherhood among professional women. *Sex Roles*, *9*, 391–397.

Zimbardo, P., & Gerrig, R. (1996). *Psychology and life*. New York: HarperCollins Publishers.

ADDITIONAL READING

Abma, J. C., & Peterson, L. S. (1995). *Voluntary childlessness among U.S. women: Recent trends and determinants*. Population Association of America Paper, Centers for Disease Control and Prevention, National Center for Health Statistics, Hyattsvile, MD.

Ambry, M. K. (1992). Childless chances. *American Demographics, 14*, 55.

Anderson, D., & Clandos, R. (2003). Dating after divorce. *Psychology Today, 36*, 46–47.

Anderson, H., & Goolishian, H. A. (1988). Human systems as linguistics systems: Preliminary and evolving ideas about the implications for clinical theory. *Family Process, 27*, 371–393.

Archer, S. L. (1990). Females at risk: Identity issues for adolescents and divorced women. In C. Vandenplas-Holper & B. Paiva, *Interpersonal and identity development: New directions* (87–102). Porto: ICPFD and Louvain-La-Nueve: Academia.

Bachu, A., & O'Connell, M. (2001, June). *Fertility of American women* (Current Population Reports, P20-543RV). Washington, DC: U.S. Census Bureau.

Berardo, D. (1982). Divorce and remarriage at middle age and beyond. *Annals of the American Academy of Political and Social Science, 464*, 132–139.

Bing, E., & Coleman, L. (1980). *Having a baby*. New York: Bantam.

Blatter, C. W., & Jasper Jacobsen, J. (1993). Older women coping with divorce: peer suppport groups. *Women and Therapy, 14*, 141–155.

Bloom, D., & Bennet, N. (1993). Childless couples. *American Demographics, 34*, 34–35.

Boggs, J. E. (1994, August). The course of delayed parenthood: A cross-sectional study of selected psychosocial variables. *Dissertation Abstracts International B: The Sciences and Engineering*, 56(2-B), 1100. (University Microfilms International)

Bogulub, E. (1991). Women and midlife divorce: Some practice issues. *Social Work, 36*, 428–433.

Bram, S. (1984). Voluntarily childless women: Traditional or non-traditional? *Sex Roles, 10*, 195–207.

Cain, M. (2001). *The childless revolution*. Cambridge, MA: Perseus Publishing.

Callan, V. (1984). Childlessness and marital adjustment. *Australian Journal of Sex, Marriage, and the Family, 5*, 210–214.

Caplow, T., Hicks, L., & Wattenberg, B. J. (2000). *The first measured century: An illustrated guide to trends in America, 1900–2000*. LaVergne, TN: AEI Press.

Christensen, H. T. (1963). Timing of first pregnancy as a factor in divorce: A cross-cultural analysis. *Eugenics Quarterly, 10*, 119–130.

Crispell, D. (1993). Planning no family, now or ever. *American Demographics, 15*, 23–24.

Daniels, P., & Weingarten, K. (1982). *Sooner or later: The timing of parenthood in adult lives*. New York: Norton.

Davis, B., & Aron, A. (1988). Perceived causes of divorce and post divorce adjustment among recently divorced midlife women. *Journal of Divorce, 12*, 41–55.

DeGarmo, D. S., & Kitson, G. C. (1996). Identity relevance and disruption as predictors of psychological distress for widowed and divorced women. *Journal of Marriage and the Family, 58*, 983–997.

deShazer, S. (1991). *Putting difference to work*. New York: W.W. Norton and Company.

Diedrick, P. (1991). Gender differences in divorce adjustment. *Journal of Divorce and Remarriage, 14*, 33–45.

Dixon, C. S., & Rettig, K. D. (1994). An examination of income adequacy for single women two years after divorce. *Journal of Divorce and Remarriage*, *22*, 55–71.

Doherty, W. J. (1983). Impact of divorce on locus of control orientation in adult women: A longitudinal study. *Journal of Personality and Social Psychology*, *44*, 834–840.

Dolan, M. A., & Hoffman, C. D. (1998). Determinants of divorce among women: A reexamination of critical influences. *Journal of Divorce and Remarriage*, *28*, 97–106.

Ebaugh, H. R. F. (1988). *Becoming an ex: The process of role exit*. Chicago: University of Chicago Press.

Faux, M. (1984). *Childless by choice: Choosing childlessness in the eighties*. New York: Anchor Press/Doubleday.

Frankel, S. A., & Wise, M. J. (1982). A view of delayed parenting: Some implications of a new trend. *Psychiatry*, *45*, 220–225.

Gardner, M. (2003, March 19). One and one makes a family. *Christian Science Monitor*, 15.

Garvin, V., Kalter, N., & Hansell, J. (1993). Divorced women: Individual differences in stressors, mediating factors, and adjustment outcomes. *American Journal of Orthopsychiatry*, *63*, 232–240.

Gatewood, J. (1993, September). Women and midlife divorce: Developing autonomy. *Dissertation Abstracts International*, 54(3-B), 1649. (University Microfilms International)

Gerson, M., Posner, J., & Morris, A. M. (1991). The wish for a child in couples eager, disinterested, and conflicted about having children. *American Journal of Family Therapy*, *19*, 334–343.

Gerstel, N. (1988). Divorce and kin ties: The importance of gender. *Journal of Marriage and the Family*, *50*, 209–219.

Gigy, L., & Kelly, J. B. (1992). Reasons for divorce: Perspectives of divorcing men and women. *Journal of Divorce and Remarriage*, *18*, 169–187.

Goethal, K. G., et al. (1983). Facilitating post divorce adjustment among women: A one month follow-up. *Family Therapy*, *10*, 61–68.

Gold, J. H. (1988). *Divorce as developmental process*. Washington, DC: American Psychiatric Press.

Goodbody, S. T. (1971). The psychosocial implications of voluntary childlessness. *Psychiatry*, *41*, 426–434.

Griffith, J. D., Koo, H. P., & Suchindran, C. M. (1984). Childlessness and marital stability in remarriages. *Journal of Marriage and the Family*, *46*, 577–585.

Haffey, M., & Cohen, P. M. (1992). Treatment issues for divorcing women. *Families in Society: The Journal of Contemporary Human Services*, *73*, 142–148.

Hardy, K. V. (1993). Live supervision in the post modern era of family therapy: Issues, reflections, and questions. *Contemporary Family Therapy*, *15*, 9–20.

Heaton, T. B. (2002). Factors contributing to increased marital stability in the United States. *Journal of Family Issues*, *23*, 392–409.

Hittelman, G. J. (1993, August). Enrichment of identity: The midlife transition in women following a non-traditional path. *Dissertation Abstracts International*, 54(2-B), 1121–1122. (University Microfilms International)

Hoffnung, M. (2004). Wanting it all: Career, marriage, and motherhood during college educated women's 20s. *Sex Roles*, *50*, 711–723.

Houseknecht, S. K. (1982). Voluntary childlessness: Toward a theoretical integration. *Journal of Family Issues, 3*, 459–471.

Hughes, R., Jr. (1988). Divorce and social support: A review. *Journal of Divorce, 11*, 123–145.

Iwanir, S., & Ayal, H. (1991). Midlife divorce initiation: From crisis to developmental transition. *Contemporary Family Therapy, 13*, 609–622.

Jacobsen, C. K., Heaton, T. B., & Taylor, K. M. (1988, Fall/Winter). Childlessness among American women. *Social Biology*, 186–197.

Jamison, P. H., Franzini, L. R., & Kaplan, R. M. (1979). Some assumed characteristics of voluntarily childfree men and women. *Psychology of Women Quarterly, 4*, 266–273.

Kuchner, J. F., & Porcino, J. (1988). Delayed motherhood. In B. Birns & D. F. Hay (Eds.), *The different faces of motherhood. Perspectives in developmental psychology* (259–280). New York: Plenum Press.

Kuh, D., & Hardy, R. (2002). Lifetime risk factors for women's psychological distress in midlife. *Social Science and Medicine, 55*, 1957–1973.

Langelier, R., & Deckert, P. (1980). Divorce counseling guidelines for the late divorced female. *Journal of Divorce, 3*, 403–411.

LaNock, S. (1987). The symbolic meaning of childbearing. *Journal of Family Issues, 8*, 373–393.

Letherby, G., & Williams, C. (1999). Non-motherhood: Ambivalent autobiographies. *Feminist Studies, 25*, 719–729.

Lewis, K. G. (2001). *With or without a man: Single women taking control of their lives.* Palo Alto, CA: Bull Publishing Company.

Longres, J. F. (1990). *Human behavior in the social environment*. Itasca, IL: F.E. Peacock Publishers.

Ludtke, M. (1997). On *our own: Unmarried mothers in America*. Los Angeles: University of California Press.

Mansfield, P. K. (1988). Midlife childbearing: Strategies for informed decision-making. *Psychology of Women Quarterly, 12*, 445–460.

Marshall, C., & Rossman, G. B. (1995). *Designing qualitative research*. Thousand Oaks, CA: Sage Publications.

Mattes, J. (1994). *Single mothers by choice*. New York: Three Rivers Press.

Millet, K. (1971). *Sexual politics*. New York: Equinox Books.

Morell, C. M. (1994). *Unwomanly conduct: The challenges of intentional childlessness.* New York: Routledge.

Morgan, S. P., & Rindfuss, R. R. (1985). Marital disruption: Structural and temporal dimensions. *American Journal of Sociology, 90*, 1055–1077.

Neugarten, B. L. (1979). Time, age and the life cycle. *American Journal of Psychiatry, 136*, 887–894.

Norman, W. H., & Scamarella, T. (1980). *Midlife: Developmental and clinical issues.* New York: Brunner/Mazel.

O'Rand, A., & Henretta, J. C. (1982). Women at middle age: Developmental transitions. *Annals of the American Academy of Political and Social Science, 464*, 57–64.

Polonko, K. A., Scanzoni, J., & Teachman, J. D. (1982). Childlessness and marital satisfaction. *Journal of Family Issues, 3*, 545–573.

Poston, D., & Trent, K. (1982). International variability in childlessness. *Journal of Family Issues, 3*, 473–491.

Queralt, M. (1996). *The social environment and human behavior.* Boston: Allyn and Bacon.

Rainwater, L. (1965). *Family design: Marital sexuality, family size, and family planning.* Chicago: Aldine.

Reece, S.M. (1993). Social support and the early maternal experience of primaparas over 35. *Maternal-Child Health Nursing Journal, 21*, 91–98.

Rindfuss, R. R., Morgan, S. P., & Offutt, K. (1996). Education and the changing age pattern of American fertility: 1963–1989. *Demography, 33*(3).

Roosa, M. W. (1988). The effect of age in the transition to parenthood: Are delayed childbearers a unique group? *Family Relations, 37*, 322–327.

Rowland, R. (1982). The childfree experience in the aging context: An investigation of the pronatalist bias of life-span developmental literature. *Australian Psychologist, 17*, 141–150.

Schlesinger, B. (1987). Postponed parenthood: A Canadian study. *Conciliation Courts Review, 25*, 21–26.

Schlesinger, B., Danaher, A., & Roberts, C. (1984). Dual career, delayed childbearing families: Some observations. *Canada's Mental Health, 32*, 4–6.

Schlesinger, B., & Giblon, S. (1985). *Postponed parenthood.* Toronto: Guidance Centre, Faculty of Education, University of Toronto.

Schlesinger, B., & Schlesinger, R. (1989). Postponed parenthood: Trends and issues. *Journal of Comparative Family Studies, 20*, 355–363.

Schultz, T. (1979). *Women can wait: The measures of motherhood after thirty.* Garden City, NJ: Doubleday.

Seccombe, K. (1991). Assessing the costs and benefits of children: Gender comparisons among childfree husbands and wives. *Journal of Marriage and the Family, 53*, 191–202.

Shafer, R. (1992). *Retelling a life: Narration and dialogue in psychoanalysis.* New York: Basic Books.

Shotter, J., & Gergen, K. J. (Eds.). (1989). *Texts of identity.* London: Sage.

Simon, R. W. (1997). The meanings individuals attach to role identities and their implications for mental health. *Journal of Health and Social Behavior, 38*, 256–274.

Smerglia, V. L., Miller, N. B., & Kort-Butler, L. (1999). The impact of social support on women's adjustment to divorce: A literature review and analysis. *Journal of Divorce and Remarriage, 32*, 63–89.

Soloway, M. N. (1986, January). Antecedent factors associated with late birth timing decisions of dual career couples. *Dissertation Abstracts International*, 46(7-A), 2090. (University Microfilms International)

Soloway, M. N., & Smith, R. M. (1987). Antecedents of late birth timing decisions of men and women in dual career marriages. *Family Relations, 36*, 258–262.

Somers, M. D. (1993). A comparison of voluntarily childfree adults and parents. *Journal of Marriage and the Family, 55*, 643–650.

Speed, B. (1991). Reality exists O.K.? An argument against constructivism and social constructionism. *Family Therapy, 13*, 395–409.

Spivey, P., & Scherman, A. (1980). The effects of time lapse on personality characteristics and stress on divorced women. *Journal of Divorce, 4*, 49–59.

Sprenkle, D., & Bischof, G. (1994). Contemporary family therapy in the United States. *Journal of Family Therapy, 16*, 5–23.

Stanley, S. M., & Markham, H. J. (1997). *Marriage in the 1990's: A nationwide random phone survey*. Denver, CO: PREP.

Stanton, G. T. (1997). *Why marriage matters: Reasons to believe in marriage in post-modern society*. Colorado Springs, CO: Pinon Press.

Streib, G., & Penna, M. H. (1982). Anticipating transitions: Possible options in "family" forms. *Annals of the American Society of Political and Social Science, 464*, 104–119.

Stroup, A. L., & Pollock, G. E. (1994). Economic consequences of marital dissolution. *Journal of Divorce and Remarriage, 22*, 37–54.

Tangri, S., & Jenkins, S. (1987). Stability and change in role innovation in life plans. *Sex Roles, 14*, 627–662.

Uhlenberg, P., Cooney, T., & Boyd, R. (1990). Divorce for women after midlife. *Journals of Gerontology, 45*, S3–S11.

Wilkie, J. R. (1981). The trend towards delayed parenthood. *Journal of Marriage and the Family, 43*, 583–591.

Willen, H., & Montgomery, H. (1996). The impact and wish for children and having children on attainment and importance of life values. *Journal of Comparative Family Studies, 27*, 499–518.

Wineberg, H. (1990). Delayed childbearing, childlessness, and marital disruption. *Journal of Comparative Family Studies, 21*, 99–110.

Zeiss, A., Zeiss, R., & Johnson, S. (1980). Sex differences in initiation of and adjustment to divorce. *Journal of Divorce, 4*, 21–33.

Ziman Tobin, P. O. (1998). *Motherhood optional: A psychological journey*. Northvale, NJ: Jason Aronson.

Index

D

E

M

T

Y

U

V

W